THE
PARENT
BOOK

To our wives, Pat and Ginny, and our children, Katherine, Peter, and Tim, and Tom, Joe, Regina, John, Matthew and Elizabeth.

Acknowledgement

Deep gratitude is due to Dr. Vincent E. Mazzanti, teacher, co-author, and long-time friend for sharing his practical wisdom, his experience and guidance, and for the countless hours he gave in patient discussion of the ideas presented in this book.

Book Design by Vivian Blackstone

Cover by Caroline Carter

Editorial Consultant, Roberta Ridgely

Photos by Bill Reed

Suggested Children's Literature compiled by Craig B. Hallenstein, Ph.D., and Kathryn E. Hallenstein, MAT. MEd.

Published by JALMAR PRESS, and Psych/Graphic

Distributed exclusively by
JALMAR PRESS, INC.
6501 Elvas Ave.
Sacramento, CA 95819

ISBN 0-915190-15-X

Printed in United States of America

THE PARENT BOOK

The Holistic Program for Raising the Emotionally Mature Child

A Source Book
by
Harold Bessell, Ph.D.
and
Thomas P. Kelly, Jr.

Published by:
JALMAR PRESS, Inc. and Psych/Graphic

Distributed exclusively by:
JALMAR PRESS, Inc.
6501 Elvas Avenue
Sacramento, CA 95819

Contents

8

Preface

This is a book about feelings—yours and your child's—and how they affect your role and effectiveness as a parent. Its aim is twofold: to help you create and maintain a *loving relationship* with your child and to foster his *Emotional Maturity*. Simple in concept, this is no small task. Every parent wants to do his very best when raising his child. But most of us approach that critical task with little knowledge, less training and, despite high hopes, a gnawing fear of failure. This book is designed to remove those fears and to help you realize your best hopes.

Emotional development is vital to your child because it is the key to his behavior and, beyond that, to his happiness and fulfillment. Emotionally mature people typically live realistic, positive, productive and happy lives. On the other hand, emotionally immature people inevitably live self-centered, irresponsible and unhappy lives. Since the stakes are so high, it's imperative for you to know how to help your child become Emotionally Mature.

In these respects, THE PARENT BOOK is different from many other books for parents:

FIRST, it focuses on your child's emotions and how they develop and mature.

SECOND, it offers a systematic, comprehensive approach to your child's emotional maturation.

THIRD, its central thrust is developmental rather than remedial. It is not intended for solving severe problems or for curing neuroses but for preventing their occurrence in the first place.

FOURTH, it deals with everyday problems you and your child must face together. It tells you What to do, Why to do it and How to do it.

What is Emotional Maturity? The concept has been defined in many ways and in many contexts. As used in this book, Emotional Maturity has specific and precise meaning. It means positive development in the major areas of Awareness, Relating, Competence and Integrity through a loving parent-child relationship.

AWARENESS is knowing yourself and others—what is felt, thought and taking place at any moment.

RELATING is knowing how to get along well with others.

COMPETENCE involves the ways to develop your abilities to solve life's problems.

INTEGRITY is the self-affirmation of the person who lives by high ethical standards and good self-discipline.

To the extent that your child achieves the best possible development in these four areas, he will be emotionally mature. The extent to which you help your child achieve this maturity will be the best measure of your success as a parent. Such success can come only through daily, stage-by-stage, issue-by-issue efforts in which you act as loving guide to your child.

THE PARENT BOOK will help you through the crisis stages in your child's emotional maturation in each of these four major areas. The book describes Awareness, Relating, Competence and Integrity as each comprising a sequence of steps and issues that underlie your child's behavior. In all, there are 69 issues that affect your child's Emotional Maturity—issues such as fear and anger, acceptance and approval, effort and risk-taking, responsibility and self-control. You will find them charted on pages 46-47. They are the common, everyday issues you and your child are likely to face as you try to help him mature.

You can use this book, then, in two ways. You can read it through to gain knowledge and insight about your child's emotional development. Or you can use it as a source book, a reference for handling specific problems. In this regard, please note that Index B includes a number of behavioral problems which have their roots in emotional issues of one kind or another. This index will refer you to the central developmental issue. For example, a lying child may need a climate of openness for telling the truth; an irresponsible child, the freedom to develop responsibility. By using the developmental steps suggested, you may be able to eliminate the problem altogether. Needless to say, if the problem is so severe that it persists, you should obtain professional help.

It's important to note that the concepts and techniques described in this book apply mostly to children between ages three and fourteen. Or, to put it more specifically, to children who are verbal, children with whom you can carry on a meaningful dialogue. For some children, this is possible at two and a half; for others, at age four. This does not mean, however, that you should wait until your child's third birthday to concern yourself about emotional development. You cannot start too soon after conception to be concerned about your child's emotional well-being. In recent years, a steady stream of research has confirmed how important to the unborn child are its mother's physical and emotional health. For many years, we've known that even the easiest delivery imposes some degree of trauma or shock upon the newborn infant.[1] Emotional development starts early.[2] Even though your infant child cannot speak in the conventional sense, his emotions are very

active. From the outset, he experiences warmth and cold, hunger and thirst, pleasure and pain, dampness and dryness, the comfort of being held and the discomfort of not being held when he wishes. Often, he experiences fright or is on the verge of it. And he experiences anger, frustration and desire. Sometimes your infant will seem to be on an emotional roller coaster, high with joy one moment, overcome with misery the next, for as yet he has acquired no buffers against the painful or pleasurable stimulations of his environment.

Your infant's greatest need is for a relatively steady stream of pleasure, safety and physical comfort. He often will feel best when being held. Many parents have found by instinct that, when they don't know what is troubling their baby, just picking him up often makes the problem go away. When you are available to your child in a very consistent and reliable way to give him the comfort and support he needs, he builds up a generalized feeling that "things are O.K." He will come to feel a sense of security; feeling good most of the time will be pretty well assured.

An important facet of every person's emotional life is spiritual development. There is no inconsistency between the system presented in this book and the beliefs of any of the major religions. Raising a child isn't easy. Nor is it easy for a child to grow up emotionally. No one truly matures without many serious confrontations with his parents. THE PARENT BOOK is planned in detail to help you manage these confrontations in a loving and constructive way. The book's ideas, methods and model confrontations are designed to help you guide your child's development with the least amount of pain to either of you—and to preclude mistakes that could require expensive therapy later on.

---

[1] The contrast between a sudden, traumatic birth and a slow, gentle one is sensitively described in Dr. Frederick LeBoyer's book, *Birth Without Violence* (Alfred A. Knopf; New York, 1975).

[2] Readers who want to understand the emotional life of the child from birth to age three are referred to Burton L. White's excellent study, *The First Three Years of Life* (Prentice Hall; Englewood Cliffs, New Jersey, 1975).

PART I
The People

I   The Parent as a Loving Guide

Your Feelings as a Parent

Becoming a parent is a moment of joy that begins a lifetime of challenge . . . and opportunity. Your life will be filled with the pleasure of simple things . . . holding your child in your arms, marveling at his liveliness and exuberance and the simplicity of his innocence, witnessing his discoveries about himself and the world around him, treasuring him as a companion, feeling pride in his accomplishments.

Your child will add meaning and fulfilment to your life in many ways, and rearing him will give you opportunities to enrich yourself every day.

But you also will suffer. You will feel guilty about bringing a child into this uncertain and often painful world. You will feel inadequate because, like most parents, you will be torn between your desire to do the best you can and the hard realization that you are almost totally untrained to raise a child. You will feel the pain of uncertainty and self-doubt. "Can I do a good job?" "Will I have the patience?" "Will my child survive my mistakes?" You will feel frustrated by your ignorance. You will agonize, "What do I do now? What's best in this situation for each of us? What does his behavior mean? How can I be sure?" You will be pulled in two directions, between your own interests and his. And you will wonder whether you're being selfish or too self-sacrificing. In all these feelings, you are not alone. All parents suffer the same doubts, the same uncertainties and, often, the same lack of knowledge. Parents have always suffered such burdens, hinging primarily upon our common lack of training and our need for the basic facts about child-rearing.

For a number of years now, information about the physical care and intellectual growth of children has been broadly available to parents. But the essential element in child-rearing—Emotional Development—usually has been overlooked or treated in piecemeal fashion. Today, based on more than three quarters of a century of research and the experience of countless therapists, a body of commonly accepted knowledge about Emotional Development is emerging.

THE PARENT BOOK attempts to provide you with a systematic, comprehensive guide to these theories and concepts of Emotional Maturity—what it is and how it happens. The book advances the philosophy that a thorough knowledge of your child's feelings, coupled with your goodwill, is the best formula for building a sound parent-child relationship and your child's Emotional Maturity. At the same time, THE PARENT BOOK will help you to understand and resolve most of the conflicts you will have with your child, conflicts that arise out of the eternal struggle in every child—the struggle of "I will grow up/I won't grow up."

Tyrant or Guide?

Nothing is so important to your child's emotional development as your basic concept of parenthood. What do you believe is your fundamental role as a parent? How "should" you relate to your child? The most-common role parents assume is that of a "benevolent tyrant." These parents usually view their role in terms of one basic function: to prevent the child from doing anything "wrong" and to punish him when he does. This essentially negative approach to parenthood ultimately damages the child and impairs his development. The negative feelings created by this approach produce negative behaviors. Unintentionally, these parents defeat their own earnest efforts to raise strong, mature children.

A healthier approach is to see yourself as a guide, ready to assist your child's natural processes of growth. You cannot totally control those processes but you can affect them for better or worse. To the extent that you believe in your child's capacity for growth and development and apply yourself to fostering it, you will become an effective parent.

The parent who acts as a loving guide is affirmative and is concerned with opportunities and possibilities for development, not just with problems. At the same time, this kind of parent is realistic about his expectations of himself and his child. The affirmative parent warns of dangers and rebukes transgressions, just as the strict parent does. But in addition, the affirmative parent is committed to being available when truly needed. This kind of parent leads the way only when necessary but is available to offer support and encouragement when the going gets rough. Parents who arm themselves with righteousness and a strap to punish misdeeds are expressing the frustration that comes from not knowing more-constructive approaches. The punishment orientation magnifies the child's fixation upon the dark side of life—upon pain, guilt and recrimination. The affirmative-minded parent emphasizes the other direction and focuses the child's view beyond mistakes and present limitations, orienting him to become the better-developed person that he can be.

Being Affirmative with Your Child

Many parents are afraid to be positive with their child because they imagine it smacks of permissiveness. Their uncertainty about the meaning of affirmative attitudes and actions feeds their notion that any such attitude will reduce their values. Therefore, they tend to stick to the only values they know: those conveyed by "No" and "You can't." But being affirmative does not mean letting your child misbehave or run roughshod over your feelings. Nor does it mean that you as a parent have to sacrifice what you think is right.

Being affirmative and not negative means focusing your attention on two critical factors in your child's development: good feelings and self-confidence. In fostering good feelings, let your child know that it is possible and desirable for both of you to feel good at the same time. Tell your child that this may be difficult but that you are fully committed to this goal. One way to begin to stress the positive is to emphasize those things that your child does that make you feel good:

1. *Each Day, Tell Your Child Something He Did That Pleased You* It may have been something thoughtful, funny or helpful. Coming from you—the most significant person in his life—this recognition will make a very strong impression upon him. It will make him feel positive about himself and life in general, and encourage him to want to please you more. As often as you honestly can, say such things as:

   "I appreciate the way you straightened up your room."
   "Do you know what you did today that made me feel best of all? It was the way you were patient when I was busy with the baby."
   "I saw you showing the new boy next door how to put his kite together. When you do kind, friendly things like that, you make me feel good. I'm really proud of you."

2. *Show Him How Much You Believe in Him* The second facet of being positive is to build your child's self-confidence, his sense of "I-can-do-it." Every child needs assurance that he is, in fact, becoming a capable person. But it is not enough that he does well. He must be told. Whenever

he does a reasonably good job at something—and it doesn't have to be something special—tell him how capable he is and how proud it makes you feel. All you need to say is, "You did that very well." You can't tell him this often enough.

3. *Avoid Suppressing Your Child* Avoid constant barrages of "No," "You can't" and "Don't you do that." Consistently negative statements on your part will quickly blunt his incentive to become mature. The drive to become mature is based on positive desires and goals, or on the desire to be and have something better. It cannot be developed by the use of negative tactics.

4. *Never Ridicule Your Child* Ridicule opens a door to emotional disaster. By stressing your child's mistakes and inadequacies, you will confirm his self-doubts and undermine his hope of coping effectively with all the challenges he faces. Only honest, compassionate confrontation will help him grow.

Getting to Know Your Child

Although most parents will tell you how well they know their own child, when the child misbehaves you frequently hear them say:
"I don't know why John does things like this."
"I don't understand Andrea. She's beyond me."
"How can Dirk do something like this? Who would expect it?"
These parents feel trapped and betrayed by their children's conduct. But the real reason for their surprise and confusion lies in their limited knowledge of their children.
Your child can't readily tell you who he is. He must be taught how to tell you. It is not an easy job. For one thing, from month to month, children are constantly changing as they grow. And, although you can see evidence of their physical and intellectual development, you will find it almost impossible to discern all the changes in their emotional growth. Emotions are more subtle and less easy to know. Sometimes your child

will hide his feelings deliberately. Other times, without realizing it, he will subconsciously hide them from himself. You will need to train yourself to peer through this veil so you can recognize the half-hidden feelings revealed in a tone of voice, in a posture and in facial expression. How can you become good at this?

Observing and Listening to Your Child

This set of methods will sharpen your powers of observation, and help tune you in to him:

1. *Observing*
Once a day, merely observe your child. Watch what he is doing and ask yourself, "What is he feeling?" Once you've decided, don't do anything about it. Next ask yourself, "What is he thinking?" After determining this, ask yourself, "What does he think he's doing?"
Check Your Observations by Asking Once you've made your observations, check their accuracy by asking your child, "What are you feeling? . . . thinking? . . . doing?" Try to avoid opening with questions that suggest answers: "Are you feeling lonely?" "Are you making a paper airplane?" Suggest possible answers only after your child has drawn a complete blank. At first, he may not have anything to say. But in time he will develop the language to respond. And, because of your interest, he will feel especially good. Your reward will be in getting to know your child, in discovering who he is. This will put you in a better position to act as a knowledgeable and helpful person when the next problem comes up, as it surely will.
Another important way to know your child is to assure him that you're available to listen to anything he wants to tell you. Obviously, you won't always be available. Sometimes you will have to explain to him that other commitments mean you'll have to listen later. But this will not be a problem once your child has experienced the caring

behind your willingness to listen to him. The paramount thing is for your child to start out life knowing that you want to know how he feels and that he is important enough to be heard. In other words, "Little children should be seen and heard."

2. *Listening*

As an art, listening must follow a few simple rules. If you apply them patiently, you can become an effective listener. This is the way a psychotherapist listens to his patients: *Give Your Child Undivided Attention* Put aside the dress you are sewing or the newspaper you are reading. Even if only for a few minutes, concentrate on what he has to say, face to face. *Focus on His Feelings* Ask yourself, "What feeling is he trying to convey? What does he really want me to know about how he's feeling?" His words will give you some information. But you can learn his basic feelings from his tone and inflection of voice. HOW he says it will tell you what he's feeling. *Formulate His Problem in Your Own Words* Once or twice in the conversation, use your own words to try to express the problem as you think he has experienced it. "Now, let me see. I think you're trying to say that you feel . . . because . . ." *Show Him That You Understand His Feelings:* "I understand. I've felt that way myself." *Get Feedback* Check your understanding of what your child is saying by asking questions that will help verify what you "think" he's telling you. Practice these methods often. Let him do most of the talking while you listen.

One-to-One Time

Once you become a parent, there never will seem to be enough time for you to do all the things you think you should. The experience is a common one and it may cause you to feel guilty that you don't spend more time with your child. Quite often, you'll feel this way even though you probably spend many hours of each day working for his benefit. There is no need to feel guilty about the limits on your time. The thing to remember is that the quality of the time together is what counts, much more than the quantity. Time spent together with your child on a one-to-one basis without any distractions or competition will build a positive, lasting relationship. One-to-one time is the ultimate in parental attention. To your child, having your devoted and undivided attention is worth hours of competing for your recognition against other children and against all the other distractions in a busy household. Your child needs exclusive time with you and will benefit from the powerful message it conveys: "I care about you."

The Magic Meeting: Ten Minutes of One-to-One Time Every Day Try as best you can to give each child at least 10 minutes of one-to-one time every day. It won't always be easy but, even if you do it only four or five times a week, it will have a positive.effect on your relationship. In spending this time, you can play a game, read him a story or listen to him. Actually, the activity is less important than the fact that you are there with him. Parents often lose sight of what this means to a child. To him, the underlying issue is, "How are things going between you and me?" When you give him one-to-one time, he knows the answer is, "Fine!"
You should expect relatively little verbalization from a child under six. He will probably prefer to engage you more or less silently in an activity that interests him. You will find that 15- or 20-minute periods often are required because the younger child generally assimilates at a slower rate.
A word of caution. You may be tempted to use this time to confront your child about some misbehavior. If you yield to this temptation, you will put him in a difficult bind. He will want very much to spend the time with you but also will want to avoid the confrontation and unpleasantness that go with it. Although confrontations about misbehavior are necessary for your child's development, don't disguise them as one-to-one time. Instead, *keep this time with him free of criticism and controversy*. Let it be a time for you and your child to be together here and now, sharing your experiences and concerns, your needs and hopes. It is a time

to show your child that you're genuinely interested in his concerns in an intimate and private way. *The content should be only affirmative, your attitude always supportive.* If for some reason you can't spend this time with your child on a daily basis, you might consider spending three or four hours with him once or twice a month. Be sure to plan this time together in advance. Be especially sure it's planned around some activity your child enjoys, one that is relatively pleasant for you, too. You needn't become upset if a brother or a sister makes a jealous fuss. Simply say, "Your turn is next." Do not confuse One-to-One Time with togetherness. Two people separately doing the same thing—such as going to a movie—are practicing togetherness. But it does not, cannot, give the Magic Meeting's deeply implied messages: "I care about you." "I am available to you with all my attention." "Nothing is more important to me than you and your concern." "My interest in you is warm, positive, personal." *Just listen completely nondefensively to all his bragging and complaining.*

The Philosophy of Confrontation with Support, the C/S Method

If a quarter of a century of clinical practice has yielded one consistently effective method of dealing with young children, it is the concept of always confronting the negative with an even-larger measure of loving support.
Confrontation is a general term for challenge or criticism or any other kind of complaint that produces some negative feelings. Loving support supplies good feeling. The combination of Confrontation-with-Support has been found to be the most civilized way of combining the challenge with the security that every child needs. It is like the trellis upon which the vine can grow.
By using this approach, you will assure your child's maturation and also you can be certain that a good mutual relationship will develop.
If your child receives only support, he will

inevitably remain weak and spoiled, self-centered and incompetent.
If your child receives only challenge, and possesses an active temperament, then he will inevitably become rebellious and act out his resentment.
If your child receives only challenge, and possesses a passive temperament, then he will inevitably become crushed.
The C/S method must not be confused with the Magic Meeting because, in the Magic Meeting, for 10 minutes you will never be anything but totally supportive.
The philosophy of the C/S method may be stated as, "Although I am calling your attention to this disagreeable matter, I want you to know that I have good feelings about you. I care about you and want you to do well. You are the smaller person, the less experienced and less developed one. I understand this and will not hold it against you. But there is a problem, one which is producing bad feelings in you or in someone else. Your behavior is immature and it's causing this problem." When this approach is used consistently with your child, he will not be prone to see you as his "enemy." He will experience you as his friend and supporter, no matter how much he may complain at the surface. You cannot use this method too often.

Your Five Basic Methods for Fostering Emotional Maturity

Because these methods interrelate with one another, they are presented here in a diagram that graphically illustrates this easily comprehended program. Listening to your child's feelings is step one, because his feelings (step two) are your most important clues to understanding him. Understanding his feelings will almost inevitably reveal the basic issue or concern. This points the way to the third step: a constructive action plan that is mutually agreeable to both you and your child. The core of the positive action plan will usually be the application of a combination of confrontation with support (step four). The fifth step in the sequence involves giving one-to-one time, which improves the positive bond with your child and opens up his concerns in such a way that you automatically return to the first step—listening to his feelings. By studying the diagram for a few minutes you will quickly see how the basic steps, or methods, unify the process of simultaneously building your child's maturity as well as a strong, positive relationship with you.

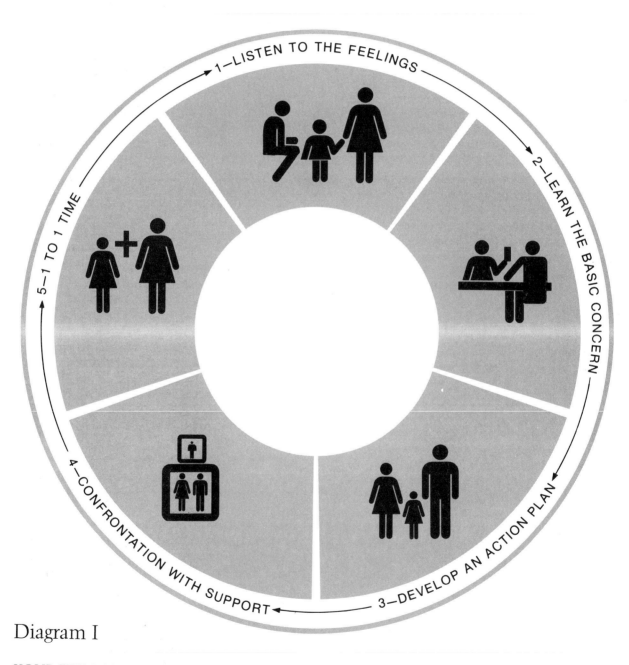

Diagram I

YOUR FIVE BASIC METHODS FOR FOSTERING EMOTIONAL MATURITY AND BUILDING A STRONG POSITIVE RELATIONSHIP AT THE SAME TIME.

*Your Five Basic Methods For Fostering
Emotional Maturity And Building A Strong
Positive Relationship At The Same Time*

1. *Listen To The Feelings*

   When you listen to your child, listen
   behind the words to the feeling. Words
   can mislead, but feelings seldom do. Ask
   yourself and your child if there is sadness,
   or desire, or frustration. This will give you
   important information essential for
   understanding your child.

2. *Get An Accurate Understanding Of The
   Basic Concern*

   Your child's feelings will lead you and
   him to the basic concern. He will then
   know that you understand what the issue
   is, and he will experience you as being
   with him and for him.

3. *Together Develop An Action Plan To
   Deal With The Basic Concern*

   An agreed upon plan has the best chance
   of working. Every action plan is based
   upon giving a fairly well defined
   combination of confrontation and
   support, varying according to the
   specific need.

4. *Apply The Confrontation With
   Support Formula*

   The formula: Emotional Maturity is
   roughly equal to N (C/S), where N is the
   number of times, C is confrontation and S
   is support. As this method is used it is
   inevitable that your child's emotional
   maturity will increase. So will the
   strength of his positive relationship
   with you.

5. *One-To-One Time Is Your Guarantee Of
   Good Results*

   Every one-to-one time session builds the
   conviction in your child that you care. It
   convinces him that you have his best
   interest at heart. It is the best rapport-
   builder known. It is always 100%
   supportive. If your child knows in
   advance that he will get your time, and if

he knows when, it will be the most
effective. The focal interest must be
either your child's concern or your child's
interest. Personal involvement is best.
Being together during a passive-consuming
activity is the least beneficial.

"What Did You Really Mean When You Said That?"

Communication is, at best, a difficult art. A
child's inexperience, impatience and lack of
vocabulary frustrate parental efforts to
communicate with him. You too may feel
some limitations in your ability to
communicate to him how you feel.
In the beginning, you should expect many
missed messages and miscommunications.
Your child frequently will say something
that means one thing to him and another
thing to you. Before he learns the necessary
language, you nevertheless can manage to
communicate effectively if you keep in mind
several things that are universal in children.
Take the issue of "needless" questions: the
child who asks for a drink of water when
obviously he isn't thirsty. What does such a
demand really mean? The safest
assumption—even though it may be an
educated guess—is that the child needs and
wants attention. Yet many parents will tell
you, "Don't give him any notice. He only
wants some attention." They fail to
recognize this is a legitimate need, just as
important to a child as food and drink. The
"needless" question, then, is a clue that your
child probably needs attention.
Next, try to keep in mind that most of your
child's communications have to do with
letting you know something he wants or
fears. Here, you want to learn what his basic
need is. For example, your child may ask to
use a hammer or electric saw. If you focus
your concern on the hammer or saw, you
may be missing his basic desire. What he
really feels may be just the urge to build
something with his hands. This underlying
need is important to know and recognize
because it can help you meet your child's
essential needs in a safer way. You may not
want him to use the hammer or saw for fear

he'll hurt himself. But knowing he wants to build something gives you options in the situation. While refusing the use of the tools he's asked for, you still can meet the same need in a safer way. In the process, you keep your communications and relationship with him positive.

Communicate About Feelings

Most of us never learned very much about describing our feelings. Largely our talk is about what we think and do. Yet our feelings are essential and affect every communication we attempt. Here are some phrases that will help you and your child talk with greater accuracy about feelings:

"How are you *feeling*?"

"Do you *want* me to listen to you?"

"Is there anything you *need*?"

When you are having difficulty understanding what your child is trying to tell you, it's always a good idea to find out how he is feeling. As early as age two, your child with only a little help will be able to let you know whether he's feeling good or bad. The way to help him is to ask a few times each day, "Are you feeling good or bad?" At first expect uncertainty or confusion; however, over a period of weeks, you will find that your child will very quickly and easily be able to answer you correctly. Knowing how he feels will help you discern what his basic need or concern is. So ask him often.

Another thing to keep in mind is that you cannot have good communication or a good relationship with your child unless he understands and takes into account that you have feelings, too. Since you are important to him, your feelings are important to him. They are a contributing factor to the way he functions. Instead of trying to be diplomatic and hide your feelings, tell him candidly how you feel. His understanding will surprise you if you give him a chance.

Routinely Let Your Child Know How You're Feeling

On a regular basis, use such expressions as:

"I'm feeling tired right now."

"You make me feel angry when you do that."

"That noise is making me nervous."

"I'm glad you're helping with the yard work."

Being in tune with one another's feelings brings people closer together and greatly reduces the chances for miscommunication and misunderstanding. Consequently, when you tell your child something you want or need, let him know which of your feelings is prompting the request:

"I want you to stay out of the street. It scares me to think you might be hit by a car. I can relax if you play in the yard."

"You have the TV turned up too high. It's giving me a headache. You'll make me feel better by turning down the sound."

Incessant Demands

Children literally will bombard you, sometimes legitimately and sometimes not, with a barrage of requests and demands for food, drink, toys, entertainment and information. And they'll want it all "right now." Needless to say, you can't dance to this never-ending tune. Even if you wanted to, you wouldn't have the emotional or physical stamina to keep up with the demands.

Under this stress, parents often react in one of two ways. One kind of parent feels compelled to grant every wish. The other refuses to grant any demand unless it is directly and obviously related to some immediate physical need. In either case, there are potential dangers.

Indiscriminately giving children everything they want simply creates more demands that will leave parents exhausted and bitter. At the same time, the children gain nothing. They end up with a set of expectations about life that is distorted and doomed to disappointment.

On the other hand, parents who consistently refuse to grant any request run a different risk. There is the possibility that their child will think he is being denied because of being "unworthy."

Fortunately, there is a way to protect your child's self-worth without granting every wish. When you refuse him, tell him the reason why. When he asks you to find his socks while you're in the bathtub, say, "I'm sorry. I'd like to help you but I'm taking a bath now. This is a bad time for me." Refused in this positive, honest way, he can take the rejection without losing his sense of personal worth.

Children's demands also represent an attempt on their part to find out what the limits are to getting what they want. While trying to find their limits, they also are testing yours. They are trying to learn how much power they can exert over you, how much they can get from you before you resist. This is seldom malicious. It's more likely to be part of the natural growth necessary for their development. Once you catch on that many of the demands are actually a form of reality-testing, you can begin to deal with each demand and request on its own merits without feeling threatened or guilty.

Make Only Realistic Commitments to Your Child Never accede to unfair demands or threats. Agree when the request is in the best interest of both you and your child. Give a definite time when his request will be granted.

Promise Only What You Are Sure You Can and Will Deliver If later you cannot keep a promise you've made, explain why. Then tell him when you'll be able to do it. If you disappoint your child often, he won't trust you. Most of all, your child will learn from your example that commitments are not important enough to keep. This kind of experience can be seen as a free ticket to irresponsibility. And there is an even deeper implication: Children can feel secure about themselves, life and their relationship with you only if they know they can count on you. Your promises are part of that security. If disappointed too often, your child will feel anxious, uncertain and insecure about everything.

Parents are Human, Too

As parents, we would like to do more for our children than we possibly can; consequently, we are apt to expect more of ourselves than we possibly can deliver. This is a common mistake. In the process, we leave ourselves emotionally exhausted and feeling guilty because we can't conform to some improbable, idealized notion of what we "should" be doing for our children. Avoid this kind of self-torture. There is no need to feel guilty or inadequate simply because you can't provide your child with every advantage imaginable. Your limits are very real. You get tired and hungry. You feel uncertain and dejected just like everyone else. To expect yourself to transcend your limits is unrealistic and can only leave you feeling frustrated, guilty and disillusioned. In self-defense, you're entitled to make an honest assessment of your talents and capabilities for being a parent. Once you do, you can set about developing more-realistic expectations for yourself as a parent:

Accept Your Limits Children ordinarily attribute godlike qualities to their parents—a reason why they seem to expect so much from us. But as a parent you are not perfect, inexhaustible, omnipotent nor all-knowing. So try to know your limits and live within them. You will save yourself needless guilt and anguish.

You might share with your child some of your well-intentioned self-expectations that fall short. This is one of the best possible ways for him to learn that you are human, too. As you talk to your child, be sure not to burden him with problems that are beyond his understanding or that will cause him to worry. The more emotionally mature he becomes, the more you can safely share.

Establish Realistic Expectations for Yourself as a Parent As a parent, you need to develop a set of possible guidelines and expectations for yourself. These should define what you can and cannot do in terms of time and effort to further your child's maturity. Both you and your spouse should discuss and decide upon these goals together. Let your promises to your child come from realistic guidelines rather than the wish to be and do everything for him.

You Too Are Still Growing Do not forget that growing up emotionally can and should continue into and throughout adulthood.

Every time your efforts achieve further maturity in your child, you should realize you too become a more-competent and mature adult.

The Fast-Time Imperative

Every parent is plagued with doubts about his adequacy for the role. As a result, you are a setup for the Fast-time Imperative. This is a compulsion for quick proof that you're doing a good parental job. But Emotional Maturity does not happen overnight. You must remember this process takes many years and requires literally thousands of experiences. For parents, there are no shortcuts or panaceas. There is only the difficult day-in-and-day-out job of giving your child positive emotional inputs: specific acts of encouragement, support, affection and confrontation. As he experiences these positive inputs, Nature will begin to take its course. Slowly but surely, your child will start to show signs of maturity. In the beginning there may be nothing spectacular. Maybe he'll surprise you by making his bed or by playing peacemaker to siblings about to fight; and so on, little by little. By letting go of the need for quick results, you will feel less anxious about your dealings with your child. This easing of tension will make him feel more secure that things are all right between you.

The Enemy Trap

Pain is your child's enemy. And so is anything or anyone associated with it. That's the rub: In your child's mind, you are often the cause of his pain. You're the one who tells him that he can't skateboard in the street and that he has to go to bed when he doesn't want to. Every day you interfere with his desires, as quite often you must. He does not see the danger of climbing roofs. All he sees is the fun. You and your warning are resented.
The result can be the Enemy Trap.
Frustrated at not having what he wants, your child looks around for something or someone to blame for the way he feels.

Because you are the one who denied his wish, you must be the cause of his pain and frustration. In his view, you become the "enemy." It makes no difference that you may have saved him from a serious accident. He's too inexperienced and too close to the way he feels to understand your motives. It's ironic: Even as you protect your child, he comes to regard you as his personal enemy. Whenever he tries to deal with his pain and frustration by making you the cause, you should deny any liability. The truth is that all of us must sustain pain and frustrated desires in order to grow up. It's no one's fault. You are merely a guide, an information-giver to your child. He needs to understand that you do not create the rules of life.

In the beginning, you can avoid the Enemy Trap by letting your child know that, when you deny him something he wants, you are trying to help him avoid getting hurt. You can do this by telling him:

"I can't let you play ball in the street because I don't want you to be hit by a car."
"I'm sorry but I can't let you climb that tree. You can easily fall off and hurt yourself."

Here, keep two points in mind: First, if you put too much stress on the dangers involved, you can give your child a fixation about danger and pain, an irrational fear or concern even about crossing the street. You easily will be able to tell if he begins to overreact to your warnings. You should then slack off. Secondly, the most important part of your explanation is the way you do it. It should be done in a calm, reassuring manner. The tone of your voice should show your child that you care. As he senses that you are denying him because you care about him, he eventually will recognize you for the friend and helper you are.

The Enemy Trap also can occur later on when your child is confronted with the pain and discomfort associated with developing patience, self-control, consideration and other traits of maturity. Because you're the one who keeps insisting that he work at these things, once again you can be misread as the villain. Be prepared.

"Here, Let Me Do That for You . . ."

Every parent worries about his child's competence. We tend to fret over many things—his handwriting, his table manners, the sloppy way he keeps his room, even his batting average as an eight-year-old. Somehow we're afraid that, if we're not careful, he won't learn what he needs to get a good job or to cope with life's problems. All of our concern is normal but of itself can create more problems.

This can happen when, out of anxiety, we step in to offer solutions which the child should arrive at himself. Watching him do a puzzle, for example, can be an excruciating experience. Every time he can't fit a piece, you'll be sorely tempted to show him where it goes. But focusing on his struggle and faltering efforts may cause you to miss the main point. His struggle is his way of trying to demonstrate to himself that he is becoming more competent and better able to solve problems. Quite often, this need for self-assertion is subconscious and therefore not apparent to either of you. But it is a safe assumption that your child is always concerned to some extent about how well he can cope with problem situations.

As he struggles with the puzzle, he is exercising a healthy assertiveness that shows his drive to become self-sufficient. Whenever you intervene to solve the problem for him, you deprive him of a chance to improve his self-image. If this happens often, your intervention may convey the negative message, "You're incompetent. You'll never be able to become self-sufficient or solve problems by yourself." It's your job to fight off the temptation to intervene, however strong.

Although it is best to let your child try to solve the problem with his own resources, he may feel deserted if you carry this to the opposite extreme and never help him at all. You can prevent this from happening by making it clear to him that you are available to help if and when he exhausts his ability. In this way, you can provide him with the best of both worlds—the chance to prove himself and the help he needs when he absolutely requires it.

Becoming Process-Oriented

Another developmental issue related to competence is the often-excessive concern many parents have about the results achieved by their children. All of us want our children to do well, to succeed at whatever they undertake. Yet, to focus merely upon the results of their efforts is to miss something else that is perhaps even more important. We overlook the process by which a child solves a problem.

You will want to teach your child HOW to tackle problems and bring them to a resolution. In the beginning, the actual results are not so important. Notice the methods he characteristically uses when working or wrestling with a dilemma. Ask yourself if he gathers all the facts and tools he needs, makes a plan, is careful or untidy. Does he anticipate and prepare for foul-ups and such eventualities? Instead of scolding him when he fails because of using an ineffective method, ask him if he would like to be shown another way to do it, a way he might prefer. If he's agreeable, teach him how.

Freeing Your Child to Become Your Friend

Perhaps the most common personal problem that plagues parents is the Silver-cord Complex. Probably every parent is affected by it to some extent. This complex explains the resentment parents feel toward a child trying to function independently of them. It is a mixture of martyrdom and extreme possessiveness: "I've given all of myself to you. I've sacrificed my life for your benefit. And now you're neglecting me."

It's normal to expect some kind of reward for your efforts as a parent. There's nothing wrong in wanting your child's respect and appreciation for all you've done for him. It's natural to worry about whether he notices and appreciates your efforts on his behalf. But it's not normal to expect, as some parents do, that your child should repay you by remaining completely dependent upon you and your judgment. ["I gave you all my attention and I expect you to give it all back."]

Parents who live entirely for a child expect him to supply all their happiness and fulfillment in return. This is more than any child should be obliged to provide. These parents neglect themselves and, later on, suffer for it. You can avoid that pitfall by developing interests other than your child. You need outside interests, time by yourself and for yourself, if you are to be a fulfilled person. Community activities, a hobby, continued education—these are just a few pursuits that can make it easier to free your child so he can become his own person. You will also liberate yourself from your own unreasonable dependency upon him. If your child grows up emotionally mature, inevitably he will appreciate and respect you. You can be sure of his lifelong friendship; you will be able to count on a reasonable amount of attention. But this attention will be prompted by feelings of love, not of guilt.

Passing on Your Values

One of the matters that worries parents and causes many conflicts and tensions is the question of values: "Is my child adopting my values and being true to them?" All parents have sets of values they subscribe to, try to follow and want to pass on to their children: a religious belief, a personal philosophy or simply a kind of folk-wisdom derived from life-experience. Because a child is subject to so many other influences—school, peers and television—many parents think they've lost control.

You have more influence than you think. Because you are the first and closest adult your child relates to, you become his model and often his ideal. You are the one he imitates. You have no choice in the matter. He learns how to behave by imitating your behavior. At this very moment, your child is subconsciously copying you.

What You Are, He Will Tend to Become

For some parents, this may be ominous news. For others, it will be reassuring. Long before—and even after—your child is exposed to outside influences, you are his chief influence. Every interaction you have with him teaches him how to feel and behave. If you genuinely want your child to be considerate, you yourself must be considerate. If you want him to keep commitments, you must keep yours—especially the ones you make to him. Telling or commanding him is not enough. Nor can you ever expect results by directing him to "Do as I say, not as I do." Like it or not, the way you are—how you act toward your child—is the most likely way he will turn out.

II   Your Child's Emotional Needs

Factors That Influence Your Child

Your child is the product of two powerful forces, his genes and his environment. How these two factors interact, especially when your child is very young, determines the kind of person he will become. It's not necessary here to resolve the question as to which of the factors is more compelling. Philosophers, theologians, social scientists and psychologists have debated that question for centuries. And the debate is likely to continue for some time to come. As a parent, the essential thing for you to recognize is the significant roles which *both* your child's genetic background and his environment play in his emotional development.

Most of us readily recognize our child's physical endowment. His height, weight, body build, eye and hair color are the most-obvious genetic effects and the ones we first notice. Do you remember the first time you held your infant daughter and compared features? "She has my brown eyes and your nose and ears, Heaven help her." Later, we recognize the temperamental heritage. "You're stubborn like your father." "He's easygoing like Dad." "She's vivacious like her mother." We hardly need any prompting to notice these similarities. But there are other inherited tendencies that are less perceptible. In addition to physique and temperament, our children also inherit predispositions to physical strength, intelligence, special talents and a vulnerability to certain diseases.

Parents often assume that a child born with certain characteristics will always be the same. This is not necessarily true. Your child's experiences will influence his inborn characteristics. For example, weight and physical development can be influenced by diet. A consistently calm living environment can quiet the behavior of a hyperactive child, just as a chaotic, noisy environment can overstimulate an average child.

Another related issue is the fact that none of us really knows what our children's genetic possibilities are. Modern science hasn't yet given us the tools to measure most of these potentials. When it has, as in the case of the I.Q. test, the results often have been controversial. As a result, most of us too often guess about our child's interests and talents. Overly optimistic, ego-involved parents expect too much. Negative, pessimistic parents never expect enough. Meanwhile, vibrant possibilities lie within every normal child, waiting to be developed. How do they become developed? That is the essential question. The answer lies in the interaction between experience and genes. Although you can't change your child's genetic make-up, by and large you can control—or at least strongly influence—his environment and many of his daily experiences. Your task, then, is to manage your child's environment and experience so he can become the person Nature prepared him to be.

Love and Affection

Your child's most important emotional need is for love and affection. He needs these more than anything else. Most parents know this instinctively, but many parents have difficulty showing how they feel. Some believe that it's wrong or inadvisable to display affection. Others assume the child already knows how they feel and that showing him isn't necessary. Nothing could be farther from the truth. Your child needs to be told and shown that you love him. On this issue, there is no such thing as benign neglect. If your child doesn't experience your affection directly, he could conclude that he must be unlovable. Once this happens, the door to his development begins to close.

The most impressive way to demonstrate your love is by natural and spontaneous physical contact—the hug, embrace, pat on the back or silent holding. Being held or touched affectionately delivers four vital messages to your child simultaneously: "I notice you, include you, endorse you and, most of all, love you." In this way, your loving embrace gives your child's self-image a powerful boost.

Another way to show your child you care is by your interest. All it costs is a little time to listen. Each evening, ask your child to tell you how the day went, and then listen to what he has to say. Pay particular attention to the emotional concerns that underlie what he says, revealed by his tone of voice. Once he's certain you're really interested, he'll begin to tell you what went well and what didn't; his dreams and wishes; things he'd like to have; what he's looking forward to and what he's dreading. It isn't necessary to get into involved discussions or to solve problems at that time. Just let him tell you what he's feeling and experiencing. The fact that you're interested and willing to listen will make him feel better about the day, and especially about himself.

Emotional Nourishment

Every child needs to feel wanted. Knowing you want him gives your child a basic feeling of security. It tells him that everything is all right and, most of all, that you care enough to consider anything that does go wrong and to try to make it right again.

From his earliest years, your child will sense how you feel toward him. You will not be able to convince him for very long that he is wanted more than he really is. Because he can't read your mind, he'll focus on what you do. If you give him attention when he needs it, accept him when he fails and are generous with your affection, he'll feel genuinely wanted. But if you rarely listen to him, scold him constantly for his mistakes and rarely display any affection, nothing you say will convince him that he is wanted.

Obviously, not all your feelings about your child can be positive. Children are demanding, frustrating and often unable to show their gratitude. They can be a nuisance. They are always a responsibility. And they can cause you endless worry. It's inevitable, then, that at times you will become angry and tired. Sometimes you'll experience what every parent occasionally feels—the urge to give the baby back. These feelings are entirely normal. Go easy on yourself. You will not be able to give your child the acceptance he needs unless you first accept yourself. The earlier you accept your limitations, the better.

Your child may resent you for not giving him everything he wants. But that phase will pass as he grows older. As long as he knows he is wanted, he gradually will become more forgiving and understanding. The essential thing is for you to demonstrate—and for him to know—that you care.

Positive Experience

For many children, childhood is a mixed blessing, a time of carefree fun and newfound discovery but also a period filled with feelings of uncertainty, helplessness, fear and vulnerability to pain. This is more than enough for any child to have to cope with. Many, raised by misguided parents who try to force maturation, sustain a long series of negative experiences.

With the best of intentions, these parents stifle their child's natural interests and possibilities. Instead of nurturing his genetic potential, they bury it beneath criticism, anger, scoldings and physical punishment. When the child expresses his honest anger, he's called "bad." When he resists some of the impersonal demands of the school system, he's told he's "incorrigible." When he shows a natural curiosity about sex, he's accused of having "a dirty mind." All this criticism, salted with anger and sarcasm, damages the child emotionally. His inborn potential seldom emerges past the scars.

Your child needs positive experiences to help him achieve his potential. In short, he becomes what he lives. If he experiences love, he'll feel worthy. If he receives encouragement, he'll do the things necessary to feel capable. If he is rejected, he'll feel worthless. If he encounters continual criticism, he'll feel inadequate and negative. Your role is crucial. How he feels about you and how he thinks you feel about him will have a telling effect on the kind of person he becomes. Basically, he's concerned about two things: his worthiness to be loved and whether he'll ever be capable to meet his own needs. Everything you do or say to him should take these fears into consideration. He needs frequent affirmation of his self-worth and adequacy.

Being affirmative is the key. This means, first of all, avoiding excessive criticism, sarcasm, physical beatings and anything else that lessens your child's belief in himself. It also means helping your child learn positive ways to deal with his everyday problems. In the development chapters that follow in Part II (pages 45-197), you will find specific suggestions on how to deal positively with a wide range of difficult situations. By identifying each developmental issue as it occurs and by following the suggested methods, you can teach your child how to deal with the common problems he's bound to meet. Then he can face the uncertainties of life and still feel good about you, himself and his own prospects for success.

Protection

Helplessness is your child's first emotional experience and, as such, it marks him indelibly for life. Suddenly, he finds himself outside his mother in a new, unknown environment, where he is utterly dependent on others for his most elementary needs. To a large extent, growing up means becoming more powerful and self-sufficient enough to meet his own needs. In the meantime, he needs protection against his basic helplessness.

For most parents, the physical dangers in the environment are quite apparent. We set up gates to keep the child from falling downstairs, strap him into a high chair and build fences to prevent him from wandering into the traffic. Later, when we're sure he can recognize physical dangers, we're willing to let him out on his own.

But your child also faces serious emotional perils that are often less obvious. These dangers feed on his sense of helplessness and tend to stunt his development. For example: finding a friend, taking on a challenge or telling the truth—all of these issues have emotional dangers your child must risk. Will he be rejected? Will he fail? Will he be punished for telling the truth? Parents quite frequently overlook these fears that are very real to the child. Because he feels helpless to begin with, he may try to avoid challenges entirely. In the process, he misses the chance to grow.

Your role here is to provide the emotional support and protection he needs in order to meet these challenges. Keep in mind that the chief threat to your child's emotional well-being lies in his experiencing too much failure.

Security

Security is the feeling that comes from knowing you are accepted and valued for being who you are and not for what you do. This is the kind of foundation your child requires in order to function effectively in the face of his own mistakes and inadequacies. He needs desperately to know that you will accept and love him even if he doesn't bring home a perfect report card or make the school team. Since he starts out being uncomfortably aware of his own shortcomings, only through the security of your acceptance will he develop the courage to overcome them. If you don't demonstrate acceptance, he will become tentative and negative, fearful and chronically insecure.

Self-Determination—Being Your Own Person

"When I was a boy, I always wanted to play the piano. I never got the chance. But you, my son, can and will play the piano [whether you want to or not]."
Every child needs to discover his own natural interests and abilities. This is an elementary step toward a satisfying career, a fruitful life. Yet many times a child is thwarted by his parents' projections of their own childhood deprivations and injustices. This is common. Many of us do it: "My kid will have all the power, success and social recognition I never had and always wanted."
If you indulge in this kind of thinking, your basic assumptions are that your child is an exact copy of you with identical tendencies and talents, and that times never change. None of these assumptions is true. Your intervention, however well intentioned, can lead only to a bad relationship. Even if he acquiesces, he is bound to rebel inwardly. Moreover, there's a certain disrespect involved in forcing a child into an activity for which he has little inclination. You will be wise to assume that your child has a real urge to become independent and a fiercer desire to be his own person. As he becomes more powerful and competent, he will want a greater role in making the decisions about his own life. Instinctively, he knows that his own personal bent is a reasonable expression of his inborn talents and strengths.
There are three things you can do to help him:

Accept him as he is. Each child should be recognized for his own unique abilities and for his individual way of seeing the world.

Help your child discover his true talents and interests. They may surprise and delight you.

Allow him the freedom to choose what he likes and does best; also give him all the backup support necessary.

Belief in His Potential

No matter how much your child may try to bluff you and others, you can safely assume he has severe self-doubts about his social acceptability and his adequacy. There's no mystery about this. He simply hasn't yet had enough experience to develop much sense of self-worth and capability. For every child, this is a tender, delicate issue which leaves him vulnerable to rejection and criticism. He easily can be made to feel worthless or incompetent if overly reminded of his failures or shortcomings.
Look back for a moment. Do you recall how you felt when someone powerful gave a lift to your hopes with an encouraging word? You can do the same thing for your child, and never too often.

Guidance and Consultation

In a very real way, your child is a stranger in a new land. Many of his difficulties are caused by a simple lack of information. In his eyes, you are an exalted person, experienced and unquestionably wiser. In his early years, he will assume you know everything. In adolescence, he'll be inclined to assume you know nothing. In the interim, there's a great deal you can teach him.
Giving advice to a child requires a sensitivity to his high degree of vulnerability. When your child comes to you for counsel, treat him as you would an adult by showing respect for his feelings and his view of the problem. "I know how you feel and, if you think this is important, then it is.
And I believe there may be a way we can solve it . . ."
Your life experience is a valuable legacy for your child; however, it's important not to impose your solution or point of view. Just be ready to provide advice on request, and your child will be more inclined to turn to you for help when he needs it.
If you can't help, simply admit it. Your child will appreciate your frankness and humility.

Challenge

Just as he must exercise his muscles through bodily activities, your child needs to form the habit of meeting challenges so he can mature emotionally. Invariably, this means learning how to face and cope with the trying and unpleasant things in life. For example, he may be put off by the amount of effort involved in obtaining something through his own exertions even though it's something he wants very much. Left to his own devices, he'll usually take the easy way He will resist gaining the knowledge and skills he needs. Nor is he apt to acquire self-control unless you require him to. He can be counted on to avoid unpleasantness wherever it occurs.

Your child, therefore, needs to be deliberately challenged. And you are the challenger. You frequently need to show him your expectations and to exact performance. The stakes are high. If you let your child slide by, if you let him fail life's emotional challenges by default, he'll be condemned to a difficult life. Undoubtedly, as you challenge him to perform, he'll regard you as a nag and a grumble. But this static is a small price. Accept it as any experienced teacher might. If you take his complaints good-naturedly, even with a bit of humor, you'll smooth the way ahead.

The most effective strategy is to draw your child into this effort as an active participant. Explain to him in simple terms that you are trying to equip him with good emotional habits, with the kind of understanding and self-discipline that are essential to having a rewarding life. Emphasize that you cannot and will not neglect this vital phase of his development. At the same time, admit that you understand how difficult it seems to him.

As at every milestone along the path of his route to maturity, he needs your support, recognition and praise as he makes the effort to face challenges. As you guide him, he will realize that the hard choices and the unpleasantness that you urge him to take on are important concerns for you as well.

Freedom

Freedom is the elbow room your child needs in order to learn how to function by himself. It enables him to explore new territory, learn new information and, most of all, become responsible. But many parents hesitate to permit their child much freedom because of the risks involved. Ironically, the risks in not giving a child enough freedom are even more formidable. An overprotected child never learns to handle difficult situations or become a responsible person.

How, then, can you strike a balance between overprotection and unreasonable risk? Use this simple rule of thumb: The more responsibility your child shows, the more freedom you can grant him. In this way, he serves as his own measuring gauge for allowable freedom, instead of being compared to other children on the basis of age or some even less valid standard. Once you grant him extra freedom, evaluate how he uses it. Is he reliable and cautious? Does he use his freedom well to accomplish the task or meet a challenge? Does he make a serious effort?

The key here is how well he keeps his commitments. Whenever you relax old rules and let him move ahead by himself, it is best to extract a promise. If you let him leave the home turf, he gives his word not to play ball in the streets or wander over by the railroad tracks. The commitment should be specific. This is how he gradually becomes more trustworthy—by making commitments and being free to prove he can meet them.

This process won't always be easy. Apart from the dangers and risks involved, your child may very well balk at commitments. Like many adults, he may want to escalate his freedom without making any commitment, and may complain bitterly when he can't have things both ways. It's a ploy to make you feel guilty. If you succumb, he eventually will finagle himself into some kind of trouble. Be firm. Later, he'll thank you for it. And all along he'll know how much you care for him.

Limits

From his earliest days, your child experiences himself as the center of the universe. He thinks the world revolves around him. When it obviously doesn't, he nevertheless believes it should. If he prefers to play with his brother's toys, he takes them without permission. If he wants a long walk, it doesn't occur to him that you might be worried by not knowing where he is. Eventually this attitude gets him into trouble. The child learns his limits by making mistakes.

To reduce the number and severity of these mistakes, explore with your child the possible consequences of his behavior. It is best done in advance, whenever he confides what he wants to do or asks for advice. Also it can be done after the fact to review some of the consequences he didn't anticipate. The procedure is simple. Sit down with your child and calmly discuss cause and effect. "Have you considered how Mother feels when she doesn't know where you are and what may be happening to you?" This kind of tactful inquiry will help your child to a better grasp of reality. The bonus is that this will inevitably lead to an open-minded attitude about alternatives he can use to avoid the trouble he otherwise might run into or create.

Most of the time your child will be grateful to you for helping him stay clear of difficulties when you point out some limitation he wasn't aware of. But sometimes he won't appreciate your information nor will it deter him from doing precisely what he wants. At such times, lay down your rules. Seeing you seriously determined to enforce them will persuade him to accept the fact that no one can have everything he wants.

At the same time, be aware that parental control most commonly breaks down when rules either are insufficiently defined or inconsistently enforced. The secret of helping your child accept reality is to define the limits in advance and enforce them consistently.

Respect

"respect, *v.t.* 1. To consider worthy of esteem."—*Webster's Dictionary*. Your child needs your respect and the considerate treatment that goes with it if he is to form a positive self-image. As we have noted, his feelings can be hurt easily because he's so unsure of himself. Any slight tends to magnify and confirm his worst fears about himself.

This would be only a minor problem if slights to children were uncommon. Unfortunately, the opposite is true. In our culture, children have been thought less important and less significant than adults and adult concerns. The popular old adage, "Children should be seen and not heard," reflects this view, implying children are not worth the consideration accorded adults. The child, already handicapped by size, inexperience and his own self-doubts, is further disadvantaged by being given second-class regard. Such treatment only can intensify his self-doubt and retard emotional development.

Try to give your child the same kind of consideration you reserve for adults or expect for yourself. Whenever practical, avoid interrupting a conversation with your child because an adult wants your attention. Never make your child wait longer for something than you reasonably would expect an adult to wait. The basic concept here is to accord your child the same consideration you would give any worthwhile person. The all-important underlying implication says to your child, "You rate respectful treatment because you are worthy."

Assurance against the Fear of Abandonment

Every child has an innate fear of being abandoned. You well know the symptoms. You're leaving for a movie with friends, and there's a scene at the front door as your child clings to you, wildly screaming and pleading because you're going away without him. Nothing you say can console him. Often you feel so guilty and upset that it's almost not worth going out. If you go, you have a hard time enjoying yourself.

You understand that the odds on your not having an accident or dropping dead are overwhelmingly in your favor. But your child doesn't know this. Because this fear that you won't come back touches his instinct for survival—for, in his view, he can't survive without you—the reaction is vehement and sometimes uncontrollable. The thought that you actually are going forever can become a terrifying obsession. Help your child cope with this basic fear. First, condition him to your goings and comings. Let him know in advance—factually, without excuses—where you're going and for how long and when he can expect to see you back.

Parents sometimes give in to their child's pleadings to stay but generally this isn't wise. At best it provides only temporary relief and defers the development of his tolerance to separations. In the beginning, it's best to have very brief separations. Avoid leaving on prolonged vacations and trips until he's mature enough to endure a long parting. Providing a baby-sitter who likes spending time with children will ease the wrench. Quite often the cries of anguish you hear at the door quickly turn into laughter and fun once you're gone.

A related issue is your being late. Here again, the child tends to think he's being abandoned or that there's been some other calamity. Whenever you're going to be late, let him know if you can. Eventually you can prepare your child to expect occasional tardiness. When he's about five, explain to him that there are times when you may be delayed and that he should expect this to happen. Give him some examples of situations that are apt to delay you so he'll be less inclined to think the ultimate catastrophe has occurred when you are late. This is a two-way street. In later years, you'll be the one at home worrying. If you give him

your consideration now, there's a better chance he'll give you his later.

In your daily conversations encourage open expression of his deeper concerns. Once in a while you may ask, "Do you ever worry about somebody in our family dying? Or going away for a long time? Or getting a divorce?" When he's willing to respond, you can discuss the extreme kinds of separation that come from death and divorce. Open discussions and the invitation to talk to you about these fears whenever he feels the need will go a long way toward reducing his anxieties.

A Sense of Humor

A healthy sense of humor will help your child survive the uncertainties and tensions of life. Humor is perceived discrepancy. It shows us the intention that backfired, the failure snatched from the jaws of success, the wrong thing said at the right time. Most of all, it shows us that everyone is fallible. Since no one feels more fallible nor takes his failures more seriously than a child, he can use a hearty laugh and he can profit from learning to laugh at himself.

Humor is the saving grace in human relations. It eases tension and relieves resentment. In its best sense, it's a form of truth-saying that tells us our soaring aspirations have been grounded due to clay feet or that our pretensions have just been exposed by our limitations. As such, it penetrates the wall of earnest seriousness we erect about ourselves and reminds us how human we are. Our laughter then becomes a proclamation of freedom that purges us of the heavy burden of pretense, self-righteousness and self-importance.

But there are different maturational levels of humor. The lowest is infantile humor, centered on jokes about toilet activities, usually out of context. At its core is the breaking of social taboos and the flaunting of the forbidden. The next level is based on witnessing the failures of others. All of us have laughed long and hard at someone else's pretensions and failings. It makes us feel better to see fallibility in others besides ourselves. But it's also a temptation that can lead to practical jokes, malicious teasing and sarcasm—all designed to provide a momentary sense of adequacy at the expense of someone else's feelings. The most mature kind of humor is the joke on ourselves; the humor here turns on our own inconsistencies and foibles. Nobody gets hurt as a lot of frustration, needless pretense and tension vanishes in laughter.

You can develop a sense of humor in your child. The most effective way is to share your laughter with him. Let him see you smile at your own discrepancies and mistakes. Never sacrifice your credibility as a fallible human being for the pretense of appearing better than you really are. Help your child recognize inconsistency, pompousness and self-delusion; point them out to him so he can begin to see through them for himself. Finally, provide him with humorous experiences. Expose him to the childish delights of Peanuts and Mr. Magoo, the subtle humor of Winnie the Pooh and the robust farce of old-time movie favorites so often revived on TV. Play riddle games with him and tell him corny jokes. Even buy him an old joke book. Then, when he's ready, help him to laugh at himself. Gently, lightly single out his discrepancies and inject humor into your encounters. His laughter will keep him close to his own reality and make his frailties more tolerable.

Acceptance, affection, challenge, respect, freedom and laughter create a positive and caring atmosphere for your child, a warmly supportive climate, a home where he can feel good about himself and his chances for becoming a productive, loving person. Persist faithfully in reminding yourself of your child's emotional needs and you can make him this precious gift.

III Encounter: You and Your Child

The Art of Gentle Confrontation

Every day you and your child will engage in a series of encounters. Some will be perplexing, tiresome and frustrating; others, rewarding or exciting or downright funny. These critical encounters are the experiences from which your relationship with your child is formed. Hundreds of such encounters will ultimately shape your feelings and his into a mixture of pain and resentment, understanding and love. Your shared feelings either will draw you closer and closer together or will drive you apart. Some of them sound like this:

Parent: How many times do I have to ask you not to do that? You're rotten! I'm sick of you and the way you act!
Child: But Dad! Nobody's perfect.

Child: I can't do it. I know I can't.
Parent: You won't know until you try again.
Child: Yeah, but I couldn't do it the last time.
Parent: There's nothing wrong with making a mistake. But you've got to keep trying. That's how we learn.

Child: Gee, Mom, thanks for making this cake. It's great . . . Mmmm . . . delicious.
Parent: Well, thank you for helping. When you try to be helpful, kitchen work makes me feel good instead of tired. It's nice to feel I have someone to depend on.

For Better or For Worse
The feelings you and your child experience together during these encounters determine the kind and quality of relationship you build. Their force is irresistible. If the feelings are good, the relationship will satisfy you both. If bad, both you and your child are in for a stormy ride. Whether the encounter is a simple "Good morning!" or a complicated disagreement, it is essential that the confrontation be constructive.

You are the bellwether. The feelings you express carry impressive messages to your child. Because children are inclined to follow your lead, their feelings will reflect your own. Good begets good; bad begets bad. For this reason, however severely any encounter tests your own feelings, try to convert it into an affirmative, supportive experience for your child.

What is the parent-child relationship all about? Primarily, it is a bond of mutual involvement and dependence that touches our deepest personal needs and feelings. As such, its richness consists of the satisfactions it provides both parent and child. As a parent, you will derive your satisfactions mainly through your role of caring, protecting, nurturing and teaching your child. This makes you feel needed and respected. Your child will receive the satisfactions of feeling wanted, of being protected by your support, of being encouraged to explore new experiences when bolstered by your companionship and his own developing knowledge and power. Each of you gets something essential from the other.

Your style of relating is crucial. It determines the feeling quality of the relationship—how you feel about each other. If your involvement is personal and warm, if you respect your child's individual viewpoint, the feelings will be good and your relationship will grow. But a relationship characterized by detachment, coldness or arbitrary authority will frustrate and alienate your child. Most parent-child relationships fall into the broad middle ground between these extremes; that is to say they are neither as bad nor as good as they might be. If you treat your child positively, if you show him that you care and support his efforts to become responsible and mature, he will be highly motivated to try to meet your needs and expectations. In this way, your relationship will evolve from continual one-sided giving to become a shared, equal partnership in which each of you looks after the other. This is what the ultimate parent-child relationship is all about.

A Confrontation a Day
Practice the Art of Gentle Confrontation with your child every day. You will be most successful when there is no chance of public embarrassment. Therefore, meet in private.

1. Sit down with your child. Ask him to tell you the things you did that day which made him feel bad. Say, "I want you to tell me how the things I did today made you feel."
2. Listen without comment, excuse or moralizing.
3. Then, tell him the things he did which made you feel bad. "Today you forgot to feed the dog again. It makes me feel bad when you don't remember her." "You made me very angry when you argued with your sister."
4. Next, tell him what made you feel good. "You made me feel proud of you when you did your chores without being reminded." "I felt good when I saw how thoughtfully you included your brother while you were playing with your friends."
5. Finally, discuss what each of you can do to make the other feel better.

Repeat this process every day. It will take real determination. Do not personalize what he tells you, or act defensively or express anger. Instead, regard his recitation as a normal release of tension. After all, this is what your child truly feels. If he does not tell you his bad feelings directly, you will be feeling the effects indirectly. At the same time, be honest with him. Discuss your own feelings in a matter-of-fact way. If ever you believe you were wrong, be ready to admit it and apologize; this will serve as a forceful model and help him admit his own mistakes.

You Can Be Honest and Warm at the Same Time
In confrontation, it's the style that counts:
"You probably didn't realize it but you left your muddy shoes on my bed."
"You'd really be great to have around if only you would take a shower."
"Nobody's memory is perfect so I thought you'd like to know you forgot to take out the trash again."
"When you do something for me, I say 'Thank you.' I'd appreciate it if you would do the same."

Politeness

"Please . . . take the dishes off the table."
    . . . get ready for bed."
    . . . don't interrupt me when I'm talking."
"Thank you . . . for your help."
    . . . for waiting so patiently."
    . . . for making me feel good."

Politeness toward your child is a potent way of showing your respect. Politeness is respectful consideration. Its exercise will have tremendous bearing upon his development and upon the tone of your relationship. No matter what you say, your child cannot experience it as excessive or as a put-down if you render it politely.
Your politeness has to be sincere; your child will know if it is not. The voice, indicating true feeling, is the unwavering indicator of genuine politeness. Politeness in word, deed and tone of voice will win your child's appreciation. He will clearly interpret the message they convey to him. When you say, "Please," he will hear, "I respect you." When you say, "Thank you," he will hear, "I value your worth."
Sooner or later—probably later—the cumulative effect will find expression: The

experience of repeated acts of politeness directed toward him will overcome his inertia and forgetfulness. He will begin to act politely as a matter of course. But the initial stimulus must come from you. Eventually he will become as polite as you are to him. If he feels he has your respect and appreciation, he will feel respect and appreciation toward you. This is the foundation of politeness.

Mutual Support

The best way to build a good relationship is by mutual support. This means that each person is actively dedicated to the well-being of the other. For both you and your child, it is a matter of proper focus, of dealing with essentials first. Mutual support is an acknowledgment that no relationship can survive or grow unless there is a shared effort to help each other.

In the early years, you will do most of the supporting. Your superior strength and experience will enable you to recognize and satisfy your child's needs; for quite some time, those needs will be his major concern. If your relationship is to mature, he must gradually assume his role as an effective partner and begin to support you as well. That day will not come quickly nor will it arrive without pain and considerable effort. You will make mistakes and so will he. This is how you both learn. But you can avoid one mistake by never confusing affirmative, positive treatment and support with permissiveness. Positive treatment is balanced. It is neither harsh nor weak; it insists upon commitments but forgives mistakes.

To help your child grow up and develop a genuine relationship with you will require daily effort. As quickly as he is ready, you, the author of his being, can patiently show him how to become your fellow collaborator. To make clear your eagerness for a more balanced, equal relationship, openly express your pleasure when he assumes initiative and responsibility. In this way, he can begin to experience what he needs to know and to do in order to reciprocate your support with his own. Your relationship then will have two legs to stand on instead of one. Mutual support is the tie that will bind you together. During your child's development, your support will have two primary objectives: As a parent, you will underwrite your child's efforts to become his own person and to discover and do his own thing. Your child, when he is able, likewise will support your efforts for better personal development and self-fulfillment. This is what is deeply meant by mutual support.

Helping Him to Understand the Relationship

To participate in meaningful relationships, your child will have to develop the necessary inner strengths. Consequently, you will need to marshal your resources and support in order to help him. This process of fostering emotional development is the primary task of parenthood. It's where the significant action is, where the components of your relationship come together.

Your first objective in raising your child will be to concentrate your support and attention on ways to help him become his own, better-developed person. Children usually are too naive to grasp the significance of their experience. For this reason, an important aspect of awareness training is to help clarify your child's experience, thereby helping make him aware of the basic elements in your relationship: his feelings, your feelings and how they interrelate.

Help Him to Clarify His Experience by asking Him:
What he's feeling.
What you're feeling.
How your relationship is going.

Ask Him What He's Feeling toward You
Ask him about his feelings—if necessary, suggesting what the emotion is, until he can name it himself:
"Are you feeling happy with me? Or unhappy with me?"
"Are you feeling mad at me?"
"Are you worried about me?"

Ask Him If He Knows What You Are Feeling
Ask your child if he knows what your feelings are. If he can't tell you, you tell him.

Tell Him What You Feel Is Happening in the Relationship
Let your child know what you believe his behavior means as it affects your relationship. In this way, he will become more aware of what actually is happening around him: "Your baby sister is taking a nap. Do you know it will make me very upset if your noise wakes her up? Play quietly, please!" "I'm always proud of how well you answer the phone. Everybody mentions it. And I appreciate your taking the calls all afternoon while I've been painting cupboards."

Better Relating
No truly substantial relationship can exist if each person does not thoroughly know the other; thus your child needs to know you in a very personal way in order to establish a good relationship. Yet children invariably do not know their parents, although there is nothing a child wants more than the security and reassurance of a strong parental relationship.

Encourage Your Child to Know You Better
When your child expresses interest in what you're doing, he may be conveying two messages. The first is simple and direct: "I'm interested in what you're doing." The second message usually is less direct but more significant: "I want to know you better, in a more fundamental way. What is important to you? What are your values, goals and concerns?" He may be making an indirect overture for a deeper relationship with you. You either can shut him out or let him in. It's important to interpret correctly what he's trying to tell you. Otherwise you may reply, "Don't bother me! Can't you see I'm busy right now? Stop being a pest and let me alone!" This brush-off tells him: "I don't want a deeper relationship with you. I'm too busy. Stay away." It decisively shuts him out. If you want a deeper relationship, confide in your child how you are feeling: "Look, I'm paying the bills now and I'm not in a very good mood. I'm just worried. Are you interested in my worry?" If he says yes, discuss your feelings with him to the extent that he can understand.

Invite Your Child to Help You Become a Better-developed Person

One of the best ways to let your child assist your development as a person is to accept his valid criticism. Many parents with fragile egos deny not only the child's criticism but the reality on which it is based. "Look, don't tell me I'm driving too fast. I'm not. I know how fast I'm driving and I don't need you to tell me. So sit still and be quiet. I work all day for your benefit and all I get is complaints about how fast I drive."
What the parent's denial really says is: "Don't attack my fragile ego. If you do, you are a disrespectful and ungrateful child." Such a thin-skinned, defensive posture weakens the relationship and retards the child's development. It denies the child opportunity for a better relationship. Therefore, when your child criticizes you, Listen carefully. He may be right.
Thank him, if the criticism has merit.
Explain your reason for rejecting his criticism if it doesn't seem logical or relevant. Tell him, "When your criticism is reasonable, I'll be happy to consider it. After all, I'm not perfect and I know it. But this time I don't think you're right."

Your Changing Role

As your child develops, your role as a parent will change. Your child's infant needs will cast you in a role different from the one you will assume in his pre-teens or adolescence. Your role function will reflect the degree of self-sufficiency and responsibility your child acquires.
The following are changing parental roles you will fulfill during his development:

When Your Child Is	Your Function Mostly Will Be As
A Baby	Protector, Nurturer
A Young Child	Protector, Nurturer, Guide
In Mid-childhood	Protector, Nurturer, Guide, Teacher, Friend
An Adolescent	Guide, Teacher, Friend, Consultant
An Adult	Friend, Consultant

Transitions in your role will range from protector of his helplessness to being a friend to the new adult he becomes. His passage from infant to adult involves gradually loosening the parental reins as you see him become more ready to function for himself. How willing and how well you make the transitions from role to role will go a long way toward forging an effective bond of friendship with your child.

Adjust Your Role to His Degree of Self-sufficiency

Your relationship with your child should be flexible and graduated. It's vital to be aware you can infantilize your child if you persist in a role unsuited to his advancing capabilities. When he is a baby, you will need to tie his shoelaces. But it is unwise to intervene and put him down by acting for him once he learns the task. Having demonstrated a capacity and responsibility, he should be allowed to make it his alone in order that he may grow.

Showing Him Your Limits

Your relationship with your child will need some boundaries. Otherwise, your feelings will have a way of colliding in unintentional but nonetheless painful ways. For his part, your child has very high expectations of you, since you are hero, ally, protector, teacher and guide. Because he sees you in such overwhelming roles—virtually the entire dramatis personae of his existence—it's obvious to him you must be inexhaustible, untiring, an unlimited source of everything he needs and wants. So he thinks and thereby sets his demands.

You, of course, know better. You do have limits which both of you should recognize and live by.

Every parent should give a thoughtful answer to the question: "How much time can I allocate for my child's development and still have time for my own needs?" Decide just what you can and will do for your child and spell out your limits.

Knowing how much involvement he can expect from you will give your child an extra measure of security. At the same time, it will provide you opportunity to plan and upgrade the time you spend with him. This can be particularly beneficial to fathers and working mothers who have less time to share with their children. If you know you are reserving three hours of one-to-one time for your child monthly, it's the quality of the time, the quality of the experiences you share that counts. Therefore set your limits and let your child know what they are.

Things Go Better with Definite Rules

"You never told me I couldn't do that."
"Yes, I did."
"No, you didn't. Honest . . ."
Dialogue sound familiar? Chances are the child is right; he wasn't told the rules. You can avoid this hassle by a simple procedure: Establish a definite, realistic set of guidelines and rules for your child's conduct.

These rules should be agreed upon by both parents, who together then present the rules to the child so that he clearly understands what they are. As he develops further, he should be included in the rule-making process. The rules he helps make are the ones he will most likely keep. Let him know explicitly what your expectations are for his conduct and performance.

Keep those guidelines and rules realistic by relating them to your own needs—even to your idiosyncrasies—as well as to his. Avoid arbitrary standards: "That's the way it is because I say so." Instead, supply him with a concrete reason.

Make Only Realistic Rules

Never lay down a command or rule that you cannot or do not intend to enforce. You damage your credibility with your child whenever you do. Some rules are simply unenforceable and therefore meaningless. Telling your child not to buy chocolate bars at the movies or not to throw snowballs on the way to school will be useless if you have no way of knowing whether he obeys you. In such situations, it's better to appeal to his desire to please you than to impose your authority. If you set your rules by your child's abilities to meet them and by your own power and willingness to enforce them, your credibility is less likely to be questioned or tested.

Enforce Your Rules Consistently
Never permit a broken rule to go unnoticed or without comment. It is damaging to your child's development when he is not confronted with a broken rule. Tell him of his violation and that it has hurt your feelings. Do this consistently. Here it is vital that both parents support each other; undivided is unconquered. If your child is allowed to deal with two sets of rules and two codes of enforcement, he will be confused and resort to testing both of you to find out what the real limits are. Even worse, he will try to play one of you against the other.

Avoid a Power Struggle
Avoid presenting your authority as a challenge to your child. If you threaten him with your authority, he may take it as an opportunity to prove his power to defy you. "Get yourself a haircut or I never want to see you again!" "If you don't straighten out your room, I'll throw everything away!" "You'll do what I tell you because I'm boss around here!" These statements represent authoritative postures that invite challenge. When you put your authority on the line, back it up. If you don't, you'll have difficulty getting it back. Authority is best kept hidden from view. It is most effective when it is rarely used.

When He Tests Your Limits
Intelligence makes it possible for us to manipulate. It is natural and inevitable for every intelligent child to test and, if possible, to manipulate whatever forces in his environment he can. This may be an electric switch, a TV remote control, the family pet or even his parents. Every day, your child is trying to learn how much control he can extend over his environment and the dynamic forces within it—including you. Be prepared to expect manipulative testing. It will help you be less angry and upset when it

occurs. The most effective strategy for dealing with it is simply to confront your child with his attempted manipulation. A common form of manipulation is his claim, "I'm sick," when in reality he is lazy, uncaring or afraid. Tell your child gently but firmly that you will not let him maneuver you into believing something that is not true: "I don't believe you're sick and I don't appreciate your attempt to mislead me. I think the truth is that you're lazy or uncaring or afraid. Which is it? If we talk about it, maybe we can work out the problem together."
At the same time, it is important to recognize that much testing is not manipulative but only a natural attempt by your child to learn the dimensions of his power and yours. Don't always assume he's trying to con you into something you would be unwise to do. Instead, look for implications other than those of behavioral manipulation. He may be studying your limits—the limits of your conviction, consistency or, sometimes, how much you care about him. ("If you let me ride my bike after dark, you don't care what happens to me.")

Expect and Accept Your Child's Attempts to Test Your Limits
For the most part, it is natural and necessary for your child's social development that he attempt to test your limits. They present an opportunity to teach your child basic lessons about your patience, consistence and conviction.
Although you accept his testing, it is not necessary to accept his manipulation. A child continually tries to con parents into believing his version of reality: "It's not raining out, Mom." Or his estimate of his powers and responsibility: "Sure, I can do it. I won't get hurt." Don't be taken in. Be firm. Let him know that you will not accept his attempts to manipulate you:
    "You're not ready yet to do something as dangerous as that—even if you think you are."
    "I disagree. That is not what happened. You hit your sister first."
When he tries to manipulate you with such standard put-offs as "I'll do it later," or "I

didn't hear you," confront him gently. Ask, "Are you trying to get me to let you do something? Or are you trying to get away with something you'll later regret?" Ask yourself the question: "Is he trying to manipulate me or is he just trying to learn my limitations?"

Hidden Messages

In every interaction with your child, there is a latent message. A simple statement like, "You don't know how to do that," can have serious ego implications for your child. His ego—the essential feeling he has about himself—is based on his perceptions of what you and others think about him, his awareness, acceptability, competence and character. These perceptions are personal evaluations that touch his very core. They involve basic questions about his existence:
   "Am I in touch with myself, with others and with reality?"
   "Am I acceptable to others and worthy of their caring?"
   "Am I capable and productive?"
   "Am I trustworthy and dependable to myself and to others?"

What Are You Telling Your Child about Himself?

The answers he receives to these questions are crucial. They largely determine whether his development will be healthy or neurotic, whether he eventually will develop a good self-concept or a poor one.
Realize that nearly everything you say or do to your child can imply something positive or negative about his realism, worthiness, competence or integrity. This is the latent message, what you imply about his ego. Common, everyday words that often pass between parent and child carry these implications:

Statement	Implication
"I can't count on you."	(You don't have any character and never will.)
"You're a dreamer."	(You don't know reality.)
"Don't bother me now."	(You are not important.)
"Let me do it for you."	(You are incompetent.)

If your latent messages are consistently negative, you will destroy your child's ego. You will be setting the stage for neurosis by teaching him to experience himself as a failure.
In each of the following instances, the implied positive message is not missed:

Statement	Implication
"I like the way you answered the door when our new neighbor called."	(You please people.)
"You did a good job cleaning your white shoes."	(You are competent.)
"You got dressed very well all by yourself."	(You are competent.)
"It was good of you to change the light bulb."	(You are capable and nice, a worthy person.)
"I like the way you told that story."	(You are competent.)
"You're fun to play checkers with."	(You are a desirable companion.)
"It was nice of you to lend me that money from your bank so the paperboy won't have to call back again."	(You are good to people, a worthy person.)
"You understood my feeling."	(You are a caring person.)

The basic implications are never missed at the deeper, unspoken level: "You are a capable person, likable and good to have around." There is no better way for you to help your child to believe he is effective and socially acceptable.

Encouraging Competence

Your child frequently will attempt things that will send shivers of fear up your spine. Some dare-devil acts may not be so much intended to flirt with danger as to demonstrate your child's competence to himself. How you react to such behavior can have important implications. So try to look for a possible power-proving element, and if it is there that facet of his action should be approved. Help him to see the difference, and to find a safer way to demonstrate his growing competence.

It's all too common for a parent to say, "What's the matter with you? Are you stupid or something? Haven't you any sense at all? You'll cut yourself. Give me that knife and don't ever let me see you with it again." This response does not foster competence. While saving him from cutting himself, you cut up his feelings and ego in the process. What you really are saying (and he understands all too well) is, "You will never be able to do anything for yourself. You lack basic judgment." The results are predictably negative.

Another approach is to confront him with your feelings in a positive way. Tell him: "Look, you're making me very nervous the way you're handling that knife. I'm worried that sooner or later you will cut yourself. I would prefer you to stop carving until you can learn how to use that knife without hurting yourself. Are you interested in learning a better way? I can show you if you like. When you cut with the knife, cut away from yourself . . ." Here you describe the danger without damaging his ego. His sense of competence, of being able to do things well by himself, remains intact.

Building Integrity

Polonius' advice, "To thine own self be true," is the psychological cornerstone of integrity. Still, all of us have a personal bag of tricks and dodges to violate this precept and its character implications, and your child is no exception. You can help him develop and maintain his integrity by making him aware of his self-contradictory behaviors, and by showing him how they lessen his self-respect. Once again a positive approach is essential. For example, let's consider a situation in which your child is lying to you and you both know it. The evidence is unmistakable. He's feeling uneasy, knowing he's trapped. What do you do?

Some parents overreact with self-righteous anger as if they had never told a lie in their lives: "I never thought any child of mine would be a liar. You're not telling me the truth. Now I'll never be able to believe anything you tell me!"

An emotional outburst like this harms the child. He lied, after all, mostly out of fear of just such a reaction. The real danger in such a response is that he may believe what you say. As he hears it, you are telling him emphatically and forever, "We can never have an honest relationship. I won't believe you." By blasting his hope for a good relationship, you undermine the principal motivation for his being honest. Remember that, without an honest foundation, the prospects for a growth relationship are meager.

A more constructive approach is to confront him with his lying: "Now listen to me. Your sister is crying. I can see bruises. She says you hit her. And you're the only person who could have, unless she hit herself. I feel almost certain that you did it and that you're lying to me. I feel disappointed. We can deal with the problem between you and your sister in a minute. But first, we have to solve this problem between you and me about being honest. Why did you lie to me?"

At this point, the child usually will admit he lied. "O.K. I did hit her. But she broke my airplane . . ." "All right. I understand. But, in the future, if she causes a problem that's too hard for you to solve alone, come to me instead of hitting her. Then, the two of us can iron out the problem together."

In this positive way, you can deal with the issues forthrightly without damaging your child's ego. You confront the basic issue of lying while offering a chance for a satisfactory solution to his problem with his sister. Your child can leave such an encounter without feeling he is innately evil.

Pain and Effort Are Essential Parts of Growing Up

Your child will want the acceptance and feeling of self-worth that come from dealing effectively with others but he will usually be unwilling to accept or endure the pain and discomfort necessary. And you are the one who keeps demanding that he work at learning patience, self-control, consideration and other traits of maturity. Consequently, your child may develop a prisoner-of-war complex in which he regards his parents as unfriendly, hostile captors whose principal functions (and pleasures) are indoctrination, enforced servitude and the prohibition of every pleasant, "natural" impulse.

He may blame his pain on your "meanness" instead of upon reality. Like those ancient messengers who were executed when they reported bad news, a parent can be considered the bad guy simply because he must remind his child of the effort and pain that are required to grow up, to become more effective and respected. Naturally you, the parent, are not the villain. The truth is that all of us must sustain unpleasantness in order to become more effective. It is not your fault that this is so. It's nobody's fault. It is merely Nature's way. You are mostly an information-giver to your child. You do not formulate the rules of life, and he should understand this fact. Reject any attempt by your child to pin the blame on you.

"Look, why do you make me out to be the bad guy? Why me? I didn't invent the rules. I'm only trying to help you understand them. It's a law of the universe, like gravity, that if you want to be good at something, you have to work at it. If you want friends, you have to learn to be considerate. If you want others to respect your feelings, you have to show respect for their feelings first. If you want people to give you good feelings, you often must give them good ones first. That's the way it is. The rules are just as tough on me as they are on you. But in the long run I wouldn't be kind to you if I didn't remind you of this often."

Communications such as these, repeated frequently, will help your child understand that reality—not you—is limiting him, that reality extracts a measure of pain as the price of gaining valuable powers and skills. You can reinforce these communications by recounting your own experience with things you had to do to obtain the results you wanted: "My best friend and I got together when we were kids simply because she was lonely and I was willing to listen. She got someone to talk to and I got a friend." "It took me three months' work to earn enough money to buy myself my first bike." "I used to feel left out, too. But I kept trying to be friendly and soon I wasn't left out." Whenever you can, relate your experience to the problem at hand and the feelings involved.

But What about Discipline?

What do you do when your child refuses to respond to your positive efforts? What do you do when he resists growing up?

Always Focus on the Feelings
During your encounters with your child, it will benefit you and him to focus on his feelings and yours. Usually, parents are behavior-oriented because behavior is tangible, whereas feelings are not readily seen. But always dealing with symptoms rather than causes can make parenthood a frustrating chase from one behavior to the next without ever coming to grips with the basic issues—the underlying feelings. Feelings cause behavior; they are the motive force. Concentrate your attention on them and you will understand the larger truth about what is happening to your child at any given moment.

Deal with the Feelings
Help your child understand what the feeling behind his behavior is or might be: "Were you angry when you did that?" "Were you afraid I'd leave you out . . . ?"
Every child is susceptible to being dealt with through his feelings. He carries a bundle of forces with him wherever he goes—these are his feelings of hope, anger, pride, curiosity; fear of failure, rejection, loneliness; and the desire for esteem, caring, approval and acceptance. By tapping into these dynamic forces, you can help your child develop in positive ways. You do this by meeting his feeling needs as they occur. An unmet emotional need almost certainly will lead to some kind of behavioral problem.

Two Ways to Help Your Child Become More Aware of Your Feelings

Make an Appeal for Fair Treatment
Make a direct appeal to your child's sense of fairness: "I treat you with consideration. Why don't you treat me the same way?" Here you compare your good treatment of him with his bad treatment of you. Of course, the credibility of your appeal depends greatly upon how well you have been treating and respecting his feelings. This appeal is an opportunity for your child to initiate a solution to the problem.

Role-Reversal Increases Empathy
An effective way to promote empathy is to use role-reversal. In this simple technique, you ask your child how he would feel if something he did to someone were to happen to him. It can be used almost every time your child does something that disturbs you.

Constructive Discipline

Sooner or later, you will be faced with the necessity of punishing your child. When should you do it and how? The first rule is never punish your child in anger. This does more harm than good and eventually will destroy your relationship. You cannot effectively correct your child's behavior by losing control of yours. A second rule is to punish as seldom as possible. Frequent punishment will brutalize your child. It seldom is fair and it generates hatred instead of respect. A third rule is to avoid physical punishment. Hitting a child may seem like a quick solution but the bad effects linger for a long time. Child-beating is a national epidemic. There's no need to contribute to it. Isolating your child in his room is more effective than hitting. It will not harm your relationship as would the trauma of a beating.
Before resorting to isolation, be sure you have followed these steps:

1. Make it clear to your child what he can and cannot do.
2. Let him know how you feel if he does what you want and how you will feel if he doesn't.
3. Emphasize that he has the power to make you feel good or bad.
4. Tell him that you believe he would prefer to make you feel good, just as you prefer to make him feel good.
5. Until he is able to respond to your appeals for mutual consideration and fair play, give him a specific consequence for any infraction of the rules.
6. Don't make any rules you will not enforce.
7. After discussion has been tried and does not work, begin to apply more pressure. The first measure is to take away some specific privilege for a specific infraction. This method usually will make an impression, but only to the extent that it is very consistently enforced.
8. If taking away privileges does not work, then you can punish him with isolation in his room. Tell him why you are doing this: "I'm punishing you because you don't have a feeling understanding of what I've been talking about. You don't see the reason why you should consider my feelings. You still don't understand that there are certain things we have to do to make each other feel better . . ."
The door to his room should be closed but never locked. Release him from his room as soon as he is willing and able to explain how he will try to do better in the future. One way to help an older child understand the issues involved is to have him write a note describing them. The note should describe: (1) what he did that aggravated, upset or worried you; (2) what the meaning of his action was— that is, what he was after; (3) what he thinks his action meant as you see it; (4) how he plans to deal with this kind of situation in the future.
Make it clear to him that his note must be detailed, not vague or general, and it must convince you he really understands what is at fault and seriously intends to do better. When this task is completed and

you are convinced, the child can then be released from his room. This effective way of being gentle but firm raises your child's level of consciousness about his behavior and your feelings. It's superior to any other form of punishment.

9. If none of the above measures work, professional help is indicated.

The Bond of Caring

The Bond of Caring means you actually like your child for who he is, and he likes and values you in return. This mutual caring springs from the experiences you share together, especially the difficult ones. Those shared experiences with your child as he struggles to grow up will fuse your deepest feelings into a lasting bond that will withstand time and trouble. Strengthening this bond should be your prime concern, coloring all your parental decisions and actions: "What can I do to show my caring?" Caring is the expressed feeling that your child's well-being, happiness, success and good feelings are important to you and motivate your behavior toward him. Warm and positive, it is best expressed in all the words and actions that support and affirm his worth and value to you even under trying, irritating circumstances. Caring is loving, but it is firm. It does not include surrender to childish demands. It has a dark, serious side, too, sometimes compelling you to say no because you truly do care. Despite his protests, these are the times your child learns you really do care deeply. He will learn to care for you by experiencing your supportive, caring treatment. The first returns that complete the bond will not come quickly, but when they do they will last for a lifetime.

PART II
The System

TABLE I

Comprehensive Table of Emotional Maturation

AWARENESS		RELATING	
A-1	Being in Touch	R-1	Self-interest
A-2	Decoding Experience	R-2	Attention
A-3	Safety for Openness	R-3	Acceptance
A-4	Denial	R-4	Approval
A-5	Mixed Emotions	R-5	Affection
A-6	Curiosity	R-6	Social Responsibility
A-7	Desire	R-7	Empathy
A-8	Fear	R-8	Friends
A-9	Anger	R-9	Peer Pressure
A-10	Projection	R-10	Confrontation with Support
A-11	Frustration, Discouragement	R-11	Mutual Support
A-12	Feelings of Inferiority	R-12	Sharing in Decisions
A-13	Worries	R-13	Promises
A-14	Reality Testing	R-14	Fighting
A-15	Imagination	R-15	Rivalry
A-16	Daydreams	R-16	Becoming Likable
A-17	Fear-fixation, Wish-Fulfillment	R-17	Ambivalence Toward People
A-18	Dreams, Nightmares	R-18	Response to Opposite Sex

TABLE I

COMPETENCE	INTEGRITY
C-1 Energy and Effort	I-1 Self-control
C-2 Knowledge and Skills	I-2 Patience
C-3 Planfulness	I-3 Truthfulness
C-4 Initiative	I-4 Coping with Unpleasantness
C-5 Creativity	I-5 Perseverance
C-6 Realistic Expectations	I-6 Fairness
C-7 Self-sufficiency	I-7 Neatness
C-8 Willingness for Challenge	I-8 Reliability
C-9 Caution	I-9 Genuineness
C-10 Self-confidence	I-10 Blaming
C-11 Responsibility	I-11 Stealing
C-12 Ambition	I-12 Work
C-13 Goal-directedness	I-13 Drugs
C-14 Standards of Performance	I-14 Sex
C-15 Cooperation	I-15 Leadership
C-16 Flexibility	
C-17 Developing One's Own Interests	
C-18 Problem-Solving	

A HOLISTIC PROGRAM FOR RAISING THE EMOTIONALLY MATURE CHILD

Part II   The System

How to Use the System

To help you use THE PARENT BOOK more effectively, there are a number of things you should know about it. As noted earlier, this comprehensive system designed to foster Emotional Maturity in your child is built on the four major areas of emotional growth and functioning: Awareness, Relating, Competence and Integrity, *(see Table 1. p. 46)*. As your child matures in these ways, he will become more aware, know how to get along with others, have self-confidence and a positive self-image based on his behavior as a decent human being.

The various issues within each developmental area are roughly in chronological order. They range from problems of less to those of more maturity, from the skills your child needs as a four-year-old to those he will need as he approaches adolescence. Chronological sequencing is most applicable to Relating, Competence and Integrity, but less so to Awareness, an area where various issues begin to manifest themselves simultaneously. Since no two children are totally alike, this sequencing should not be viewed as exact and ironclad, but rather as a general indication of your child's progress. Each sequence forms a general pattern of growth that suggests how well your child is maturing within each developmental area. If, for example, the most common problem you have with your child is his selfishness, you can locate that problem under "Self-interest" in Relating. Because selfishness is the first issue in Relating, you will know that your child has a long way to go before he can relate well to others.

After a month or two of observation and application, you can tell how your child is progressing in each sequence. When you determine this level, you will have located his "growing edge." Children's growing edges are the emotional issues where the greatest development can be gained through concerted application and emphasis. As you watch your child trying to make friends, you know the time has come to concentrate on that area of development. Gradually, his readiness will shift to more-advanced issues within any sequence. As it does, reinforce your child's earlier gains, and challenge him to deal with more-advanced emotional issues.

It's important to note at the outset that these issues form a continuum of emotional skills or abilities. But they are not separate divisions. Like rainbow colors, they overlap and blend together in a harmonious spectrum. We divide them artificially only to study and better understand them. There is much overlap. These issues are charted so you may be certain no crucial developmental area will be left to chance.

Within THE PARENT BOOK system itself, each emotional issue usually is treated with basic information, a dialogue and practical suggestions for dealing with the issue. Quite often, the first dialogue will present a typical but "wrong" way of dealing with the problem. A second dialogue, using questions or statements as a wise parent might, indicates a "right" way to discuss the issue with your child and suggests a vocabulary to use in the parent-child conversational give-and-take.

The "How-to" section summarizes the methods and techniques you can use to help your child cope with the particular issue. Tested by years of experience, the basically simple methods are those used by therapists. These methods can be managed by any parent who will take the time. As you follow the indicated steps, you and your child can grow and mature together.

A word about praise: Throughout the system you will be advised to praise your child for desirable behavior. Some parents occasionally attempt praise by saying, "You are a good boy." Such a global statement can be misunderstood by a child as representing a total assessment of himself as a person. Also be advised of another possible implication: If your child makes a drawing at school and brings it home to show you, and you say, "That's a very good drawing," he may perceive this as a sweeping universal judgment rather than your private reaction. He may even read into such a statement the idea that you are sitting in judgment over him. Or your approval may so impress him that thereafter he will go overboard to seek it. Even worse, he may come to feel he always needs someone to let him know he is an O.K. person.

Although under ordinary circumstances none of these possible side effects is likely to pose any threat to your child's development, it is wisest to praise his specific action or effort and avoid possible misinterpretation. For example, when your child makes his own bed, instead of saying, "You are a good helper," it would be wiser to say, "You did something nice for me. I appreciate it."

A word of caution about using this book: Don't become impatient with yourself or your child. You will need to persevere in using THE PARENT BOOK system. Results will be in direct proportion to your persistence. Over the years countless parents have proven the value of the methods this book endorses. If you skip about from system to system and—almost inevitably—are dissatisfied with results, you never will be able to pinpoint where things went wrong. It's the Tortoise and the Hare all over again: Patient fidelity, coupled with consistence, will pay off in the long run. There are no shortcuts leading to your child's emotional development. You must expect much repetition and many false starts before the finish line is crossed.

A mature person is like a large and magnificent tree that has reached maturity over many, many years of slow, painstaking growth. Your child's emotional development will take considerable effort and a great deal of time. If you are patient, positive and very persistent, the results most assuredly will be gratifying.

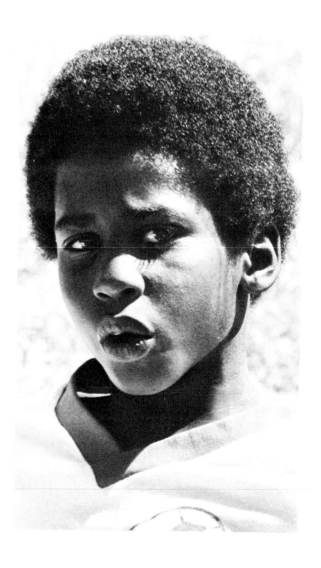

IV Awareness

How to Have Children Who Know How They Are Feeling,
What They Are Thinking and What They Are Doing

Are We Emotional Illiterates?

Because we never were taught to communicate our feelings—indeed, many of us were taught not to—we lack vocabulary to express them with any degree of accuracy. When describing how we feel, we're usually vague or uncertain. This lack of language is like the proverbial nail that lost the shoe, the horse and the battle. For lack of the right words, many of us remain cut off from the most significant part of our own experience. Awareness refers to our consciousness. It is the knowing of oneself. When we are aware, we know what we are feeling, thinking, doing. In the very young child, this experiencing of self is pure feeling alone. As yet, the infant has no language. The ability to think out and describe behavior will come later. All infants experience their feelings simply, directly, immediately. But this is a two-edged sword. The infant is in absolute touch with himself but lacking any buffers against stimulus. Pleasure is experienced as great delight. Pain is felt as great misery. He is fully receptive to his feelings, which are neither diluted nor protected.

If there is a "wish" common to all infants long before they can verbalize it, that wish is to experience only the ecstasy, never the agony. But it isn't possible to escape intense hurt in the beginning months of life.

In time, many simple and even complex mechanisms will be utilized for evading unpleasant, unwanted feelings. Most of these mechanisms, when used in a very limited way, do help reduce the little child's pain.

Yet, as with everything else, there is a price to pay. As your child learns to hold back his tears, he will feel a little less misery. He will also be a little less in touch with the full extent of all his feelings. If the evasive process is repeated often enough, your child automatically will suppress his crying. He will be pushing out of his awareness both his fury and his sadness. Tragically, these alienated feelings will still remain a part of him. They will seek and find expression in unintegrated ways. Over the years, the anger may turn into an unrecognized bitterness and cynicism; the sadness, into an underlying depression, reducing his overall zest for life.

The more in touch he is with the full range of his emotions, the more emotionally healthy your child will be. Because to a very large extent this awareness spells out the difference between his having a satisfying life or a miserable one, it should be seen as a pivotal point in his adjustment. As his loving guide, you then have the task of helping your child preserve his natural awareness. He will want and need little help with his good feelings. But you will have many occasions to help him to avoid a particular pitfall—his own natural inclination to escape from feelings of pain.

Such escapism, while being experienced as adaptive at the moment, each time takes its toll of the child's emotional maturation. But with your help, given at the right time and in the right way, he can learn instead to make constructive use of the many painful facts of life.

TABLE II

Awareness Issues of Emotional Development

A-1   The Vocabulary of Awareness: Being in Touch

A-2   Decoding Experience

A-3   In This House It's Safe to Be Open

A-4   Denial

A-5   Mixed Emotions: Taking the Bad with the Good

A-6   Curiosity: The Drive to Know

A-7   Desire: Need, Want or Deprivation Complex

A-8   Fear: It's a Scary World

A-9   Anger

A-10   Projection: It's Not My Fault

A-11   Frustration and Discouragement: I'm in a Bad Mood

A-12   I Am Different, Therefore Inferior and Unworthy

A-13   Worries

A-14   Real and Make-believe: Separating Symbols from Reality

A-15   Imagination: Exploring the Possible

A-16   Daydreams: Planning or Escape?

A-17   Hysterical Fantasy: Fear-fixation, Wish-fulfillment

A-18   Dreams and Nightmares

A-1 The Vocabulary of Awareness: Being in Touch

Your child needs to express his feelings in simple, meaningful words that accurately describe the full range of his emotions. He needs a vocabulary of awareness with which to communicate his experience. Like all language development, such a vocabulary involves a gradual learning process. It starts with simple concepts and simple words and grows toward more complex and sophisticated ones. At each stage, your child will need time and plenty of repetition to master the concepts and the language. Don't back away from "big" words. If they are explained and used often in proper context, your child will readily add them to his vocabulary.

You can start this development in a general way when you make it a daily point to ask him how he feels. The mere fact that you are interested enough to ask such a question has tremendous reassurance for your child. Very often, children feel insecure and inferior simply because no one ever discusses their inner feelings with them; consequently, they often assume their feelings are unique or "wrong" or even unimportant.

Once he's mastered answering your daily question in simple terms, you can move on to the more specific emotions of fear, anger, desire and pleasure. Then he will learn to connect his feeling to an event or experience: "I'm afraid when it's dark." "I get mad when you don't listen." "I want you to talk to me." "I feel good when I have someone to play with."

Ambivalence, or the problem of mixed feelings, is the next step. You can help your child identify mixed feelings he has about a particular event: "I feel good and bad about going to school. I like the teacher but I don't like some of the kids." "I like to go to Grandma's but her dog scares me."

The final stage involves more-advanced concepts that reflect your child's increased awareness of himself and the people around him. As he masters concepts such as attention, coping, acceptance, self-respect and many others, he will develop an even more accurate vocabulary to communicate his feelings and his total experience of events.

Helping your child master the words to match his feelings will add immeasurably to his perception of himself and others. In this sense, an emotional language—the vocabulary of feelings—is an indispensable tool of Awareness.

A Word About "Good" and "Bad"

Before we continue, we should arrive at an understanding about the meaning of the terms "good" and "bad" as used in the text. "Good" merely means that the particular experience produces a pleasant feeling. "Bad" means that the experience produces an unpleasant or painful feeling, ranging from discomfort to real suffering as from an actual injury.

Both terms refer to the way the person having the experience feels about it. "Good" and "bad" do not mean "moral" and "immoral" when referring to a feeling. This is not intended to downgrade the concepts of ethics and morality. You always will want to encourage considerate and decent behavior. Actually, your child's awareness of "good" and "bad" feelings is the best way to ensure his considerate behavior, which will increase as he comes to recognize the value of behaviors that make him and others feel good or bad.

Moralizing creates needless guilt, damages parental credibility and fosters a conflict of values between parent and child. As we are about to see, there are many better ways to socialize your child.

How to Practice the Language of Feelings

Listen to what your child says. Repeat the feeling he expresses. Concentrate first on good feelings. Then introduce the notion of bad feelings. To dispel his fear or reticence, you might start by mentioning a bad feeling you have had. Say, "Sometimes we have bad feelings, too, as well as good ones. I had a bad feeling today." Describe it. "Did you have a bad feeling today, too? Can you tell me about it? Can you remember some other bad feeling you once had?"

Don't press for answers when first discussing

bad feelings. Point out to your child that it's hard to remember them and talk about them but, before long, he'll be able to do it. The same kinds of discussions should be held about thoughts and behaviors. Explain that "bad" behavior (that which makes someone feel bad) is sometimes a matter of opinion: What is "good" for one person often is bad for another.

A-2 Decoding Experience

Liza, an active four-year-old, brims with ideas and "projects," frequently to her parents' dismay. Mother has just discovered Liza's latest project, a crayon mural on the family-room wall.

Mother: Look at that! You've just ruined that whole wall. You're a naughty, naughty girl!

Liza: (At first surprised, she quickly catches Mother's tone and shrinks under the onslaught.)

Mother: Don't you have anything to say? I wish you'd tell me what makes you do things like this!

Liza: (Still silent; now the tears begin.)

Mother: Go ahead! Cry! A lot of good that will do. I give up, Liza. I'll never understand you, never.

Such a response, although common, usually is both ineffective and damaging. Mother proceeds to injure Liza emotionally by: labeling her as "bad," therefore "worthless" in the child's mind; asking her why, a question almost impossible for anyone—let alone a child—to answer; and cutting Liza off from the hope of meaningful communication.

The real problem here is merely Liza's lack of awareness of Mother's feelings. Like every young child, she is essentially self-centered. Liza hasn't yet learned about psychic fallout, the effect her behavior has on other people's feelings. She was happy while drawing, and totally unaware her mother had feelings that surely would be affected by the wall "mural."

Mother needs to broaden Liza's awareness to include other people's feelings. Here is where the most effective solution lies. But, without suitable language that Liza comprehends, there can be no communication about how each one feels.

To develop this verbal link, every child first needs the skill to categorize and evaluate his experience. He has to be able to "name" what's happening outside in the world around him and inside in his own mind and body. As a parent, you instigate this process by teaching your child about the kinds of experience and how to evaluate them: at any given moment, he is experiencing a *feeling, thought* or *behavior.*[3]

Every experience has a value based on the feelings it produces. With this kind of information, your child can begin to recognize his different kinds of experience and to verbalize them. Ask easy questions that put you in touch with your child at his level of Awareness. The replies he gives will be revelations to understanding him and his behavior. Expanding your child's Awareness in this way is a gradual, often tedious process without immediate results. The same diligence and persistence required to teach him how to talk are necessary to develop his vocabulary of feelings.

It's likely, in the beginning, that you won't get any answers at all:

Mother: Liza, are you having a good feeling or a bad one?

Liza: I don't know.

Mother: That's all right. I wondered what you were doing and how you were feeling.

Liza: Oh, I was just playing.

There is nothing to be gained by pushing for an answer at this point but don't write off the exchange as a waste of time. Your questions demonstrate your interest in your child, always a plus. In addition, you focus attention on his favorite subject—himself. Little by little, the process of decoding his experience will begin to take hold. At this stage, remember that it is your questions which activate and keep the process growing.

---

[3] Actually, he feels, thinks and behaves simultaneously, although one facet of his experience may be more dominant or apparent than the others.

Let's revisit Mother and Liza to see how that unsatisfactory encounter might have gone had Mother the vocabulary and technique to expand Liza's awareness:

Mother: Liza, do you realize what you're doing?

Liza: I'm playing.

Mother: Does drawing on the wall make you feel good?"

Liza: Yes.

Mother: Can you guess how it makes me feel?

Liza: (Cautiously) Bad?

Mother: Yes, it really does, Liza. I'm happy you want to draw. But NOT on the wall. Let's clean if off together. Then we'll find a way you can have a good time without making me feel bad.

How to Help Your Child to Express His Feelings

Listen to your child's feelings.
Do not disapprove of his feelings. Allow your child the right to honest feelings expressing what life is like for him at the moment. Help him see how his actions affect your feelings. You then will be encouraging continued access to his experience, and he will be in a better position to understand what is happening and to share it with you.
Prepare your child to expect pain and unpleasantness, and let him know these are unavoidable parts of life. Encourage him to remain open to all his feeling experiences by telling him that he cannot close off pain without also closing off pleasure.

A-3 In This House It's Safe to Be Open

One of the remarkable things about young children is their sheer aliveness. They delight in things we adults somehow have overlooked or forgotten. One reason is that the senses of young children are finely tuned to themselves and the world around them. Without emotional barriers to stimuli from the environment or their own emotions, young children absorb experience immediately and accurately. This receptivity to external and internal stimuli is your child's openness.

Openness is a needed part of your child's emotional development. It enables him to perceive the world and how it affects his feelings and well-being. As long as he is open to his inner feelings, he knows exactly where he stands and how well he's getting along. In the sense that it lets in the experience of the outer world and lets out the feelings thereby produced, openness is a double door serving the two basic facets of human existence—experiencing and expressing.

The problem is that the door can be shut. A child who suffers bad experiences or an unpleasant environment will try to cut himself off from painful reality. Or, what is worse, he may block himself off from his own feelings in order to shut out the different kinds of pain. In either case, he grows less alive and can become emotionally disabled. This loss of openness is called denial and is a serious problem.

As a parent, you can't avoid your child's feelings. You run into them all day long. But how do you handle them? And what about his negative feelings and the trouble they cause?

Letting your child vent his anger or frustration is unpleasant, to say the least. But blocking expression of his negative feelings invites denial. It tells him he has one set of feelings and experiences you will accept and another set—equally important to him—which you won't. How, then, can he solve fears, anger, frustrations, bad moods and intense desires if he can't express them? To whom can he turn for help if not to you? Unable to get away from his intense feelings yet desperately wanting your approval, he is caught in a trap.

If he keeps his bad feelings to himself, repressing them into his subconscious, they can become emotional time bombs.

The notion that your child will behave "better" because you won't let him voice his negative feelings is mistaken. The opposite usually happens: He will act out his suppressed feelings indirectly in some negative, self-destructive way. Assure him he can tell you what he's feeling, even when it's

56

negative. Letting him tell you how mad he is at his kid brother will let some of the steam out of his system and make him feel better. He still may want to punch the little guy, but he'll have a less intense desire to do so. Meanwhile, you will have time to solve the conflict before it escalates.
A basic guide is:
• Accept the Open, Free Verbal Expression of Any Feeling Your Child Tells. Feelings are innate and emerge spontaneously.
• But behavior is another matter.
• Never Accept Any Destructive Acting Out of Your Child's Negative Feelings.

Holly, seven and constitutionally prone to be excitable, is particularly keyed up because she has invited three girls from school to celebrate her birthday today. Now Holly can't find her favorite blouse and is in a rage. Her emotional excitability affects Mother, who tends to overreact:
Holly: (Screaming at her mother) What's happened to my yellow blouse?
Mother: Calm down. Little ladies don't get mad. Or, if they do, they don't ever show it.
Holly: I don't care what little ladies do. I can't find my blouse! What did you do with it?
Mother: You shouldn't lose your temper over such a little thing. Wear something else.
Holly: I don't want something else. It's my birthday and I want to wear my yellow blouse!
Holly's mother communicates some strong negative messages to her child that threaten to stunt Holly's emotional growth. By conveying the idea that anger is bad and implying Holly lacks the conscious control she "should" have over how much anger she experiences, Mother abandons Holly when the child needs acceptance and emotional support. Holly's mother further abandons her daughter by failing to offer any actual help in finding the blouse.
Holly's feelings are trying to say: I'm easily frustrated and quick to get angry . . . I'm emotionally upset . . . I wish I felt less angry. Holly is intensely aware of these uncomfortable feelings. What she needs is

someone who will listen, understand and give emotional support. None of these will help her to find the blouse. But they will reduce the intensity of her unpleasant feelings. Consider how the interchange might have gone if Holly's mother knew what to do:
Mother: You sound frustrated and angry, Holly.
Holly: Well, what's happened to my blouse? I want to wear it to the party!
Mother: I'm sorry to see you so unhappy. What would make you feel better?
Holly: Finding my blouse would.
Mother: Will you feel less miserable if I help you?
Holly: (Calming down) Yes, please, Mother.

Just a few words can carry a totally different meaning. Instead of making Holly feel that she's a bad girl, Mother now conveys some very positive messages:
• It's natural to have strong negative feelings and it has nothing to do with your worth as a person.
• I am interested in your unhappiness and what causes it.
• I care enough about you to want to help you get over your bad feelings.
With such positive messages, Holly's mother actively promotes her daughter's emotional maturation. Mother is helping Holly develop a more natural and tolerant attitude about having negative feelings. The next time Holly is angry or frustrated, she is less likely to regard herself as an innately bad person. She will feel less socially isolated, for now she has evidence from her mother that another person can be interested in helping reduce Holly's feelings of misery. The little girl thus can retain her awareness and grow up with positive expectations about coping with unpleasant feelings.
Many parents believe that to recognize and accept emotional displays from their children will encourage more of the same. This is true if the child's angry display draws only an agitated response from a parent. If a parent acknowledges the feeling as an unhappy experience and shows the child that expressing it won't destroy their

relationship, the child learns to reduce his bad feelings by sharing them with others. Such sharing, even when the feelings are intense, will not encourage new temper displays but will in fact lessen them.
Suppose Holly experienced such great anger that her feelings spilled over beyond words and she actually threw and broke some things in her room:

Mother: Holly, what in the world have you done? All your things are tossed around and you've broken this pretty little vase!

Holly: (Scared, defensive, screaming, counterattacking) You've put my yellow blouse someplace where I can't find it! I've looked and looked till I'm sick of looking. But you don't care!

Mother: (Slapping Holly) You can't talk that way to me. Your birthday party is off!

Here Holly's mother undermines her child's growth process. In a moralizing way, Mother implies Holly is not a good person.
What might have happened if Mother were more enlightened about the importance of expressing feelings while controlling behavior?

(Hearing Holly yelling and throwing things, Mother enters the room.)

Mother: What's happening?

Holly: I'm mad, that's what. I couldn't find my yellow blouse, so I threw all those things off the dresser.

Mother: Did that help?

Holly: Yes. But I'm still mad . . . Are you going to punish me?

Mother: Not if you're willing to learn about a better way to deal with your angry feelings.

Holly: You mean you won't spank me?

Mother: Not if you listen carefully. First of all, maybe you can learn how to be less angry. You can do that by coming to me next time and telling me how angry you are. I'll be glad to listen if you'll be sure not to make it seem like it's my fault.

Holly: Will that really make me less angry?

Mother: It works for me. Holly, there's nothing wrong with having angry feelings. We all get mad. That can't be helped. But we can control our actions. Today you're excited about your party and it's annoying not to be able to find your favorite blouse. I won't punish you for what you just did but I expect you to straighten up this mess.

Holly: All right.

Mother: You do need your blouse, Holly. And if you ask me, I'll help you find it.

How to Eliminate the Negative

Don't moralize about feelings. Soften the emotional upset by telling your child his intense feeling is natural and that you're interested in what caused it.
Offer your help in solving the problem. Instead of dealing with the event as a disciplinary matter, offer your genuine help as a friend. Don't let him set you up as the antagonist. Keep the focus on his feelings. If you can't help or don't want to, tell him what prevents you. The knowledge that you care—and would help if you could—will comfort him. Always let him know of your sympathetic interest.

A-4 Denial

"Who spilled all the milk?"
"Who left the window open so the rain came in?"
Every day of the week, you ask questions like these, and the likelihood is an answer that appears to be a lie:
"Not me."
"Must have been somebody else."
The fact that you know your child is responsible makes his denial infuriating. Yet he may not be lying. He may be denying. There's a difference—an important one. Whereas lying is a conscious process by which we deny to others the truth about ourselves, denial is an unconscious process in which our subconscious withholds the truth from us. As far as we consciously know, we've not failed in our performance. A child commonly will deny what he's done if he's afraid of punishment or of being experienced as inadequate by his parents should he admit the truth. What is even more damaging, he may deny what he feels. Denial is one of the most widespread

emotional disorders in both adults and children. Less apparent but equally as devastating as polio or multiple sclerosis, it can become crippling.

The child who first denies his feelings of inadequacy and later denies feelings of other kinds eventually becomes a "blindman," cut off from his emotional experience. He lives inside a double shell. The outer shell protects him from the disapproval and punishment of other people. The inner shell shields him from the pain of his own negative opinions of himself. Cast adrift in a hostile environment, with little emotional connection to himself or his world, a child can become an emotional cripple living in a state of chronic defensiveness. He slips into a grey, twilight existence, consciously experiencing little of either his pain or his joy—a stranger to family and friends and, most of all, to himself.

Obviously, one incident of denial doesn't make a neurotic. Denial doesn't happen overnight. It feeds and grows over a period of time during which the child is subjected to parental punishment, putdown and threats. Do prevent denial, for—once it becomes extreme and constitutes a neurosis—it is very difficult to cure and often requires lengthy therapy. You can forestall this by creating a warm, secure atmosphere in which your child feels safe to be himself. Give him a place where he can grow without being penalized for his mistakes, where he knows he is respected and accepted.

Eric, as a baby more shy and slower than most children in coming out of himself, by age four was showing some spontaneity, curiosity and assertiveness in quite normal ways. He might have told you what he felt but unfortunately his parents never asked him. They both believed that life should be a businesslike affair, that emotions disrupt normal functioning; consequently, they discouraged any display of strong feelings on Eric's part. When he vented his anger, he was told he was bad, that out-of-control temper was for savages. When he exhibited sadness at disappointment, he was told he should not feel sad and ought not to have held such high expectations. When he showed normal tearfulness, he was told not to act like a baby but to "be brave and keep a stiff upper lip." Even when he showed a great deal of pleasure, he was discouraged. For several years, Eric sustained this steady blanketing of his natural feelings.

During the past few years his interests and involvements have been few. Now reports have been coming from school that Eric, eight, is not performing. After much parental avoidance of the problem, the school principal finally was able to persuade them that an expert opinion should be sought from a psychologist. Eric's testing indicated above-average intelligence but a lack of enthusiasm or willingness to communicate. His parents, who came into frequent contact with adults and children who were much more emotionally expressive, always had secretly suspected that they themselves might be missing out on something. With insistent prodding from the school and confirmation by a professional, they reluctantly accepted the idea of family therapy.

After a number of sessions, it became clear to Eric and his parents that feelings perhaps weren't so harmful after all, and efforts were made to get in touch with them.

Eric has just arrived home from school. He has the usual dull expression on his face and seems preoccupied:

Mother: Remember what the doctor said, Eric. You're supposed to tell me what kind of a day you had at school.

Eric: Oh, it was all right.

Mother: Dr. Day says that we're always feeling something even if we're not aware of it.

Eric: David is having a birthday party on Saturday and I think he's invited all the boys except me.

Mother: How is that making you feel?

Eric: He should have invited me too.

Mother: Are you telling me how you feel or what you think?

Eric: I'm kind of mad at David. But I guess I don't care. I didn't want to go anyway.

Mother: Dr. Day says that, when we think we're a little angry, we're probably a lot more angry than we are able to admit to ourselves.

Eric: I guess I really am mad at David. But I only feel it a little.

Later that week, Eric's father notices his son staring out the window:

Father: Eric, is there something interesting out there?

Eric: No.

Father: Do you know what you're feeling right now?

Eric: I'm not feeling anything.

Father: Then you are thinking something?

Eric: I'm thinking that I'm not going to be at David's birthday party Saturday and all the other kids will. But I don't care.

Father: You mean you don't have any feeling about it all? I would think you'd be sad. At least, that's what our therapist says.

Eric: Yeah, well, I didn't want to go anyway.

Father: You look sad to me, son.

On Friday night, Eric, whose silence ordinarily would have been considered a sign of normal behavior, is observed by his parents to be preoccupied still:

Mother: You're very quiet, Eric. I want to know what you're feeling.

Eric: Not anything.

Mother: If you don't know what you're feeling, then at least tell me what you're thinking about.

Eric: About how I don't have any friends.

Father: What kind of a feeling does a thought like that give you?

Eric: Not good. So I guess it must be bad.

Father: I guess you're afraid that you never will have a friend.

Eric: Yeah. That's what I'm thinking. I suppose that's the way I feel, too.

Father: I've met David's father. If you want, I'll phone to see if he thinks his son would be willing to invite you to the party tomorrow. David may have just forgotten.

Eric: O.K. But don't say I want to be invited.

Father: (*After making a short call*) His father said David meant to invite every one of the boys in the class. He's sorry he missed you and hopes you can come.

The family now is struggling successfully with its denied feelings. Without the therapist's intervention, Eric almost certainly would grow into adulthood unaware of most of his feelings and unequipped to cope with the emotional problems of living. In size and age, he would appear to be a grown man but, because of his limited awareness, emotionally he would still be a child.

How to Deal with Denial

Watch closely for signs of denial and challenge them. Create a secure atmosphere for your child's expression of his feelings, by the simple device of discussing them with him every day. If you spend one-to-one time with him each day, denial will be all but impossible.

When your child denies something he's done, or draws a blank when asked how he feels, use this basic strategy to raise his awareness:

Accept his denial patiently. Don't become angry with him for his denial or accuse him of lying. Remember, denial is the simplest, most immature and frequently used emotional response to what your child experiences as an overwhelming threat. It is automatic and beyond his awareness. In effect, your child is trying to wish away some unpleasant feeling of failure or rejection.

Confront the denial. Tell your child what you think he's feeling. Gently disagree with him: "I know what you said. But I think you did drop Cam's glass. You were the only person around." Or, "You say you don't know how you feel about not being invited to Mario's backyard campout. But I think you feel left out and bad, so bad you don't even want to think about it. Isn't that true?"

Focus his attention on his bad feeling. If your child doesn't become aware or can't recall how he feels or what he's done, don't push too hard. It's sufficient for the time being that you've confronted his denial and told him what you think he is experiencing. End the episode with something like, "I find it hard to believe that this situation isn't making you feel bad."

A-5 Mixed Emotions—Taking the Bad with the Good

For young children who can deal with only the simpler experience of separate good and bad feelings, mixed emotions (or ambivalence) will pose a dilemma. How can you help your child deal with the matter? Mixed emotions is another way of experiencing. As noted earlier, experience is made up of feelings, thoughts and behaviors. When we give them a value, we have the basic building blocks of awareness—nine categories of experience that we live with every day of our lives:

Good Feelings	*Pleasant Thoughts*	*Positive Behaviors*
Bad Feelings	*Unpleasant Thoughts*	*Negative Behaviors*
Mixed Feelings	*Mixed Thoughts*	*Mixed Behaviors*

Adam, eight, is still in pajamas and reading the morning comic-strip page. Mother, who has an anxious eye on the clock, thinks he's taking a bit too much time. She's right. Adam's stalling.

Mother: Adam, put the paper down and go get dressed, right this minute!

Adam: (Mumbling) Aw, gee.

Mother: If you're not out of here in five minutes you'll be late for school.

Adam: Mom, I'm sick.

Mother: You don't look a bit sick to me.

Adam: But I am. Really!

Mother: (Feeling his brow) You're not feverish and you certainly haven't lost your appetite. So what's wrong with you?

Adam: I don't know.

Mother: (Changing her tack) Adam, tell me how you feel about school lately.

Adam: I'm not sure. I like school sometimes. But today I don't. I'm mixed up. I don't know how I feel.

Mother: Maybe you both like it and don't like it. In that case you're having mixed feelings about it. Can you tell me what it is about school that makes you feel bad?

Adam: Arithmetic tests. There's a test today.

Mother: Is there something happening today that you feel good about?

Adam: Darren and I were gonna play dodge-ball after school.

Mother: So your feelings make you want to go to school and yet make you want to stay home?

Adam: I guess so.

Mother: I think I understand. We all have mixed feelings now and then. When I get them I'm confused and don't quite know what to do, just like you. But I'm not letting you run away and hide from your unpleasant feelings. So put your clothes on. Off you go to school. Have a good time with Darren. When you get home, we'll discuss what to do about bad feelings about arithmetic.

Mixed feelings like Adam's are inevitable. Prepare your child to have them about almost every person and event he encounters: you, his sisters, brothers, friends, interests and activities.

You will ease his confusion and concern by focusing your efforts on discussing your child's bad feelings and letting his accompanying good feelings take care of themselves. Talk about possible solutions for the bad way he feels. Keep the channels of communication open. Your child then will feel more secure in such situations because he knows you're available and willing to help.

How to Deal with Mixed Emotions

Teach your child the basic concepts of mixed feelings, thoughts and behaviors, and how common and natural they are to everyone. Help him recognize ambivalence. Discuss mixed emotions with him, using a variety of cues. Give him personal examples of your own to start off with: "Something makes me feel good and bad both, at the same time." Tell him about it and have your child name the good feeling and the bad one. "Something happened to me that was good in one way but bad in another." Discuss. Explain that the prelude to learning something worthwhile often involves pain or effort or having to deal with some challenge we're not sure we can meet. And tell your child that for most of the good things in life we should be prepared to pay some price.

A-6 Curiosity—the Drive to Know

Every normal child comes into the world with a desire to know and to understand his new environment. This curiosity is a part of genetic endowment and begins to operate at once. As an infant, he will study things with his eyes. After he has discovered his hands, he will begin to explore everything within reach, absorbing every impression. These impressions are stored in his nervous system and constitute a fund of information he can use to know and understand his new surroundings.

As he grows, your child's curiosity steadily will press him to learn even more about his environment so that he can have some control over it. This leads to those wonderfully profound questions little children ask, "Daddy, why do you love Mommy?" "Why do people grow old?" "Where did yesterday go?"

Once he becomes mobile, first as a crawler and later on foot, his curiosity will cause him to seek even more-direct knowledge of his new world. And then trouble begins.

Curiosity is so consuming and single-minded in a young child that it often will lead him into physical danger and conflict with others. And yet . . . *your child cannot make a good adjustment to life without finding out.*

Mother, preparing dinner, realizes Tessa, an inquisitive six-year-old, has been missing for about half an hour. In between the meat loaf and potatoes, Mother searches for Tessa, finally locating her in the master bedroom. Tessa, dressed in one of Mother's best dresses and partially dragging it on the floor, is busy applying mascara to a face already smeared with rouge and lipstick. Some bottles have spilled on the floor.

Mother: Tess, are you out of your mind?

Tessa: I'm just playing.

Mother: Just playing?

Tessa: I didn't mean to hurt anything. I was just playing.

Mother: Take that dress off right now! Hurry up! (*Grabbing Tessa, starts to pull off dress. Then stops, smelling smoke.*) Dammit! The dinner is burning! Now see what you've made me do? Don't you ever come into this room again! (*As she bolts out, she gives Tessa a hard slap.*)

This is a typical conflict. Mother rightfully doesn't want her possessions mussed up. Her anger is just as normal as Tessa's curiosity. Inquisitive Tessa was trying to learn what it's like to be Mother. From Tessa's point of view, Mother is fascinating: She's tall, attractive and very important to Father; she can do so many things and knows how to answer so many questions. Tessa, who wants to share in these powers, wonders how she can acquire them. This urge to know is totally natural.

How can Mother support this curiosity without sacrificing things she values?

Mother: Tessa, whatever are you doing?

Tessa: I'm just playing.

Mother: And I suppose you're having lots of fun.

Tessa: Oh, yes, this is so much fun. How do I look?

Mother: Well, Tess—different. Does it make you feel good to look like that?

Tessa: Oh, sure. I look just like you now, Mommy.

Mother: And how do you think I feel?

Tessa: (*Sensing trouble*) Bad?

Mother: That's right. Bad and mad!

Tessa: I didn't break anything.

Mother: Perhaps not. But you easily could have. These things are important to me and you're making a mess of them. Just look at what you've done!

Tessa: I'll clean it all up.

Mother: Fine. I'll let you. Tessa, I don't mind you dressing up when I'm around to help you. But don't do it with my good things when I'm not here. And I really do get mad when you spill things.

Tessa: O.K.

Mother: All right. You're forgiven. After we eat, you and I are going to clean this up together. And then I'll show you what each thing is and why it's important to me, what you can play with and what you can't.

In this instance, Mother tries to reinforce Tessa's curiosity while maintaining the integrity of her personal possessions. By focusing on the feeling, she is able to help Tessa understand the implication of what has happened. At the same time, Mother keeps open the door for Tessa to learn more about clothes, jewelry and cosmetics. Mother is direct and honest. She expresses her anger but doesn't use it to destroy Tessa's curiosity, nor does she make it unsafe for the child to learn.

How to Confront Curiosity

When your child's curiosity conflicts with your interests, you can deal with it effectively if you . . .

Tell your child that curiosity is normal and understandable. Explain that it is through curiosity we learn about the world. .

Describe the conflict to him. Say that you can see what he's after. Show him how it is causing a conflict:

"I'm glad that you like music so much. But if I let you experiment with the piano right now, I'll worry that it will waken Daddy."

"I understand how thrilled you were to see that beautiful butterfly, but I can't answer your questions about butterflies right now. I'm in a hurry to pin up the hem of your sister's skirt."

Seek a mutually satisfactory solution. Ask your child to suggest a way that will satisfy his curiosity without causing you any disagreeable feelings. If he cannot come up with a good solution, you suggest one:

"If you'll stay right beside me, and hold the pin box for me carefully, without spilling any, then I can work fast and still answer your questions about butterflies."

Curiosity and Learning
There will be times when your child's curiosity will charm you and make you feel proud. Each time he exhibits curiosity is a special opportunity to excite his desire to learn. You can give your child this precious gift in his early years when you—
Encourage his curiosity. Ask him if he wonders about certain things, if he has any questions. Praise him for seeking new knowledge: "It makes me so glad when you want to learn."

Answer his questions. Don't put him off or down but try to give the best answer you can, or refer him to another source. If you don't know, say so; make it a joint project to learn the answer together.

Arrange events and field trips based on his expressed interests and what you think he might like. Take him to new places where he can meet new people and situations. Provide a wide range of learning materials, simple things like paper and pencil, crayons, blocks, educational toys, magazines and books—a wide variety of things he can enjoy as he develops his skills and knowledge. Making learning easy and fun for him in his early years, even if it is an effort for you, will pave the way to success in life. It's well worth your time and energy, for your child never will be so eager to learn as when he is young.

A-7 Desire: Need, Want or Deprivation Complex?

Every parent knows the hassle of dealing with a child's desires. It begins with the first two-o'clock feeding and never seems to end. There is a perpetual stream of "gimme this, gimme that," leaving you confused and exhausted. Coping with these desires and demands is plainly one of the most difficult and draining tasks parents face.

It is critical that you become aware of the many different meanings behind an expressed desire. Otherwise, in responding, you may take his request or demand at face value and miss what he really wants.

Basically there are four kinds of meanings behind expressed desires. When your child asks for something, he may be . . .

Asking for something he needs.

Saying he wants some material object because he consciously seeks personal involvement with you.

Asking for something he wants, in order to explore the limits of his power over you.

Saying he wants some material object because he subconsciously suffers from a deep gnawing sense that he is missing something. This is the mark of the deprivation complex, seen in the child who has had insufficient personal attention.

Essentially, desire concerns getting the things we need. But a lot of confusion can exist between what your child needs and what he wants. The distinction is an important one:

• A need is something your child must have for his well-being. Without it, he might suffer dire consequences to his physical, intellectual or emotional development.

• A demand is a desire for something pleasant but unessential to your child's well-being. He can live without it.

Ordinarily, parents try to satisfy a child's every need. Most of us work hard, struggle and even sacrifice things we want or need ourselves rather than let our child do without. But when we confuse our child's wants and accept them as though they were needs, we can subject ourselves to needless guilt.

Meet your child's needs. But don't consider it necessary to satisfy all his demands. If they're reasonable and important, attend to them. If they're unreasonable, say no. Otherwise, the sheer number and intensity of his requests will wear you out and spoil him, thereby compounding the problem by increasing his expectations for more.

Children often ask us for things just to test the limits of their power. Remember that your young child's essential state of being is one of helplessness. One of his main tasks in life is to overcome that helplessness by acquiring power. When he tries to learn the limits of how fast he can run, how far he can jump and how high he can climb, he is getting information about the dimensions of his power.

Therefore, it's natural for your child to explore the limits to his desire by asking for things. He'll try every tactic from politeness to wheedling to tantrums to find out how far he can push you before running into your resistance. That's how he learns to test the limits of what he can get; that's how he develops realistic expectations about satisfying his desires. As he presses for them, he's not trying to aggravate you. You are the testing ground on which he must prove his mettle. The harrassment is a by-product, part of the price you pay for his development.

Another kind of desire has to do with emotional needs. This is sometimes so severe that it may be called a deprivation complex. Quite often, when your child calls for a glass of water at bedtime, he wants your companionship and involvement more than he wants water. But these are intangible concepts he may lack the language to express. So he uses the best possible approximation he knows: "Can I have a drink of water, please?" He subconsciously senses that, if you bring him the water, there will surely be some kind of personal contact which may give him the attention he craves.

Children's desires are particularly intense. This intensity can lead to problems for both child and parent. Brian, full of life and curiosity, with the voracious eight-year-old appetite, wants to do everything, have everything and eat everything in sight. It's 5:30 p.m. and he's hungry:

Mother: Get out of those cookies, Brian. Dinner will be on the table in 20 minutes.

Brian: But I'm hungry right now.

Mother: I want you hungry for dinner, too.

Brian: I'll eat all right.

Mother: I've heard that before and I know what happens.

Brian: When? When did I ever not eat dinner after having cookies?

Mother: I don't have time to argue. I said no.

Brian: All I want is a couple little ones. Huh? Please?

Mother: I said no. That's final!

Brian: (Grumbling) Aw, you never let me have anything good.

Mother: I'm too busy to have you underfoot causing trouble. Out of here, now, Brian! Before I really get mad.

Every mother will recognize this encounter. But you may not recognize the possible hidden emotional message that could make this seemingly innocuous exchange potentially harmful. Mother and Brian really may be saying:

Mother: I don't want you to do what you want to do.

Brian: You don't want me to feel good. That means you don't like me.

Mother: You're irritating me by doing something I don't want you to do. You're beginning to make me feel inadequate.

Brian: You don't trust me. And you're against me.

Mother: I'm against you because you're against me.

In this classic conflict—deeper interpersonal implications aside—Brian is attracted by the prospect of eating some cookies and satisfying his immediate hunger. But his desires blind him to the larger issue of saving his appetite for dinner. Mother feels pressured by his insistence. And his push to get what he wants threatens her feelings of effectiveness as a parent.

The solution to Brian's desires lies in looking beyond cookies to the interaction of feelings. Had Mother known:

Mother: Get out of those cookies, Brian. Dinner will be on the table in 20 minutes.

Brian: I'm hungry right now.

Mother: You can have cookies after dinner. Please save your appetite.

Brian: Can't I have just one? One cookie?

Mother: I wouldn't like that. I'm trying to get dinner ready and you're making me feel that it's a waste of time. Because getting what you want would make you feel good, you haven't thought that I might want something, too. I'm cooking a nutritious meal. I realize how much you love those oatmeal cookies, Brian. But I don't want you stuffing yourself with them before mealtime.

Brian: It wouldn't hurt to let me have just one.

Mother: You're thinking about right now. But I'm thinking about what's going to happen later. You'll miss the benefit of a nutritious meal.

Brian: I'll eat my dinner if you'd let me have just one little cookie. And I wouldn't bother you any more.

Mother: Let's settle it this way, instead. Wait until after dinner and then have some cookies. That way you get what you want and I get what I want.

Brian: How soon did you say dinner is going to be ready ?

Mother: If you leave me alone now, I'll hurry and serve you in 15 minutes, Brian. You can wait that long, I know.

Brian: All right. I'll try to wait.

Mother: Fine. I appreciate it when you're willing to listen to what I think is important.

This way Mother manages to get through to Brian by translating the situation into a language he can understand—good and bad feelings. By contrasting her feelings with his, she makes him aware of an aspect of the conflict he simply would not have noticed in his drive to satisfy himself. She focuses on solid reasons for how she feels, then bargains for a solution they both can life with.

How to Deal with Strong Desire

Acknowledge the intensity of your child's desire. Tell him that you understand how much he wants what he's after. This recognition blunts the intensity of his desire by relieving the feeling of deprivation that often makes desires more urgent; you lessen his desire a little and make it easier to postpone immediate fulfillment.

Determine the kind of desire. When confronted with his demands and desires, ask yourself, "What is he really asking for? Is it something he greatly needs or something for his amusement or pleasure? "Is he testing my endurance, trying to find out his limits and mine?" "Is there a disguised message? Does he really want what he's asking for? Or does he want my attention and personal involvement?"

Deal with the particular kind of desire. If your child is asking for something he needs, you will want to provide it.

If he is asking for a mere frill, you may want to deny it.

If your child is incessantly testing limits by asking for things, help him by setting definite, consistent standards regarding his requests. The sooner you set and communicate these standards clearly, the less he will need to test you. Chances are, however, that he will continue to challenge the limits to push them back if he can. Your task is to maintain the reasonable limits you've set.

If he is constantly asking for things but nothing seems to satisfy him, you have reason to suspect a deprivation complex—a child's feeling that he's being seriously neglected and not getting satisfaction for his deeper needs.

If your child is truly deprived, his constant requests may be his way of saying, "I need to feel that life and the world are good to me." The solution is to define his needs and meet them. Much one-to-one time is indicated.

If yours is a disconsolate child handicapped by a downcast, disagreeable inborn temperament, he may feel deprived even when he has everything. He doesn't feel good but has no language for his unfortunate temperament. "Give me a lollipop" can be his way of saying, "I feel miserable and I want to feel better. It's been my experience that, if I suck on a lollipop, I will feel better, at least for a moment or so. So let's try that." You have to be patient and recognize that some children are finicky, cranky and melancholy, difficult to satisfy. The physiological causes are not yet known. If this applies to your child, all you can do is to give him plenty of acceptance and caring to lessen his built-in bad feelings.

Tell your child there is something you want very much, too. Explain what your conflicting desire is, and why it's important to you.

Ask your child to suggest a reasonable solution that will satisfy your conflicting desires. If it is agreeable to you, follow it. If your child cannot come up with a mutually satisfactory solution, offer and enforce your own. But give him your reason for selecting this solution so that it does not seem completely arbitrary. Even though your child does not get what he wants, at least he will have been heard and shown why he was denied. Consequently, he will be less likely to feel he's being treated in an offhand way or mindlessly discriminated against.

Keep your promises. Ordinarily, if there is no conflict, you will want to grant your child's wishes. But it's critical for your credibility as a parent that you promise him only what you fully intend to deliver. To do otherwise will set you up for future trouble. Never give in to your child merely to silence him.

A-8 Fear: It's a Scary World

Many parents regard their children's fears as a sure sign of cowardice or congenital weakness. But fear is natural and beneficial. It's Nature's way of warning us of real dangers. And it touches all of us—adult and child alike.

Without his fear to protect him, your child would burn himself at the fireplace, cut himself with a carving knife or leap off a roof while imitating some TV super-hero. As it is, these injuries do occur to many children whose normal, instinctive fear is not sufficiently developed.

Before age four or five, the best protection for your child lies in child-proofing his environment. Removing poisons to a locked cupboard, capping electrical outlets and putting away sharp-edged objects of all sorts—these are ways to make the home environment safe for curious and fearless youngsters. At age six or seven, when your child develops the power to reason, explain what dangers are and why he should avoid certain things. Thereafter, more and more he can serve as his own guardian.

It's also important to distinguish between fear and phobia. Because they seem alike, parents often mistake one for the other. They're not the same. Fear is a normal pattern of caution. Phobia is an extreme, deeply felt fear that lacks justification; the actual danger doesn't warrant the amount of fear. Phobias are abnormal, yet almost every child has at least one phobia. For one child, it will be an acute fear of dogs; for another, spiders; and, for still another, an intense fear of the dark.

In many cases, these intense fears gradually disappear as the child gains more experience and self-confidence. As a general rule with the young child, it's advisable to accept his great fear for the time being without making him confront the object of his phobia. Forcing a child to touch a feared dog or

66

spider merely terrorizes him and intensifies the phobia.

Nor should a young child be given a great deal of hollow reassurance: "It's all right." "Don't worry." "It will go away." In the face of his fear, such reassurance is simply not credible. Be your own best example, either by telling or showing him how unafraid you are of the dog or spider that is terrifying him. He will pick up the positive implication that, as he grows older, he probably will become less afraid too.

For several years Lee, eight, has been afraid of the dark unless there is another person in the room with him. His parents, to preserve their privacy, refuse to permit him to sleep in their room. His father, although somewhat afraid of his superiors at work, has little sympathy for such an irrational fear as terror of the dark. It's bedtime:

Father: O.K. Time for bed, Lee. Goodnight.

Lee: (Hesitant) I know. But, please, can't I stay up just five more minutes?

Father: Don't give me that. You're scared of going upstairs and don't want to face it. There's nothing up there that can hurt you.

Lee: I know nothing's going to hurt me. But I get afraid anyway.

Father: How can you know nothing's going to hurt you and still be afraid? That doesn't make sense. You're acting like a baby.

Lee: Will you come up and read me a story?

Father: Absolutely not. Get to bed!

Lee: (His body stiffening as he senses time running out) Please, Dad.

Father: (Menacingly) Lee, I don't want to have to give you something to be really afraid of.

This exchange has a number of serious implications. Like most children, Lee lacks the vocabulary and experience to articulate his feelings clearly. What he is trying to tell his father is:

I am afraid.

I know that it's probably irrational, that it doesn't make any sense.

I'm ashamed of being this way but I can't help it.

Please don't demean or desert me. It's bad

enough to be so inferior and ridiculous on top of being scared.

Lee's father is unwilling to listen to this. Instead, Father makes strong statements with profound underlying implications:

I don't understand you.

I don't know how to help you.

I find you irritating.

You are an embarrassment, a potential disgrace to me.

I will not accept your attempts to avoid the fearful thing you cannot deal with.

I'm threatening you with physical harm.

I don't like you.

I'm deserting you.

I'm helpless to cope constructively with your problem even though I'm so big.

His father's messages compound Lee's phobia with feelings of shame, inferiority, unacceptability and desertion. Here are the makings of a mutually hostile and frustrating relationship.

Let us assume the boy's father understands that most phobias eventually will be outgrown—especially if there is a strong, positive, supportive parental relationship with the child—and that he is dedicated to encouraging Lee to face other fear-filled situations in which there is only a reasonable degree of true danger. Still, Father wants to avoid overprotecting Lee from normal fears lest the boy grow into a sissy:

Father: O.K., Lee. It's bedtime.

Lee: Do I have to go?

Father: That's right.

Lee: I don't want to go up to bed. I'm afraid of the dark.

Father: Is there something specific that you're afraid of?

Lee: It's just the dark that I don't like.

Father: Most people have something that they're unreasonably afraid of, and you're entitled to yours. But you do have to go to bed, son.

Lee: Well, will you come up and read to me, just for a few minutes?

Father: Sure, I'll come up. But let's have a talk instead.

(A few minutes later, upstairs in Lee's room. Lee is in bed.)

Father: I want you to try something with me. O.K.? Tell me some horrible thing that you imagine might happen to you. And take it to its most horrible ending.

Lee: That's scary, Dad . . . but I'll try . . . Well . . . let's say that you and Mom leave. And I'm all alone. And I hear a noise.

Father: What's the horrible ending?

Lee: Like supposing it's a robber and he comes in here.

Father: Then what?

Lee: He might kill me or take me away.

Father: That would be terrible. I don't want anything bad to happen to you, you know. Now, what can you do if you hear a strange noise?

Lee: I guess maybe I could yell for help.

Father: Right. And you know I'll come in a minute if you yell.

Lee: I'm afraid nobody will hear me.

Father: I'll be sure to hear you, Lee.

Lee: Dad, is there something wrong with me?

Father: Well, it's not good to be so scared about something. But everybody is scared at one time or another. So there's nothing seriously wrong with you.

How to Deal with Fear and Phobia

Focus on you child's feeling of fear. Don't try to debate the merits of how realistic or unrealistic the fear may be.

Don't offer superficial reassurance. It merely tells him that you've deserted him to cope with his fears on his own.

Offer your sincere help: "I know you're very much afraid. And I'd like to help you find a way to get over it." Your offer is the best reassurance he can get. Reducing his sense of loneliness reduces the feeling of fear.

Ask him to specify what he fears: "What do you think the spider will do to you?" "What do you think the dog is going to do?" What's the worst thing that can happen to you?"

Ask him, "Is there anything you can think of that would make you less afraid?" If his suggestion is reasonable and possible, use it. This reaffirms your willingness to help, and is far more likely to be effective than a

Freudian investigation into the origin of his fears.

Use the principle of universalization. Assure your child by admitting that you yourself sometimes become intensely afraid, that everybody does, even his friends who say they don't. This will allow him to feel more "normal" and relieve him of the feeling he's "weak," "cowardly" or "peculiar."

A-9 Anger

All of our feelings are aspects of three basic core urges: to approach, to avoid and to destroy. The underlying feelings are desire, fear and anger. For example, pleasure, appreciation and affection flow from fulfilled desire. Anxiety and insecurity are forms of fear, apprehensions of dangers perceived or imagined. And irritation, annoyance and frustration all are closely related to anger, to the readiness to fight or destroy. As noted earlier, Emotional Maturity depends upon your child being in direct touch with his feelings, whatever they may be. This is especially true when the feeling is anger.

As a core feeling, anger is a natural, valuable part of your child's emotional repertoire. It functions as an adaptive mechanism to guard him against encroachment and threats to his well-being. When he angrily makes a stand after being pushed by another boy in the schoolyard and says, "Don't try to push me around or I'll let you have it," his anger protects him not only from bodily harm, but also from psychological mutilation that results from degrading treatment.

Nevertheless, anger is a difficult emotion for parents and children to handle or control. When your 10-year-old screams out his anger at you, it's hard to be objective or understanding. Our egos become involved and we retaliate in kind. But our angry response too often teaches our children by example that the "best way" to deal with anger is more anger.

The issue is complicated by the fact that a child's anger toward his parents often is justified: "You never spend any time with me." "Why didn't you ask me what really happened before you started to yell?" "Why do you always take his side?" "Just because she's small doesn't mean she's always right." Much as we dislike hearing such angry accusations, that is not sufficient reason to suppress them. In order to stay in touch with his feelings, your child needs to express the truth of your relationship as he sees it—even when he's angry. His anger can be safely expressed verbally. It is repressed anger that can lead to hidden resentment, psychosomatic symptoms and sabotage.

To cope effectively, your child must learn how to express his angry feelings.

But anger is not only a protective response. It also can become a self-indulgent abuse, raising false behavioral issues and obscuring real ones. This emotional smoke-screening usually takes place when a child becomes angry over disappointment or frustrated desire.

His vented anger provides relief from the feeling of frustration; but the real issue, his inability to cope with disappointment and frustration, can be overlooked and neglected. If it remains untreated, it may cause trouble at the next provocation. When your child succumbs to this handy self-indulgence, he often remains unaware of his real need and the true nature of his difficulty.

Kevin, 10, has a strong inborn inclination to regard himself as the center of the world and to believe firmly that his wishes should prevail in every situation. When he doesn't get what he wants, his self-centered and demanding nature becomes rebellious and belligerent. Raising him has been, for his parents, a running battle. Time and time again, they have had to resist his insistent demands and endure the unpleasant aftermath. Becoming desperate, they more and more are relying on physical punishment in a futile effort to control Kevin's behavior. On this Saturday, in a typical conflict, Kevin is insisting on riding his bike halfway across town in the rain to see a movie. Ordinarily, his father would drive him. But Father is away on a business trip. Mother is trying to hold the fort:

Kevin: I don't mind if it's raining. I want to go to the movies and I'm going.

Mother: You're not leaving this house. There's a downpour outside and you'll get soaked through.

Kevin: I don't care about the rain. I want to go.

Mother: Try to be reasonable for once! Can't you see you're just asking for trouble?

Kevin: You never want me to have any fun.

Mother: You'll catch pneumonia or be run over.

Kevin: You're just coming down hard on me because you don't want me to have a good time. You're always like that. You're always against me.

Mother: Dammit, I've had enough! Go to your room. And if you dare to come out of it, I'll break you in two.

Kevin: I don't care! I hate you!

This is merely one of a number of battles in an escalating war. With each skirmish, the chances for developing positive, supportive relationships are disappearing rapidly in mutual resentment. Kevin is acutely aware of his desire and his anger. But he is having trouble integrating these emotions with reality. Today, he ignores the rain and danger on the road. Tomorrow, he'll ignore something else.

What can a reasonably patient parent do with such a willful child? Not much in the short run. Instead of merely reacting on the spot to these daily episodes, Kevin's parents need to lift their sights to the planning of a long-range strategy to reduce his burgeoning egoism. As a start, they need to view his angry outbursts as a symptom of the larger problem—his self-centeredness. At the same time, they also are going to have to give up their own belligerent attitudes and accept the fact that they are custodians of a child with a severe temperament disturbance. This means removing their own egos from the scene and foregoing any moralizing. A temperamental child cannot be helped by temperamental treatment from his parents.

What Kevin is struggling with is not their authority but his own difficulty in developing a less angry outlook and a more considerate relationship with those who love and care for him. He needs a steady diet of patience, reassurance and loving-but-firm confrontation as he displays his intensely self-blinded behavior:

Kevin: I don't mind if it's raining. I want to go to the movies and I'm going.

Mother: I understand how much you want to go. I get upset too when I can't do what I want.

Kevin: Then you should let me go.

Mother: I can't let you go out in that torrent.

Kevin: Every time I want to go someplace, you say no. Well, I'm going anyway.

Mother: I've explained why I can't possibly say yes today. You're very upset, aren't you?

Kevin: You bet I am.

Mother: I want you to get over being angry.

Kevin: That's easy. Just let me go to the movies this afternoon.

Mother: We'll have to find another solution.

Kevin: That's just another way of saying no. You don't want me to have any fun, ever. You're always against me.

Mother: Kevin, you know that's not true. I really want to find a solution to this. Do you? Or don't you want to do anything but complain?

Kevin: You can bet I'm gonna complain as long as you won't let me go.

Mother: That's part of our problem today, you see. You have only one solution for everything, Kevin—to get your own way every time. Well, it won't work this time. I have concerns too.

Kevin: Like what?

Mother: I'm very concerned about your getting soaked to the bone or hurt on the road. The visibility is dreadful. And have you stopped to think how much you'll enjoy sitting in a movie theatre if your clothes are soaking wet? Now let's stop fighting and see what we can figure out. Is this movie playing tomorrow?

Kevin: I think so.

Mother: I promise to take you there tomorrow. Your father will be back and I'll have the car.

Kevin: You're sure you're not just saying that? This isn't a trick? You won't change your mind?

Mother: If I promise to take you tomorrow, I will. O.K.?

Kevin: Well, maybe . . .

How to Deal with Anger

Accept your child's anger as a natural, valid feeling. When he becomes angry over some injustice, frustration or disappointment, it is a natural discharge of energy. Never tell him, "Don't be angry." Instead, let him express his anger verbally to "get it off his chest." Accept his verbal tirade.

Do not accept any attempt on his part to act out his anger. Yelling out his feeling is one thing but throwing things or hitting people is unacceptable. As provocative as his anger may be, you must never prolong the episode by retaliating with anger and indignation. Once verbalized, his anger often will be effectively reduced.

After things have quieted down, spend a few moments considering the most probable underlying cause. Here once again, it will be easier if you have an accurate picture of his deepest concern. Look first to the most common causes. Is your child perhaps acting badly out of a clinging to his early self-centered nature, just wanting everything to go his way? Or, closely related, may he be suffering feelings of loneliness, social isolation due to an underlying shyness? If the causes are here in the social department, the answers must of course come through better relations with other people. If the problem is one of strong self-interest, you will be able to make good headway by giving more one-to-one time. This can be augmented by additional encouragement and guidance in developing more-substantial friendships.

If the anger is caused by an inability to succeed at some task or solve some problem, you know you're dealing with a competence problem. Review the competence component and, as you identify the main developmental issues, give the indicated help. Often you will find that clinging to unrealistic expectations is the root of the matter. But, rather than one specific developmental deficiency being the cause, there may be a generalized resistance to the whole idea of growing up, taking on more responsibilities, having to be held more accountable in general. You should expect such regressive behavior once in a while: a wish to return to an earlier stage, to a time of indulged dependency when there was much less expected of him. If this is so, then some extra attention and reassurance are indicated. Focus on the things about your child that you appreciate and respect, rather than dwell on the angry feelings.

Another consideration is that the underlying cause may be a deep sense of deprivation. In such a case, anger can serve as a trigger for deeper concern. Say, "Just because you're not getting your way in some small matter at this moment doesn't prove that you're being cheated out of a good life. Nobody gets everything he wants." Again, your special reassurance of one-to-one time will reduce the sense of deprivation and thereby reduce the resultant anger.

Be especially careful to avoid the enemy-trap. Do not let your child set you up as his antagonist. Get on his side. Show him how much you want to help him solve the problem that caused the anger in the first place.

A-10 Projection: "It's Not My Fault"

Suppose your child allows the water in the sink to run over, but cannot face up to this minor failure. His memory, influenced by the dread of feeling very bad for having goofed, easily can fail. It even can be so distorted that he believes "seeing brother Cass walking away from the sink after Cass did it."

This is not lying, since lying is consciously withholding the truth from another person. Your son is unconsciously withholding the truth from his own conscious awareness; thus he is the first "victim."

Actually, projection is a two-step process. The first step is denial: The unwanted truth is withheld from the self. In the second step, the unwanted truth is attributed to something or someone else. The purpose of the second step is to reinforce the first step, making it more likely to stick: "It was Cass. It wasn't me." Subsequent vehement denials are reiterations of the "truth" as your child knows it. If he doesn't feel completely safe to fail, then each failure or mistake can pose a severe threat. If he lets himself see clearly what is happening, he could feel very helpless and inadequate.

Parents find such behavior exasperating and bewildering. There he is, standing in the kitchen and chewing celery while the broken celery dish lies on the floor, and he tells you, "I didn't break that. It was somebody else, not me." Your first inclination is to kill him on the spot. How can he be so obviously to blame and then so dumb as to lie about it? The answer is that he may not be lying. Because he wants to believe it so much, he fools himself. If he is permitted frequent unchallenged projections over a period of time, he further confuses them with reality.

The solution to this possible emotional disaster is simple: Break up the pattern by gently challenging your child's projections whenever one comes up. As you do, you must show a supportive, forgiving attitude toward his mistakes and failures. If you reduce his fears of failure and rejection and help him understand that we all are fallible, he will have less need for projecting his mistakes and failings onto others.

J.J., nine, is failing in school. Rather than accept his own role in the failure, he really believes his teacher is responsible. In the deeper recesses of his mind, he knows better. At the conscious level, he misperceives himself as the "victim" instead of the cause. He has just come home with a bad report card.

J.J.: (Attempting nonchalance) Sign this for me, will you, Dad?

Father: (Studying the card and seeing the borderline grades) Hey, wait a minute! Does this mean you're failing these subjects?

J.J.: It's all my teacher's fault. She won't ever help me.

Father: But she helps the other children?

J.J.: More than me.

Father: Do you ask her to help you?

J.J.: She doesn't like me. She's always mad at me for no reason.

Father: It says here that you haven't been turning in your homework.

J.J.: I turned in some.

Father: What happened to the rest?

J.J.: Well, I couldn't do some of it. And I lost a little of it.

Father: And you made no effort to redo it or to explain?

J.J.: My teacher wouldn't believe me anyway. She never does.

Father: So you bring home a lousy report like this! All this tells me is that you're going to turn out to be a bum!

J.J.: (Feeling hopeless, he is speechless.)

Father: You listen and listen good, J.J. Until you learn to do your homework and get better marks, you're not going to be allowed to do anything—and that means playing baseball too!

J.J.: But, Dad, that's not fair! I have to play. The coach says I'm the number-one hitter on our team.

Father: I don't care whether you're Hank Aaron. If you don't get good marks, you're out. And that's how it is.

The problem here, of course, is that J.J. is projecting his failure onto his teacher. J.J.'s father is vaguely aware of the feebleness of his son's excuse but, untrained to spot this dodge and deal with it effectively, he brings all his weight to bear on the surface issue—J.J.'s grades. This is merely treating the symptom. And so the projection can go on unchecked.

At the same time, his punishment deprives J.J. of baseball, the one experience that boosts his ego and gives him some of the security he needs so he can accept responsibility for his failures. The boy also hears the implications of his father's frustration: "You're not really making an effort at school but I don't know how to discuss this constructively." "You're going to be a loser and I don't know how to prevent it except by punishment."

If he could, Father would avoid these disastrous methods. With a little training to give him insight into J.J.'s emotions, Father might deal with the boy's underlying insecurity:

Father: J.J., this report card is terrible.

J.J.: It's all my teacher's fault. She won't ever help me.

Father: You mean it's all her fault that you're failing?

J.J.: Yeah. She doesn't like me. She won't help me at all.

Father: But is she responsible 100%? Or do you have a part in this failure—something you're doing or not doing?

J.J. I got pretty fair grades last year with Mrs. Dix. She liked me. If I still had her for my teacher, I'd be doing O.K.

Father: Did you get much homework in third grade?

J.J.: No, not much.

Father: But now you do. Maybe that's the problem. More work is required of you than when you were in Mrs. Dix's third-grade class. And, from what I've seen, you don't seem to be doing very much work.

J.J.: My teacher makes it so boring. I'd rather play ball.

Father: In other words, unless the work is great fun, you won't have anything to do with it?

J.J.: Well, what good is this kind of stuff, anyway? Why do I have to study geography and history? Who needs them?

Father: J.J., the most important thing you learn at school isn't history or geography. It's developing good work habits, applying yourself, training yourself so you'll become an effective person.

J.J.: Why can't they teach me something interesting?

Father: That will come later. First, you have to learn how to understand ideas. You have to know the fundamentals—reading, writing and simple arithmetic. If you don't know these, you'll always be limited. And, if you don't learn early to apply yourself and organize your efforts, you'll never succeed at anything.

J.J.: What can I do when I've got a teacher who won't help me?

Father: There you go, blaming your teacher again. I'm not at all sure that she's your problem.

J.J.: Then you mean it's me. That's what you think.

Father: Now you've got the point. Only you can do the work, J.J. Only you can learn the basics. If your teacher doesn't like you, maybe it's because you won't work. Let's make a deal. If you'll stop blaming your teacher, I promise to help you every night to organize your homework so you can get it done in a reasonable time. O.K.?

J.J.'s father concentrates on the real cause of the difficulty: his son's unwillingness to apply effort and to accept this personal shortcoming as the real reason for his school failure. Father goes behind the defense of J.J.'s projection and zooms in on the importance of effort and good work habits. Then Father offers continued support to help J.J. develop the needed work habits, thus increasing the boy's feeling of security.

How to Deal With Projection

Prevent projection from ever becoming a habit. Once established, it can constitute a serious emotional disorder that encourages escape from the challenge of self-improvement. Your strategy is to confront gently and reveal your child's projections when they occur.

Keep in mind that it's hard on the ego to admit being the cause of one's own failure. It's easier on the emotions to attribute failure to some external cause, perhaps another person. Don't accept this projection. Confront your child. Tell him he may be doing something he isn't aware of that is contributing to the failure or mistake. Ask him to look for his possible role in creating the problem. If necessary, help him to see what his role has been. When he is able to recognize and accept his own inadequacy, say, "I know it's hard to admit making a mistake. I admire your courage in doing it." You also can work at building his basic security by giving him more one-to-one time.

Create an environment that minimizes the need for projection. Build an environment out of realistic expectations which make it clear that it is safe for your child to admit his limitations. Show your acceptance of the fact that mistakes and failures are inevitable, and you can make projection unnecessary.

A-11 Frustration and Discouragement: "I'm in a Bad Mood."

All of us have bad moods that come from many sources and are hard to shake. Your child will have his share of them, too. What are the means of getting him out of his bad moods? To learn how, consider two common forms of bad moods, or dysphoria—frustration and discouragement.

Frustration: "I'm So Dumb!"

Frustration is an inescapable part of life. There are so many things your child wants to do but can't; or can do, but not as well as he would like. You've seen it happen. He can't solve the puzzle he's working on and ends up angrily trying to force the pieces together. When this fails, he throws the puzzle onto the floor in frustration.

To an adult, all this emotion expended over a puzzle seems like a tempest in a teapot. But not to your child. In his eyes, the puzzle represents a serious challenge, an important test he wants to pass. As he sees it, his failure threatens his sense of personal effectiveness and leaves him convinced he is a born loser, helpless now and likely to remain so. It's this conclusion that frustrates him.

You can expect almost every child to overgeneralize in this way, taking each and every failure as absolute proof of his personal inadequacy. His failure to solve the puzzle is unsettling but superficial compared to the underlying possibility that he is a total failure. You will need to focus your efforts on his feeling of inadequacy. The name of the game isn't puzzle. It's ego.

Kelly, 10, hasn't yet mastered long division. The fifth-grade teacher has assigned him extra work to take home. Tormented and fuming, he sits at the kitchen table and grapples with an arithmetic problem.

Kelly: I can't do it! It's too hard!

Father: You sound awfully frustrated.

Kelly: I just can't do it! I'm so dumb!

Father: Well, long division is hard for anybody to learn.

Kelly: You're just saying that. The other kids can do it. I'm so dumb, Miss Hill gave me extra work. And I still can't do it.

Father: And how is all this making you feel about yourself?

Kelly: Stupid, that's how. I'm just too dumb for anything.

Father: Wait a minute. In one leap you've just gone from long division to being no good. Does that mean if I teach you how to do long division you'll be a complete success?

Kelly: I'd probably just turn out to be a dummy about something else.

Father: Well, I'm certainly glad I'm not you. I'd feel frustrated all the time.

Kelly's father shows him how to do the problem, emphasizing a step-by-step approach until the boy understands exactly what he is doing. Father stays with him as his son finishes the rest of the assignment:

Father: There, you've done them by yourself. And correctly, too. What do you think you've learned?

Kelly: I think I can do long division pretty well now.

Father: You've got the hang of it, all right. And what did you learn about frustration?

Kelly: I don't know. Probably that anything's frustrating until you know how to do it.

Father: And how do you feel about yourself?

Kelly: A whole lot better.

How to Deal with Frustration

Learn the Cause. When you see your child in the throes of frustration, take a few moments to find out how much his trouble is connected to the task at hand—the school assignment, puzzle, model or game—and how much to his general sense of effectiveness. If he runs himself down badly, challenge his overgeneralizing: "I don't believe that one limitation proves that you're totally stupid."

Remind him of the many challenges that thwart you because you haven't mastered them yet: "There are plenty of things that frustrate me—like when I can't start the car in the morning." Help him master the task but give only as much assistance as he needs. Then, remind your child of the overall picture: "It's part of the price we pay to learn how to do something. Just because you make a few mistakes with something doesn't mean you'll never learn it."

Discouragement: "Nobody Likes Me"

It's essential for your child to experience himself as a person others can want as a friend. But simply telling him he is worthy of friends is not enough. He has to experience this sense of being wanted, in daily contacts with others—especially his peers. It's inevitable that he'll have problems. He may be rejected, ignored, left out of games, not invited to all social events. He even may be made fun of until he thinks he no longer wants to make friends. Then, the theme song of discouragement—"Nobody Likes Me"—will threaten to become a self-fulfilling prophecy.

Jody, 11, has just been finding out how vicious some sixth-grade girls can be. She's been fairly well accepted by a loosely knit group of girls but, for the past few days, they've hardly said hello to her. Yesterday, she overheard a comment that they were planning to form an exclusive club—without her. Right now, she's moping:

Mother: Jody, something's bugging you. What is it?

Jody: Nothing.

Mother: You've been moping around. What's making you so sad?

Jody: Nobody likes me any more.

Mother: Nobody? Nobody is a lot of people.

Jody: It's not funny. Somehow I've lost all my friends. Carla and Toby won't talk to me any more.

Mother: What did you do to them?

Jody: I didn't do anything. They all just dumped me.

Mother: (After drawing out more of the details) Jody, this sounds an awful lot like what happened to me when I was around your age.

Jody: It happened to you, too?

Mother: Yes, and it seems like it's beginning all over again with you. Suddenly the girls in my class became so concerned about whether they were going to be included in things that they stopped reaching out. Some of my oldest friends shut me out and made me feel like a stranger. For a while I was convinced I was so plain and unattractive that no one would ever want me for a friend.

Jody: What did you do?

Mother: Luckily, I figured it would be smart to look for friendship from people who were looking for it too. When I decided who else probably needed a friend, I went out of my way to be nice to them. Before long, I went from feeling like an ugly duckling to actually being fairly popular.

Jody: You did?

Mother: And so can you. Be friendly and make it easy for other people to be friendly. You'll be surprised how many people will want to be your friend.

How to Deal with Discouragement

Your first task is to diagnose the symptoms: moping about, avoiding contact with others, appearing upset. You can help by asking your child if he's feeling sad about something. Listen to the source of his bad feelings until you're sure you have enough information to work with him toward a solution. Almost always, your support and helpful suggestions will provide encouragement enough to tip your child's mood toward one of hope and constructive action. Give him some follow-up interest and, after a day or two, ask how things are going.

A-12 "I Am Different, Therefore Inferior and Unworthy"

Somehow children are keenly aware of their individuality. Far from perceiving it as a blessing, they are apt to regard their individual traits as a sure sign of essential inferiority. Wearing glasses, being short, not having the latest clothes or haircut can readily create the delusion of uniqueness— the false assumption that being different is proof of unacceptability. Many children fervently believe this.

The strength of this delusion is rooted in children's emotional isolation. The real problem is not so much the braces, the cowlick or the fat nose. Children feel "different" when no one discusses their inner concerns with them. This leads children to believe that only they feel the way they do and therefore something must be "wrong" with them. Without knowledge of how others feel, the child concludes that he is the only person in the world who's terrified of garter snakes, the only child who worries about pimples, the only kid who gets mad at his mother.

Individual differences and imperfections are unavoidable facts of every life. Because most children do not realize this, they need to be informed. Otherwise, they can go through life with a false picture of themselves. You must explain to your child that everyone has his own individual differences, good points and limitations, and yet we all are very much alike.

Matthew, a short nine-year-old, is called Shorty by his classmates. The label makes him feel unacceptable:

Matt: Dad, why am I so short?

Father: There are a lot of short people in our family.

Matt: But I'm the shortest kid in my class. They all call me Shorty, and I can't stand it.

Father: (Well-intentioned) So don't put up with it.

Matt: Huh?

Father: Fight back or they'll walk all over you. If someone calls you Shorty, point out his weakness. Let everyone else know the kid is bowlegged or has a funny nose.

The next day, Matt's father returns home from work to find his son nursing a black eye:

Father: What happened?

Matt: One of the guys was teasing me, so I did what you told me. I told everybody he was fat and gross. Then he hit me.

Father: He can't get away with that. I'm going to teach you how to beat his ears off.

This kind of escalation merely begs the question. Even if other children stop their teasing, your child's enhanced self-esteem probably will be only short-lived. Indeed, by insisting on escalation, Matt's well-intentioned father conveys a series of underlying—and discouraging—messages to the boy:

You are short. Your assumption about your inferiority and lack of acceptability is probably true.

The only solution you have in this dog-eat-dog world is to fight it out, an eye for an eye and a tooth for a tooth.

There is no way that you can feel normal and acceptable and get some of the kids who tease you to become your friends.

Teasing of this kind is not healthy but it is encountered by everyone. Because each child in Matt's class is struggling to feel more adequate, nothing delights them more than exposing someone else's limitations. For the moment, the taunter can feel superior. The next minute, that feeling is gone, and the same child again is troubled by his own sense of uniqueness, inferiority and unworthiness. Without a positive solution, the chain of teasing, fighting and insecurity continues. What would happen if Matt's father thought more positively?

Matt: They all call me Shorty, and I can't stand it.

Father: Tell me, Matt, what does all this mean to you?

Matt: I don't know . . . It makes me feel bad.

Father: Let's see if we can go deeper into the matter.

Matt: Deeper? All I know is I don't like being short. And I don't want to be called Shorty . . . It makes me feel bad because I'm the smallest one. It makes me feel like I'm not as good as they are.

Father: Not as good? Is this true of the other kids, too? Are there some who aren't as good

as the others? Who's the worst reader?

Matt: Oh, that's Keith. He can hardly read at all.

Father: Then he's inferior and worthless?

Matt: Sort of. I feel sorry for him.

Father: Would you trade places with Keith? Trade your being short for his poor reading?

Matt: No way.

Father: Now tell me who's the sloppiest kid in your class.

Matt: That's easy. It's Brad.

Father: Is he teased about it?

Matt: Sure. We all call him Pigpen.

Father: Oh—then you do some of this teasing, too?

Matt: Everybody does it.

Father: How do you make Brad feel when you tease him?

Matt: Oh . . . Bad, I guess.

Father: How would you like to trade places with him?

Matt: I'd rather be called Shorty.

Father: All right, now tell me which kid is so perfect that he doesn't have anything different about him?

Matt: Well, nobody's perfect. I guess everybody in my class has something a little wrong with him.

Father: Well, which one is the most worthless?

Matt: That's kind of hard to figure out.

Father: If that's the case, what do you think of yourself now?

Matt: I . . . I guess I'm not so bad off.

Matt's father has confronted his son's delusion of uniqueness and inferiority. He shows Matt that everyone is unique and has individual characteristics that fall short of the ideal; and that everyone feels the same way about his own shortcomings or limitations. Once Matt knows that other people experience the same feelings and concerns about being different, he will begin to feel better about himself.

How to Dispel the Delusion of Self-assurance

The basic method to solve your child's

feeling of inferiority is called *Universalization:* making your child aware that other people experience the same problems and feelings he does. To accomplish this:

Dispel the illusion of self-assurance. Tell your child that, even though many other people may seem quite self-confident, they really are concerned and uncertain about themselves too. They are merely hiding their mistakes, confusion and self-doubt behind a self-assured facade. They "keep up appearances." But they still feel "different" when they make a mistake or don't know something.

Tell your child that no young child can have a lot of self-confidence. He doesn't have a big enough backlog of successful experiences.

Point out the fallacy of superiority: The more inferior and insecure young people feel, the more likely they are to hunt for someone who looks even more like a loser. But it never works. Only real accomplishment gives the feeling of genuine self-worth.

Always realize that your child's feelings of insecurity and inferiority are not automatic reflections on the quality of your parenting, but can be part of your child's growing awareness of himself as he faces the challenge of the world around him.

Emphasize that the delusion of uniqueness—which we all share—shows how alike we are rather than pointing up our differences.

A-13 Worries

For every child, growing up means meeting one challenge after another. He seldom is able to face these challenges without apprehension and worry because of his acute sense of his own limitations. He is aggravated further by his concern that he can't do anything about those limitations, that they are permanent and that he always will be at the mercy of every situation. His belief in his own inadequacy can become another self-fulfilling prophecy, preventing him from accomplishing those things necessary to prove that he can meet challenges effectively. In the meantime, he worries about two things: whether he is capable and socially acceptable.

Ordinarily, when your child brings home an "A" paper from school or finds a new friend or scores a touchdown for his team, one might assume he would become less apprehensive. Yet children quickly forget their accomplishments in the face of the next challenge. It takes a large number of successes over a long period of time before a child begins to perceive how skilled or socially acceptable he actually is. Some children—too many—never become convinced. You can help your child avoid this outcome by listening to his worries and supporting his efforts to become a capable, likable person.

Tracy, nine, is always insecure and a little more worried than most children about each impending event. She worries not only about what is upcoming but about what has only a remote chance of happening.

Just returned from a friend's house, Tracy now mopes about with a dejected look. Father deduces there is something wrong:

Father: Tracy, are you feeling all right?

Tracy: Natalia wasn't home.

Father: Is that a reason for looking like disaster just struck?

Tracy: You don't understand. Natalia's over playing with Karen.

Father: This worries you?

Tracy: Sure it does. Maybe she's not my friend any more.

Father: Did you two have a fight about something?

Tracy: No. But something must have happened so now she likes Karen instead of me.

Father: I find that hard to believe. Tracy, you have no way of knowing that Natalia doesn't like you.

Tracy: Well, she isn't playing with me, is she?

Father: Let me explain something to you. Kids your age sometimes like to make new friends as a way of finding out if other people like them.

Tracy: But I'm her friend. Why does she need Karen?

Father: That's not the point. Probably Natalia's interested in finding out whether she's likable enough to be able to make friends with Karen. It has very little to do with liking you or not liking you.

Tracy: That's O.K. for Natalia, but what about me?

Father: You still feel bad, don't you?

Tracy: Yeah.

Father: Maybe there's something you can do. Why not prove to yourself you're the kind of person who can make more than one friend, too? Is there some other girl in school you like?

Tracy: There's Eve. But I don't think she'd want to play with me.

Father: Why not?

Tracy: She's kind of popular. Why would such a popular girl want to be my friend?

Father: Everybody, no matter how popular, needs to feel wanted as a friend. Ask Eve to come over to play.

Tracy: If she says no, then I'll feel worse than I do now.

Father: You can't win if you don't try. Try three times with Eve. And, if that doesn't work, try with someone else you think you might enjoy knowing. Remember, you have something to offer that's important to every child in your class.

Tracy: What's that?

Father: You can ask them to be your friend.

Note Father's interest, his gentle probing to identify the problem so Tracy can see an important but overlooked aspect. Father is not debating with the child to prove who is right or wrong. To help Tracy find a solution he contributes from his own experience. With his encouragement, she can now test her own ability to find a new friend. The thrust of Father's talk is to give Tracy a broader understanding of her problem and of what she can do about it. Father furnishes Tracy with the support and challenge she needs in order to convince herself of her acceptability.

How to Deal with Worry

Tell your child we all worry. Assure him it's a normal aspect of human nature. Say, "I worry too. We all do." Then ask your child to tell you some of the details of his worry. Be careful not to bring up ideas that don't relate to the situation. Encourage a full discussion. It will help you to pinpoint the basic concern.

Make the cause clear. As you listen to his feelings, regard the process as one of peeling away layers of bad feelings until the core "catastrophe" is revealed. Do this by gently probing his feelings about various aspects of the problem. You can identify the basic concern more easily if you remember that the two most likely areas of worry are about not being competent or accepted by other people.

A-14 Real and Make-believe: Separating Symbols from Reality

The human landscape is littered with symbols. The Statue of Liberty, the alphabet, advertising trademarks—all these symbols and many more surround us and affect our daily lives. Your child needs to be able to recognize symbols for what they are— representations of reality. He can't truly adapt to his environment unless he's able to recognize the symbols around him. The onyx fruit on the dining-room table is not intended for nourishment but for visual pleasure. Your child is in for a surprise if he doesn't recognize the symbolism and bites into an onyx peach.

The child who confuses symbols with reality will never be quite sure what's likely to happen next. He'll be fooled and at times victimized by appearances. The onyx peach is no substitute for the real thing. The same is even more true when the symbol represents human behavior and relationships.

Ability to build realistic expectations about human behavior and relationships is one of the central issues in the controversy surrounding children's programming on TV. According to TV's simplistic dramatic conventions, the hero always wins, always gets what he wants, solves his problems by cunning or violence, usually lives in luxury and easily divides mankind into good guys and bad guys. These unrealistic messages about human nature may seem plausible to the child who is not easily able to sort out reality from the fiction he's watching. In the process, he can act on various erroneous assumptions: that there is no room for failure in his life, that he should get whatever he wants, that force is the most effective solution, that luxury is a birthright and that everyone can be classified as either good or bad.

Drama as Symbol

If your child acts on these notions or if his behavioral models are fictional and he doesn't realize their limitations, he may be headed for trouble. Given his inexperience and the countless hours probably spent watching TV, it's vital for him to learn how to distinguish between fiction and reality.

When she herself was a child, the mother of Tiffany, five, and Mike, seven, had loved the story of Peter Pan. She introduced it early to her children and it became a bedtime favorite. They also enjoyed seeing the rerun of the famous TV musical version. Now the children have attended a local theatrical production of *Peter Pan.* Before the matinee yesterday, Mother reread the story to Mike and Tiffy. She also went to the play with them.

The children have just been separated after a noisy dispute outdoors. Tiffy tried to fly off the porch roof. Her brother successfully pulled her down before takeoff but in the scuffle the little girl was somewhat bruised. Now she and Mother are alone indoors. Mother is learning that the bruise is only partially responsible for Tiffy's tears.

Tiffy: (Between sobs) I wanted to fly the way Peter Pan showed Wendy. But Mike wouldn't let me. He said Peter Pan isn't real. He says it's all lies. Peter Pan is real, isn't he? We saw him yesterday. We saw him fly.

Mother: Mike didn't want you to fall and be badly hurt, Tiffy. What we saw yesterday was a play. A story.

Tiffy: But it wasn't like TV. It was real people.

Mother: Yes, real people like you and me. But not people who can really fly.

Tiffy: They did too. They were flying all around.

Mother: There's a clever way of putting people into little jackets with wires fastened so you can hardly see them. That's how the people on the stage seemed to fly.

Tiffy: You mean Mike's right? They weren't flying? There isn't any Peter Pan?

Mother: Peter Pan is a wonderful story everybody loves.

Tiffy: (Lower lip trembling again) But I wanted Peter Pan to be real. *(Suddenly giving her mother a sharp look)* Tinker Bell is real.

Mother: No. She's part of the story too, Tiff.

Tiffy: But when Tinker was sick and Peter Pan asked us to clap if we believed in fairies, you clapped too. I saw you. Why did you do it if you knew it wasn't so? You lied, Mommy. You lied!

Mother: Tiffy, how did you feel when Tinker Bell was so sick?

Tiffy: I felt bad. I didn't want her little light to go out.

Mother: I felt the same way. You see, our feelings were real even if what we saw was a story. The important thing about the Peter Pan play was the way we felt about it— sometimes we were happy and laughing, sometimes we were sad or surprised.

Tiffy: I liked the part about Tiger Lily. It was exciting.

Mother: Yesterday I clapped my hands for Tinker Bell because I remembered all the feelings I had about her when I was a little girl.

Tiffy: Why did you feel that way if it's all a big lie?

Mother: The story of Peter Pan isn't real. But Peter Pan isn't a lie either. He's a symbol.

Tiffy: What's a symbol?

Mother: Something that makes us have certain thoughts and feelings any time we see it or think about it. Peter Pan is the symbol of all the fun children have when they're small—exploring a world so new to them it sometimes seems magical—learning to act a little more independent—having lots of unexpected adventures . . . It's a bit hard to understand about symbols, isn't it, Tiff?

Tiffy: Yes.

This conversation illustrates a child buying a fantasy whole cloth and a parent having to help her differentiate between the real and non-real. Fortunately, Tiffany's more-knowledgeable older brother was around to prevent a serious accident taking place. However, not many days afterward, brother Mike himself is discovered accepting the myth (and adopting some of the tactics) of a somewhat plausible TV superhero. Mother has to straighten Mike out:

Mother: What's going on here?

Tiffy: (Between screams) He hit me! I didn't do anything and he hit me!

Mike: She wasn't playing Tarzan right.

Tiffy: He wanted me to be a bull ape. I told him I didn't want to be any old bull ape.

Mike: We can't play Tarzan unless there's a bad guy. Tarzan always zaps a bull ape or elephant.

Tiffy: I wasn't a bull ape. I was Cheetah the Chimp. You hit your friend Cheetah, stupid!

Mike: Oh, no, you weren't. You were supposed to be the bull ape so we could fight over the secret treasure.

Mother: Let me help you understand something, Mike. Tarzan of the Apes is make-believe. He isn't real.

Mike: Sure. I know that. Tarzan's a story on TV. But it could happen.

Tiffy: (Smugly) I bet he's a symbol.

Mother: If a man like Tarzan in real life went around hitting people and taking the law into his own hands, he'd land in jail.

Mike: But it's O.K. because he lives in the jungle.

Mother: The jungle is in a country and every country has laws. Besides, if he really tried to swing from one tree to the next the way he does on film, he'd break his neck.

Mike: He would?

Mother: Yes. And all that hitting is no way to solve a problem. All it did was get you in trouble.

Dealing directly with the behavioral illusion Mike has absorbed from television, Mother brings him down to earth with this incontrovertible fact: Whether it's cartoons or an adventure film, make-believe is make-believe, especially when imaginary characters do not deal with their problems in acceptable, true-to-life ways.

Dealing with Make-believe

Point out the difference between what is real and what is nonreal: "That picture on the wall is real. But the tree in the picture is not real. It's just an artist's idea of how a tree might look."

Teach your child the concepts of what is possible and impossible: "Some things are possible to do, like going to Grandma's. That's possible. Some things are impossible, like me flying around this room." "One of the ways we know things are real is through our senses—by touching, seeing, hearing, tasting and smelling." "There are a lot of people we don't see who are working very hard right now to bring us what we see and hear on TV. But the people in the TV stories are only actors. And what they are doing, pretending a story for us, may or may not be true."

Show your child how time, place and person affect the possibility of things: "We might be able to visit the zoo on Sunday, but we can't today because you have to go to school and I have to go to work." "You can keep water in a glass but not in a sieve." "Brett knows how to play the bugle. But, because Benjy hasn't learned yet, he can't."

A-15 Imagination: Exploring the Possible

Fantasy, or imagination is really a two-edged sword. On the one hand it is essential to be able to tell the difference between reality and fantasy. Yet fantasy as a first step in problem-solving is also adaptive. So, while helping your child to clearly distinguish between the two it would be unwise to discourage the basic process of using imagination. As a first step its use should be encouraged.

A good imagination enables a child to unravel problems. The more imaginative he is, the more options he is likely to have when faced with problem-solving. Besides, the imagination that develops out of children's fantasies is the source of all human creativity. Without imagining, there would be no paintings, plays, jetliners or television sets.

Imagination, then, is the foundation of human progress and art, as well as an everyday tool for problem-solving. Encourage your child's imagination, fantastic as it sometimes is, for it has practical value for his development.

Miles, nine, has big dreams and ideas. For the past 20 minutes he has been drawing intently. Now, excited with the result, he approaches his father, an engineer:

Miles: Look, Dad. See what I did?

Father: (Putting down an engineering journal) Huh? What is it?

Miles: See, I invented a way to stop smog. This screen catches all the smog when it comes out of the smokestack.

Father: Interesting. But it won't work.

Miles: Sure it will.

Father: If you ever want to invent anything, you need to be more realistic. First of all, smog particles are too small for your screen. Even if they did get caught in the screen, they'd plug up the smokestack. It'll never work.

To be sure, imagination alone will not solve problems. There is also the chance it can become an escapist flight from reality—as with Walter Mitty. But by and large the imaginative child is better able to meet the obstacles life throws in his path. He has more flexibility, both in viewpoint and will, to seek new solutions.

Miles' father does not fully appreciate the value of imagination. After all, a lot of money has been spent to educate him to value fact over fiction. Without realizing what he is doing or even consciously intending to do it, he communicates these stifling messages to Miles' emerging imagination:

I (one of the most important people in your life) am not impressed by your imagination. My outlook about your imagination—and therefore about you—is negative.

Reality, hard fact, is all that matters. Don't show me anything you do unless it's factual, exact, correct.

As Miles suffers more of these negative reactions, he will gradually become more cautious and less enthusiastic about his imaginative ideas. Eventually he will even be cynical, and will believe as his father does that imagination—if not a sure sign of weakness—is useless at best. At this point, his creative urges will die out and, along with them, his potential for being a flexible, creative person.

Miles' father is well-intentioned enough. He wants to improve his son's sense of reality. But Father has the order mixed. Imagination comes before fact-finding. How could Father better respond to Miles' imagination and an unrealistic invention?

Father: It looks interesting. How does it work?

Miles: This screen up here stops the smog when it comes out of the smokestack.

Father: Who, knows, you may have something there. How did you get the idea?

Miles: My teacher told out class about the smog problem. And then I thought about the time you used a screen to get rocks out of sand when you fixed the back porch. Remember?

Father: Yes, I do. And I'm impressed by the way you've used your imagination.

Miles: What do you think? Will my idea work?

Father: Maybe you should take a closer look. Smog particles are very, very small, much smaller than rocks. So what kind of screen will you use?

Miles: I didn't think about that.

Father: That's understandable. It takes a while to solve every one of the problems involved in any invention. I'm glad to see you working on something so imaginative. If you have more ideas I'll be glad to hear them.

This approach reinforces Miles' imagination by accepting his fantasy as worthy of consideration. It also stimulates him to deal with some of the implicit realities. Father does not cut off his son's imagination but channels it into more-realistic problem-solving. Miles leaves the encounter feeling approved and challenged rather than discouraged or stupid; he has picked up Father's positive messages:

I am very interested in your imagination.
I'm a positive person and am pleased to see you being positive.
I want to encourage you to keep trying because I consider your ideas to have merit.
I'm willing to imagine with you.

How to Develop Imagination

Accept your child's imagination:
"I like that story you made up. It shows you have a lot of imagination." "Your drawing is imaginative and fun."
Stimulate his imagination. Encourage your child's interest in the things he likes to do. Some children prefer to express their imagination by drawing pictures, others by story-telling or dress-up or by making things. Provide materials for imaginative play. Because they are unstructured and will give his imagination more freedom, simple and inexpensive things often are best.
You can develop the problem-solving potential of your child's imagination. This comes about when you challenge him to be more realistic. Always gently point out the reality or problem he has overlooked; never criticize his failure to deal with it. Ask him to consider still other ways of attacking the problem.

A-16 Daydreams: Planning or Escape?

In our pragmatic society, daydreaming often is looked upon as a waste of time. To children, daydreaming is a practical necessity, often a form of planning or rehearsal that makes a child aware of the alternatives available to him in his school work or in new situations. When your child daydreams about a social-science class project, he is planning, selecting, making choices as a prelude to the work involved. In much the same way, daydreaming about making friends at a new school or paying a visit to relatives he barely knows will permit the child to consider the possibilities of a situation and prepare himself for its various contingencies. Without daydreams, he would be thrust—sink or swim—into new situations or tasks without any prior consideration or preparation, a possibly traumatizing experience. To avoid the shock of surprise, all of us use our daydreams to some extent, in an effort to gain some measure of control or understanding of the events we face.

Daydreaming can also be a symptom of boredom, laziness or the fear of failure. Or it can represent fantasy fulfillment for some deprivation. Every child daydreams, some more than others. A modest amount of it should be regarded as normal. But a problem may exist if your child spends a great deal of time daydreaming: He may be trying to avoid reality. If so, you will want to discover what the problem is and guide him to more effective functioning.

For the past week, Nina, 11, has spent many hours daydreaming and not doing much else. Mother decides to find out what's going on:
Mother: What are you reading, Nina?
Nina: One of my movie magazines.
Mother: Is it interesting?
Nina: It's all about how movie stars live. You wouldn't believe the wild things they do.
Mother: That would depend on how wild they are.
Nina: They meet all the In people and travel all around to Spain and Paris and Mexico. And they live in the biggest houses and drive these fantastic custom sport cars.
Mother: Sure sounds like fun.
Nina: Oh, it is. It's the way I want to live when I grow up.
Mother: It's certainly pleasant to daydream about people and places like that. But have you considered how you're going to get there?
Nina: First, I'd have to be famous too, I guess.

Mother: I'd feel better if you developed some of your real abilities while you're waiting around to be discovered.

Nina: What does that mean?

Mother: I mean nobody can live on daydreams. They won't solve any problem. They won't get you very far. They won't make people appreciate you.

Nina: I'm not doing anything wrong.

Mother: You're just not doing anything, Nina. You're not developing yourself by sitting here and reading those magazines. The movie stars and the Beautiful People you read about didn't daydream a lot. They started out early to be doers. So now how about doing something that's useful as well as fun?

Nina: Like what?

Mother: How about that new dress you've been asking for? Would you like to come with me to the fabric store and pick out the material? We could make it together.

Nina: Can I pick the pattern and color and everything?

Mother: Why not? You're the one who's going to wear it.

Nina: How soon can we go?

In counteracting Nina's excessive daydreaming, her mother uses the best diversionary tactic—productive activity. She recognizes Nina's fantasies as a symptom of boredom, a lack of stimulating things to do. Mother suggests an activity they can do together, the better to jog Nina out of her dream world into constructive involvement with the girl's real environment.

In the process, Mother doesn't emptily advise, "Find something better to do than just lolling around," or, "Go out and play." Rather, she suggests a concrete activity mother and daughter can do jointly to develop Nina's real skills and reduce her need for excessive daydreaming.

How to Deal with Daydreams

Accept a certain amount of daydreaming as natural and useful for your child's development. Daydreaming can be a method of planning or rehearsing new situations and tasks. Remember it can also be fun.

But should you notice your child lapsing into too much daydreaming, make him aware of what he is doing and the realities he may be avoiding.

Gently confront your child about his excess daydreams. Ask him to tell you what his daydream is about, what happens in it and what role he plays. The daydream will suggest what the real problem is. You will find that almost always this will concern a relationship with another person, or something that he can't do that he would like to be able to do.

Clarify the functions and limits of daydreaming. Tell your child some daydreaming is normal, even healthy, but too much of it often means that a person is not coping effectively with some need. Explain that fantasy won't solve the problem but that some kind of action probably could.

Try to learn his unmet need. If you find that he's just at loose ends, suggest a number of attractive activities: "You could work on your stamp collection." "There's a great new model-plane kit we could get." "You can call Benjy and ask if he is free to come over and play."

When the daydreaming is realistic, encourage its fulfillment. You can do this by making supportive comments and by providing any materials, information and assistance he needs.

A-17 Hysterical Fantasy: Fear-Fixation, Wish-fulfillment

Children's fantasies often are highly charged with emotion, tinged with extreme feelings of fear or desire. Your child may dread some impending event which he has overblown into a possible catastrophe. Or he may have exaggerated expectations about how perpetually delighted he will feel if you buy him some toy touted on those pervasive and persuasive TV commercials. As you know, the dread of imagined catastrophes is wasted emotion; and imagined raptures often are doomed to disappointment.

Fear-Fixation

All of us have generalized feelings of fear. The origin usually lies in a basic sense of inadequacy or insecurity. When an event is anticipated, it can trigger or crystallize these deep anxieties. An upcoming examination can present the prospect of total failure. If your subteen daughter anticipates that she might not be invited to a party she has heard about, she may regard this as equivalent to total rejection. Because these are exaggerated reactions, they are not very realistic. But they do set off very real, deep generalized anxieties.

Your young child probably lacks the concept and vocabulary with which to give clear verbal expression to a broad fear of this sort. If he did have the words to tell you the true concern, then—instead of listening to his hysterical obsession about the imminent disaster—you might hear, "When it comes to a challenge to my adequacy, I will be exposed as a total failure in life." Or, "I'm doomed to a lifetime of loneliness because I have nothing to offer in my relationships with other people." These are the true concerns. Because these deeper, broader, more generalized anxieties are what's ailing the child, it is useless to try superficial reassurance like "You'll do all right on the test." Or, "You'll probably be invited to the party." Such well-meaning attempts fall short of the mark, are not credible and don't deal constructively with the basic problem.

How to Deal with Hysterical Fear-Fixation

Acknowledge your child's fear. Tell him that you can see how very frightened he is.
Look for the deeper, more general concern. Determine whether your child can recognize that he is overreacting to the actual degree of the anticipated danger.
Help your child to solve the basic problem. If the concern is about inadequacy, then aid your child by pinpointing his deficient areas in the Competence sequence [page 130] and help him develop the specific skills he needs. If his basic concern is about insecurity in relationships, find the deficient areas in the Relating sequence [page 90] and help him relate more effectively with people. As an additional measure, you will find that spending more one-to-one time with your child almost always will bring improvement, but the time usually will have to be given over a period of several weeks or more before substantial benefits accrue.

Wish-Fulfillment

At times your child will display almost feverish enthusiasm for something he wants: the privilege to do something or go somewhere, or to obtain some one item that he is convinced will provide him with unbounded joy. Toy manufacturers, for example, recognizing that a child usually is enticed by the promise of power, cannily have made available the very popular mechanical robot. Since it is remotely controlled by the mere turn of a dial, a child absorbing its TV sales pitch is led to believe the robot is something that will reduce his feeling of helplessness and give him an extraordinary sense of power. Most children will not easily be dissuaded by a parent's forewarning that any such heady feeling will quickly evaporate.

How to Deal with Hysterical Wish-Fulfillment

Empathize with your child's desire. Agree that it does appear that the desired object (or privilege, or event) will work some wondrous change for him. But then inject your doubt about just how long such a marvelous feeling would last. Try to let your child down gently.
Help your child to greater competence and better relationships with people. Look into the Competence and Relating sequences for areas of development that will give your child a greater sense of power, acceptability and friendship. As your child's competence and friendships improve, his tendency toward hysterical wish-fulfillment will accordingly be reduced.

A-18 Dreams and Nightmares

Every night each of us passes through several dream periods for a total of between one to two hours of dreaming. Most adults don't remember many of their dreams. But children do and love to relate them. What they and their parents seldom realize is that dreams are an integral part of our total functioning.

Dreams are real, ongoing processes in our brains and are best understood as problem-solving activities. As such, dreaming has much in common with the unconscious adjustments our bodies make in certain situations. When we become overheated, our bodies automatically perspire to maintain a balanced temperature. As we shift our gaze from one object to another, the muscles that control the lenses of the eye adjust the focus without any conscious effort on our part. In much the same way, our body uses dreams to make emotional or mental adjustments at the subconscious level in efforts to maintain optimal emotional functioning and equilibrium.

Understanding our dreams is important to developing awareness and Emotional Maturity. The better we understand our dreams, the less separation exists between the conscious and subconscious parts of our mind. We become better aware of the emotional problems we subconsciously try to solve.

Jason, 12, has good retention and likes to discuss his dreams; he is learning to find out what they are saying to him. He has been guided by his father, whom he now meets at the Sunday breakfast table:

Jason: Wow! I just had a really crazy dream!

Father: What about?

Jason: I dreamed I was walking home alone from downtown. It was very dark. But I could see this man was following me. I was really scared. Then suddenly I was in a room with all kinds of weird gadgets, like some sort of laboratory. I was all alone there, like the place belonged to me. And there was this machine. And next to it was a rabbit in a cage. So I put the rabbit into the machine—I don't know why. After a minute, a small dinosaur popped out of the machine. Was I surprised!

Father: I imagine so . . . You know the dream is expressing a problem your subconscious is trying to help you solve?

Jason: I know that all right. But what would I need a baby dinosaur for?

Father: I'm not sure. See if you can role-play the people and the things in your dream.

Jason: Even the rabbit and the machine?

Father: If necessary. But first be the man following you.

Jason: O.K. "I'm about 35 years old. And I'm kind of angry. Jason's on my mind because he has something I want. However, I'm very uneasy about what Jason's going to do."

Father: Very good. Continue playing the man.

Jason: "Jason and I both sort of know what this is all about. But Jason is trying to avoid me."

Father: Now try being Jason in the dream—when he's in the laboratory.

Jason: Yeah, that laboratory. Turning a rabbit into a dinosaur—that's unreal. Though it sure would make a neat project. Hey—wait a minute. Now I think I see. It's my science project.

Father: What do you mean?

Jason: Turning the rabbit into a dinosaur must be the science project I've got to do for class. And, now that I think of it, the man who was following me could be my science teacher.

Father: Have you done any work on your science project yet?

Jason: No. And he's probably after me for it—the man who was following me. I haven't decided yet what I'm going to do.

Father: Shouldn't you be getting started?

Jason: Yeah. I guess so. You wouldn't have any genius idea for a science project, would you?

Father: Well, nothing quite as exciting as changing a rabbit to a dinosaur.

This method of discovering the problems our dreams are working on is called role-playing. When a dream is first remembered, we recall only the superficial aspects of what happened. But if we give a voice to each character and object in the dream, new material is revealed which often sheds light on the dream's meaning. We give voices to all the persons and animals and even the inanimate things that were our dream-objects. Then we describe their functions in the dream—their wishes, fears, thoughts and feelings. Out of these monologues invariably come clues to the problem our subconscious is striving to solve.

To most people this method at first glance sounds completely ridiculous. But it so often works.[4] As we grow used to it, it becomes less strange and has the enormous advantage of helping children and adults get in better touch with the subconscious parts of their mental and emotional life. Emotional problems troubling our subconscious can be raised to the conscious level where we more easily can come to terms with them.

How to Help Your Child Understand His Dreams

Raise your child's awareness of the dream itself by verbalization of its various components. The object is to make him consciously aware of the problem his subconscious is trying to solve in the dream. The process for doing this is fairly simple and, if followed, will reveal its own answers: Listen to the dream in every detail.

Do not guess what it means.

Have your child give voice to the dream-elements.

Ask your child to have each person, animal and object describe itself and its function in the dream, telling its concerns and what it thinks the problem is and giving its thoughts and feelings as the action of the dream unfolds. The experience of verbalizing the dream is often sufficient and rarely misleading. It isn't necessary for you to "interpret," nor is it desirable for you to impose your own interpretations.

The concerns your child expresses in his dream and his manner of perceiving and

[4]This method is credited to Fritz Perls and is best described in his book, *Gestalt Therapy Verbatim* (Bantam Books, N.Y., 1969).

dealing with them will give you clues to the basic problem.

Nightmares

It's hard to find anyone who has not had a nightmare but some people experience more than others. Usually these are highstrung individuals—bright, sensitive and often nervous. For children, a nightmare can be a terrifying experience. If your child has one, he will need your comfort and attention, even if it is three a.m.

Nightmares are an expression of some great fear which our subconscious is trying to resolve. Remember that the intense fear expressed in the nightmare often is disguised as something tangible—an angry dog, a speeding car or a sinister bully. For this reason, the great underlying fear causing the nightmare often is missed. You should concentrate upon your child's feeling of helplessness and the fearful vulnerability that is besetting him, rather than upon the dream's action-elements that represent the fear. Role-playing is not indicated, but reassurance is.

Polly, six, has been suffering a recurring nightmare involving a big dog that chases her. Just as it is about to catch up and bite her, she awakens in a state of panic:

Polly: Mommy!

Mother: What happened?

Polly: A big dog was after me! It was going to bite me, Mommy! *(She is shaking.)*

Mother: I'm sorry you're so frightened, but don't worry. I'm here with you now. *(Mother holds Polly close.)*

Polly: But that mean dog was going to bite me! I could see its teeth!

Mother: It's all right now. You just had a bad dream.

Polly: I'm so scared. Please stay here with me.

Mother: I'll be right here beside you till you go back to sleep.

Mother's concern is to comfort Polly. Mother does not say it is foolish to be afraid of big

dogs; she lets that issue alone, recognizing and accepting the fact of Polly's intense fear.

How to Deal with Nightmares

Hold your child while you listen to every detail of the nightmare.
Acknowledge the fear: "I know how you feel. I've been that much afraid, too."
Tell your child everybody has nightmares from time to time. Explain that perhaps the dream was trying to solve too much fear at once.
Stay with your child until he feels safe again—even if it takes an hour. If your child has nightmares more than once a month, it may be advisable to seek professional help.

V Relating

How to Have Likable Children

All the Friends You Can Earn

In our highly mobile society, it's very common for children to complain bitterly if they must move away from their old neighborhood. At the root of the tears and complaints is a sense of loss: "I don't want to give up my friends." Or there is fear: "I don't want the trouble of having to make friends all over again." These feelings are universal among children and attest to the power of human friendship and our need for secure relationships.

It is a basic fact that man is by nature a social animal—"No man is an island." And so it is with your child, who needs satisfying relationships with others in order to be happy and fulfilled.

As desperately as children need friends and companions, they often find it painfully difficult to win the acceptance of other children. Self-doubt, combined with a deep fear of rejection and a simple inexperience about the feelings and needs of others, is a mighty obstacle for any child to overcome. At the same time, the people your child wants as friends can be obstacles themselves. They too have self-doubts and fear rejection. Some are shy and not easily approached, others domineering and manipulative. In trying to satisfy his social instincts, your child faces an uncertain world. Without the proper knowledge and skills, hurt comes easily. The emotional stakes for winning or losing are very high. On the one hand, your child needs companionship for all the special pleasure and fulfillment which friends bring to our lives; on the other hand, in seeking them any child risks the devastating pain of rejection.

The solution lies in learning and practicing the skills of relating. Relating is the art of building and maintaining good relationships with other people. It embraces the entire scale of knowledge, attitudes and interpersonal skills which everyone needs in order to make and keep friends. Practicing the skills of relating enables a child to find agreeable friends and companions, deal with shy or manipulative people and understand the nature of each relationship. In addition, he will learn to cope with the problems of mixed feelings which often end many friendships. Most of all, with his skill will come a sense of personal value and contentment as new friends are made. Not only will your child satisfy his natural gregariousness, he will feel more confident and secure in having the ability to get along well in what otherwise would be an uncertain, precarious world. He will know that he can have all the friends he can earn.

R-1 "Narcissus Is My Name:" Self-interest

Every child is the center of his own personal universe. He has a built-in narcissism that focuses his attention and concern almost exclusively upon himself. Your child will start out almost totally self-centered—this is an inescapable fact. Doing and getting the things that interest him will monopolize his efforts. In the early years, this self-interest is normal and even healthy.

It's well for you to know that this childish

TABLE III

Relating Issues of Emotional Development

R-1   Narcissus Is My Name: Self-interest

R-2   The Name of the Game Is Attention

R-3   Nobody Wants to Play with Me: Acceptance

R-4   Approval: How'm I Doing?

R-5   Affection: All I Need Is Love . . . Pure Love

R-6   Social Responsibility: I've Got You in My Power

R-7   Empathy: Yourself in Other People's Shoes

R-8   Everybody Needs a Friend

R-9   Resisting Peer Pressure

R-10 Painful But Loving Confrontation

R-11 Mutual Support: the Tie That Binds

R-12 Decision-making: Sharing the Power

R-13 Promises! Promises!

R-14 Fighting

R-15 Rivalry Means Insecurity

R-16 Becoming Likable

R-17 I Have Mixed Feelings Toward My Friend: Ambivalence

R-18 The Opposite Sex: a Never-ending Interest

self-centeredness is neither malicious nor "immoral." Your child merely is trying to meet his natural needs as he sees them at any given moment. In the beginning, he almost always will be unaware of an unconcerned about the feelings and needs of people around him.

As a child develops, the tendency toward exclusive self-interest can become a social liability. His drive for self-satisfaction inevitably will collide with the interests and rights of other people. The pain he causes is real and the recriminations unpleasant; consequently, it's extremely important for every child to learn how to adjust his concern to the needs and feelings of others. It is essential that he develop a social concern to balance his self-concern. If he doesn't, his natural narcissism can deteriorate into a selfish disregard for everyone else, best described as an eat-my-cake-and-yours-too attitude. This is the formula for a life of hostility and loneliness.

The Great Supermarket Battle

Jeffrey, seven, alert, is eyeing the supermarket toy section while his mother is considering the pork chops. Seizing a brightly colored racing car that strikes his fancy, he rushes off at a breathless pace to find Mother:

Jeff: Mom, look! A Mark IV Super 8 Pucci-Puccini Bearcat!

Mother: Jeff, put that right back. You've got so many others at home.

Jeff: I want it for my collection.

Mother: I'm sorry but I haven't enough money to buy it today.

Jeff: But I just want this one. It doesn't cost much.

Mother: Put that car back before I get mad.

Jeff: No, I don't want to.

Mother: (Collaring him) Give me that car this instant! And don't you dare make a scene! You're getting to be more of a brat every day.

This situation is familiar to any mother who has ever gone shopping with a small child. It's a common vexation mothers suffer and it's understandable that this one lost her temper. A demanding child in a public place, public exposure of her uncertain skill as a parent, the possible loss of face—volatile elements that will ignite the temper of any parent.

Mother's anger overrides Jeff's single-minded insistence upon having the toy. But labeling him a brat doesn't get to the basic problem. Name-calling may give her temporary control but it merely raises false issues. And it confirms Jeff's suspicion that she really doesn't want to support his interests. He leaves the store feeling that Mother is the "enemy" who has unjustly denied and put him down. He doesn't comprehend his own role in lighting the fuse. For this reason, it's inevitable that the scene will repeat itself. The solution lies in understanding each other's feelings. Jeff was feeling and communicating at 50 megacycles while Mom was operating at 68. They missed each other completely and heard only static. Mother felt economically and psychologically threatened by Jeff's determination to have the toy. Worst of all, she feared her possible "incompetence" as a parent was being stripped naked to public view. Her self-doubt interpreted his stubbornness as a personal attack that drew her counterattack.

Jeff simply was "doing what comes naturally." At seven, this generally means vigorously pursuing the things that interest and please you to the virtual exclusion of everything else. He was making his best effort to obtain an alluring toy. The last thing on his mind was what Mother was thinking and feeling. Without any bad intentions, he was collision-bound.

How could the collision have been averted?

Jeff: Mom, look! A Mark IV Super 8 Pucci-Puccini Bearcat!

Mother: That's nice. But you'd better put it back now.

Jeff: Can't I have it, Mom? Please?

Mother: I'm sorry, Jeff. I just don't have two dollars to spend on a toy today. Perhaps some other time.

Jeff: I want it now.

Mother: Jeff, how do you suppose you're beginning to make me feel?

Jeff: I don't know. Can't I have the car? I won't ask for anything else. I promise!

Mother: You're making me feel bad. If you don't like anyone to make you feel bad, is it fair for you to do it to me? Wouldn't you rather do something to make me feel good?

Jeff: (Not too sure) Yeah.

Mother: Fine. Then put the car back where it came from.

Jeff: If I do, then I'll feel bad.

Mother: That's true. You'll feel bad about not having it. But you'll be glad because you'll know you made me feel good.

Jeff: Ohhh . . . all right.

This is the start of a continuing dialogue in which Mother and Jeff can build toward a mutually supportive relationship. Here, Mother is firm but polite. By keeping the situation focused on the feelings involved, she is able to give Jeff some understanding of the way she feels. She helps him face up to the unfairness of imposing feelings on other people he himself doesn't wish to experience. Mother offers a substitute satisfaction: relinquishing the toy for the chance to exert power over her feelings. As the toy appears a little less significant, Jeff settles for the power. Mother is able to silence his persistent request by supporting his ego, not attacking it. In terms of what he wanted, Jeff loses. In terms of discovering the power to influence her feelings, he gains something.

How to Deal with Self-Centeredness

Recognize his self-interest. In the beginning, he will be blind to and unaffected by your feelings and those of others. Ask yourself, "Is he deliberately trying to bug me, or is he simply pursuing his own self-interest?"

Give him sympathetic interest. It helps soften his own intense self-concern. Don't brush him aside; regard his desires seriously, even if you can't grant them. Your notice and daily attention will gradually enable your child to give his attention to other people. Then he'll slowly move away from exclusive self-centeredness toward a better balance between his self-interest and that of others.

Use role-reversal. Ask your child if he would like to experience the bad feelings which his behavior is causing someone else. Its value lies in his putting himself in other people's shoes. It promotes an understanding of how alike people are, and reduces his natural tendency to regard you as an antagonist locked in a battle of wills. The sequence in this role-reversal is: Tell him his behavior has hurt your feelings. Ask him how he would feel if it were his feelings that were affected. Lead him into expressing some empathy, if you can: "Do you think it's fair to make me feel this way? I hope you just didn't think, or weren't aware of how bad you were making me feel."

R-2 The Name of the Game Is Attention

Attention is everybody's most fundamental social need. In your child's early years, he will need enormous amounts of attention, far more than parents commonly assume—and you are his principal source. Later, he will receive attention from his peers. In this respect, attention-giving is a diminishing parental function. But it never really ends. The only safe assumption is that your child's need for attention is practically unlimited. Attention is notice, recognition. It says, "I know you exist, that you have feelings and needs. When you give your young child attention, you are in effect saying to him, "I know you are feeling lonely and that you rely on me for guidance, knowledge and involvement. And I know that your demands for attention show dependency on me, especially when you ask for information, things to do, reassurance or my companionship."

Because attention is so vital a need, your child will get it one way or another. Instead of denying him attention, show him more mature and developed ways to draw attention to himself. Sometimes it seems as if the rule is: All's fair in love and attention-getting. This no-holds-barred approach will create problems and conflict. You will need to show him how to obtain—and, also, how to give—attention in considerate,

constructive ways. Apart from teaching him, the most important thing you can do is to bestow on him as much of your attention as often as you can. Preventive attention, that which is given before it is sought, often goes the deepest and lasts the longest.

Problem-solving with Attention
Father has just come home from waging a pitched battle with a stubborn boss. Four-year-old Cheryl arrives as her father is settling into his favorite chair. She carries a large-sized Magic Bunny book, her current favorite:
Cheryl: Daddy, can you read my book to me?
Father: Ummmmm. What did you say?
Cheryl: Will you read me my book?
Father: Not now . . . I'm reading the paper.
Cheryl: Please, Daddy?
Father: Don't bother me. Can't you see I'm busy?
Cheryl: You won't read me my book?
Father: I said no and I meant it. Get out of here now so I can concentrate.

Here is seen in action the Law of Inevitable Attention-getting, a child's persistent tendency to pursue attention. Father is caught in the conflict which demand for attention poses for every parent: the child's enormous need for attention versus the parent's limited availability, willingness and energy to provide it.
Father's choice is to deny Cheryl's need for his own. On a regular basis this would be very damaging, though on an occasional basis it is understandable. What does her father's denial do to Cheryl here? It gives her bad feelings about herself and him. The impression he gives to her: "I don't have time to spend with you. You're not as important as the newspaper. Therefore, you're not very important to me." At the deeper levels of awareness, she is moving toward such doubts as these: "Will I receive the support and love that I require—and the toys, clothes and trips to the zoo that I want? Will all my other needs be met? Am I cared about?"
Cheryl's request for attention is untimely but thoroughly normal. She is less interested in Magic Bunny, really, than in her father's companionship. Five or ten minutes with Father might satisfy the child. Concerned with his own need for comfort, he fails to recognize her need for attention or—recognizing it—refuses to deal with it. His attitude is one of resentment, a rebellion against the amount of attention Cheryl will continue to need for some time. To admit her need to himself would mean being fully aware of the heavy responsibility and burden of being a parent:
Cheryl: Daddy, can you read my book to me?
Father: I'd love to, but Dad just got home from work and is worn out. I'd like to sit for a minute and catch my breath. Can I read to you in a little while?
Cheryl: When?
Father: First I need 10 minutes for myself. O.K.? And if you could look for my slippers and bring them to me, it would make me feel very good.
Cheryl: Where are they, Daddy?
Since Father is gentle and polite, deals directly with the issue and gives her a specific time and commitment, Cheryl can go away feeling her need will be met fairly soon. At the same time, Father suggests an interim activity, in itself a form of attention. He is willing to give in a little and will meet Cheryl's request providing he can have a few minutes first. Such flexibility is essential for solving the conflicts your child's need for attention sometimes creates.
Basically, your child needs and will seek four kinds of attention:
Companionship because he is lonely;
Reassurance because he is afraid;
Activity because he is bored; or
Answers and information because there are things he doesn't know.

How to Deal with the Need for Attention:

Assume your child's need for attention can be almost unlimited.
Accept your role as his chief source of attention in his early years.
When he is three or four, teach him the

concept of attention, so he can recognize his need for what it is and develop the vocabulary to ask for it directly. Tell him: "When you ask for things, when you demand things, often you're really asking for attention. You want to be noticed, to be recognized. It makes you feel good. So say, 'I need attention.'"

Tell your child when you will be able to give him some time.

Take some of the pressure off yourself. A good nursery school can be ideal. Once your child is in kindergarten or first grade, school provides some of the attention he otherwise would seek from you. Neighbors and relatives can also give him satisfying companionship.

Upgrade his attention-getting skills. It will make your life easier. Normally, children will use any means of winning attention, including such common negative behaviors as demanding, screaming, throwing tantrums, getting into things, swearing, teasing, hitting siblings or requesting everything in sight. Your child will be inexperienced in using positive, considerate means to achieve his ends. Help him by saying, "This way may get you attention but it irritates me very much. I can show you a better way. If you would help me for five minutes by [name something for him to do], then I'd have the time to sit down with you."

Urge your child to give attention to others around him. Remind him that you give attention to him and that he can do the same for other people. Give specific examples: "On the way to the shopping center, I stopped to talk with Mrs. Henderson because she's very lonely and no one talks to her or keeps her company. And, by the way, little Kerry's mother called and said she didn't have anyone to play with. This will give you a nice chance to give your attention to someone who will appreciate it very much." Explain that attention is "something everybody needs—you, me, all your friends and all the people we meet. And the best way to get attention from others is to find a way of being useful to them."

R-3 "Nobody Wants to Play with Me": Acceptance

Acceptance is the next step in social development. Your child needs to feel included, first by you and then by others. That's what acceptance is—inclusion. To meet this need, he has to learn how to make others want to accept him.

Your acceptance of him is special to your child and has great significance for his self-esteem. It goes beyond merely including him in your activities and conversations. Your acceptance represents a definite and positive endorsement of your child's value. It's his security.

That endorsement meets its test every time he does something that annoys you. This is precisely the moment to give him your acceptance, to show him that you are committed to him. Your acceptance of him enables you to deal with his misbehavior without attacking his sense of security. It says: "I don't like what you just did, that's true. It upsets me and I will not endorse it. But I want you to know that we still have a good relationship. I think you're O.K., even though I don't like what you did."

Through your acceptance, your child recognizes that your relationship is positive and enduring. It tells him that, if any difficulty comes up, "You and I will resolve it to our mutual satisfaction, one way or another." Having experienced this sense of support, he can set about developing his skills and feel he will not be rejected out of hand for his misbehavior.

The Dynamics of Acceptance

Kit is a typical eight-year-old. He's been feeling neglected lately, but doesn't know how to conceptualize his need for inclusion, and is therefore unable to ask for it directly. As a close approximation he experiences himself as vaguely needing something.

Kit: I'm hungry, Mom. And I'm thirsty.

Mother: I'm busy getting dinner ready. We'll be eating in 10 minutes.

Kit: But I'm hungry right now. Can't I have a little something?

Mother: I'm too busy. You've got two hands. If you want something, there's juice in the refrigerator. Don't spill anything.

Kit: (Pouring too much too fast, spilling juice over the counter) Oh, no! It spilled!

Mother: I warned you to be careful. Now you've made a mess. You're just a damn pest! Now, get away.

Kit: I'm sorry. I'll clean it up.

Mother: Oh, no, you won't. You just get yourself out of here.

This is not a glowing example of acceptance. Kit stands guilty as charged but his mother's irritation doesn't justify demolishing his ego. Mother is telling him in effect: "I don't like what you just did and I don't much like you, either." Feeling cut down, as well as left out, Kit is in shreds when he leaves the kitchen. He can salvage nothing from his devastated feelings.

Mom was involved in her own activity and, like many people, couldn't accept interruption gracefully. But the key to her response lies in her resentment of all the time and effort required for Kit's care and development. She feels mad and put upon. If Mom had been a little more tuned in to the possibility that Kit has a regular need for human involvement as well as hunger and thirst, she might have casually asked Kit if he wanted to help her get dinner ready. This offer of inclusion could have effectively bridged the gap of his inability to understand and clearly state his true need. Even if he was really only hungry and thirsty she could have shown acceptance by recognizing these as legitimate needs, rather than only an inconvenience to her.

When Kit spilled the juice his Mom might have made it clear to him that while such carelessness is not O.K., he still is. These are the ways that acceptance is conveyed.

Earning Inclusion by Peers

As a parent you will hear the sometimes tearing cry, "Nobody will play with me." Or, "They won't let me play with them." These complaints concern the second aspect of acceptance—the need for inclusion by peers and siblings. Your child needs to know how to get inclusion from others and also how to give it. You can help him.

Inclusion generally hinges upon learning to take the initiative with others. Invariably, a child who consistently includes other people in his activities will be included by others. You can encourage your child to take the risks involved in developing this skill. Start by making him aware that everyone needs acceptance and wants to be included.

The basic formula for being popular, whether you're an adult or a child, is to take the initiative to include others. The popular child is the one who extends himself to other people, who takes the first risks in establishing a relationship. Others find him approachable, a desirable person to deal with. They see that he's willing to give them the acceptance they need and want.

There are a few angry children who sometimes deliberately set out to hurt others. But most exclusion is caused by insecurity coupled with inexperience, rather than by malice. When you notice your child excluding others, remember his immaturity. Point out how bad he makes an excluded child feel. In most cases, your child will indicate a complete lack of awareness of the pain he has been causing someone else. His self-concerned pursuit of his own interests blinds him. He's merely at an immature stage in his development and tends to experience others as "interesting toys" devoid of feelings.

Role-reversal is a persuasive tool: "How would you like it if somebody left you out? Would you like to feel you're not accepted?" The answer is predictable: He already knows how good it feels to be accepted and included. Like his other lessons about life, this one will have to be repeated frequently over a long period of time before he gets the message. But get it he will, eventually, with your continuing help.

How to Deal with the Need for Acceptance

Help you child distinguish between self-interest and compassion. Say, "Everybody wants to be included and accepted because they need to be. It's a good thing to include others and accept them—especially children because they are lonely, too, just like you." *Tell him he has the power* to make other children feel included: "They often are very afraid to approach other people. They want someone else to be the first to make the invitation so they can feel included."

Use role-reversal. Make him aware of excluded children's feelings. Ask him how he would feel if he were the one excluded. When he indicates he wouldn't like it, say, "Well, if that's the case, is it fair for you to be doing this to Cass?"

Remind him of the basic rule of acceptance: You get acceptance by giving it to others.

Include your child in as many adult functions as possible. Don't ignore him nor his presence during basically adult conversations and activities. Try to include him always, unless there is a very good reason not to.

R-4 Approval: "How'm I Doing?

Your child needs to feel that you like and endorse what he's doing. Every time he does something difficult or worthwhile, he will want your approval. Here again, as with attention and acceptance, a steady diet of endorsement is essential for your child to develop a healthy self-image. Your approval also assures him that he has a good relationship with you.

Focus your approval on specific actions. Whenever he is patient, shows self-control or includes another child—these are the times to offer him your approval. Rather than telling your child that he is a good fellow, it's better to let him know that you like a particular thing he did. Then, you avoid the possible danger that your child may feel his total worthiness as a person is up for evaluation. After all, he knows that even if he is doing well today, he may do poorly tomorrow; if you refer to him as a "good boy" today, what will you think of him when he's not doing so well? This concern could keep your child on edge.

Your job as a parent is essentially one of reinforcement. Whenever your child demonstrates that he is making progress, your approval says to him, "Keep it up. You're doing fine. You're on your way to being a mature person." Your approval provides the personal affirmation and incentive to go on trying. Don't lose sight of the double benefit of giving approval to your child. It builds his sense of worthiness as a good human being and serves as a reward that will motivate him to continue his positive behavior.

One of the common mistakes many parents make is to come down hard on their child when things go wrong and to take it for granted when things go right. This raises the child's awareness of his errors, shortcomings and unacceptability, without reminding him of all the positive things he does. The tragedy here lies mostly in the fact that many parents truly believe this is their primary function and duty—to let the child know when he does something wrong. But it is the opposite that actually is true. Desirable behavior is gained by noticing, commenting on and rewarding your child when he does things right. Recognition and reward will help you win the struggle for Emotional Maturity. Punishment or scolding, rendered in a spirit of rejection, will undermine your child's sense of self-worth.

Deedee, who is nine, knows that her mother is having a party this evening. Without being asked she has cleaned up the living room. Deedee is hopeful that her mother will notice her helpful behavior and give her some recognition. But, Mother who is much more prone to notice misbehavior and comment on that fails to see that Deedee has done something that deserves her notice and approval. Many parents miss such golden opportunities to boost their child's self-concept.

Had her mother a more developmental attitude, she would take time to notice and comment on her daughter's help. "I want you to know how much I appreciate your help in cleaning the living room. It shows me how grown up you're getting." These words reward and encourage Deedee to be helpful again the next chance she gets.

Instead, Mother misses this excellent chance to reinforce Deedee's positive behavior.

Mother doesn't understand how simple approval builds a child's sense of self-worth and how praise builds positive behavior. Our children need our approval on a frequent and consistent basis. Not a day in your child's life should pass without it.

Disapproval: "I Don't Like What You Did"

Your child needs to be reminded when his actions stray from reasonable limits. No misbehavior ever should go unnoticed or without comment. Many parents find this an onerous task. And it often is. But it's nevertheless essential.

Disapproval is directed toward your child's negative, destructive behaviors. It focuses on what he does that causes you and others bad feelings. Strongly as you feel, it's vital to concentrate on the event, the deed that caused the pain, and not upon your child's person. The rule of acceptance still applies—disapproval always should be combined with acceptance: "It upsets me when you exclude your brother from playing with you. Even though I don't like what you did, I still like you. And I'm willing to try to work out this problem with you."

If all your child receives is disapproval, he'll develop a negative self-image. Accentuate the positive but do not fail to comment on the negative.

How to Deal with the Need for Approval

Your behavior will teach your child how to give and get approval. Your example is his most impressive teacher. If you make a habit of telling others how much you appreciate the things they do for you, your child gradually will learn to do the same.

Your child needs as much approval as you can give him. You are his god and his guide. He is prone to imitate you. The things you praise are the things he will want to do. The time to give approval is whenever your child does something that pleases you, particularly when his action shows good development and indicates he's becoming more

responsible, patient or aware of others' feelings. Thank him.

Point out the things he does that other people like. This will reinforce his positive behaviors toward friends, siblings and teachers. Say, "Doesn't it make you feel important and worthwhile that you can make somebody else feel good? Now they'll appreciate having you around and will want to do things for you too."

Encourage him to face others. Point out to him the value of giving feedback to other people: "You have a right to let others know how they make you feel. There's no need to suffer in silence. When someone does something to you that is unfair, tell him, 'I don't like what you did to me. How would you feel if I did something like that to you?'"

Invite and accept his disapproval of your actions. Ask him, "How did you like what I just did? How did it make you feel?" It's inevitable that he'll disapprove of some of your actions. How you react will be a test of your capacity to be a positive, open parent. Accept his disapproval and thank him for it. Say, "Thanks for telling me. I guess I didn't realize how I made you feel. I'm glad you told me." This is a potent way to maintain open communications with your child.

Being aware of his bad feeling does not obligate you to change your behavior. But it does mean that you should consider seriously how your behavior is affecting your child and whether some change is in order.

Teach him to ask others for their feedback. Their information tells him valuable things about himself and his actions and the feelings of other people.

R-5 Affection: "All I Need Is Love . . . Pure Love"

Affection is the richest kind of endorsement you can give your child. It is an act of affirmation that says to him, "I want to have a deeper personal relationship with you." If someone as powerful and important as you wants to be more closely involved with him, then he must be very important indeed. This message—that he is special, desirable and valuable as a person—is critical to his development and happiness.

Every child needs love and affection in vast amounts. One reason your child requires so much affection is that he needs to feel worthy. At the same time, he's aware that he makes mistakes, fails your expectations and misbehaves. This tends to make him feel unworthy and unlovable unless you give him frequent affection. Never say to him, "I won't love you any more if you're a bad child." Withdrawing your love and affection is simply too shattering. Your frequent display of affection says to him, "Even though you disappointed me, I still love you and believe in you." That one message, delivered often, will reduce his uncertainty about himself and will serve as an incentive to grow up.

One of the best ways to show your affection is physical contact—the hug, embrace, pat on the shoulder or silent holding. Being held or touched affectionately delivers four important messages simultaneously: "I notice you, I include you, I endorse you and, most of all, I love you."

Another powerful way to communicate with your child is by showing personal interest in him. Asking him about his activities, listening to him, helping with things that interest him—all of these demonstrate in very concrete terms that he is important to you and has been accepted into an intimate relationship with you.

Love is not an easy thing for a child to understand, any more than it is for an adult. Love entails a sacrifice and a selflessness that your child needs to know and experience. Love can be defined as caring enough about someone else to treat that person well in spite of the pain he causes you. As a parent, you understand this. After all, you try to meet your child's various needs even though at the same time you bear his anger, cope with his demands and set aside your own needs and desires in favor of his. None of this is easy or without pain. Your child needs to know that love and affection are not trifles, but the deepest and most essential experiences in human relations.

The Cold Shoulder

At five, Andrea is attractive and seemingly outgoing and self-assured. In reality, she is very insecure and uncertain. She has lots of toys and comforts but her father is among the missing, an executive who is either on the road or occupied in the den with his reports. Mother is chic and fastidious, a woman who fulfills the role of the manager's wife: an expert on table wines (for the visit of the Big Boss), bridge, hairdressers and out-of-the-way shops that feature hard-to-pronounce cheeses and salamis. Toward Andrea she is standoffish—as if Mother's hair or dress might be mussed if the child came too close.

Mother is going over a list of invitations for a club luncheon when Andrea arrives looking for something:

Andrea: Momma, have you seen my teddy bear?

Mother: No.

Andrea: What are you doing?

Mother: Don't come too close. You might mix up my addresses. I'm sending out some invitations to a luncheon.

Andrea: Am I invited?

Mother: No, dear. It's for Daddy's friends.

Andrea: Won't there be any kids there?

Mother: Just some of your father's associates and clients.

Andrea: Oh . . . Momma, could you read me my Dr. Seuss book? Please?

Mother: Not now. Perhaps later.

Andrea: Can I sit next to you?

Mother: Not now, dear. Please. You'd be in the way. Why don't you look for your teddy bear?

Andrea: I just wanted to be with you for awhile.

Mother: I know, dear. But you can see how busy I am.

Andrea: Yes . . . I guess I'll look for my teddy.

Of course Andrea isn't interested in her bear. She really wants the assurance of her mother's interest and affection. Either because it is inconvenient or because it involves a commitment Andrea's mother doesn't want to make, she rejects the child. Mother seems to have little understanding of the vast amount of affection her young child requires.

The effect on Andrea is deflating. She leaves the room feeling that, to her mother, she is uninteresting and unworthy of affection. Instead of looking for her teddy, Andrea probably is heading for her room to brood. If the rejection she feels continues, it will become a psychological time bomb. Her resentment will grow steadily until it either becomes a severe depression or erupts in explosions of anger, for the deepest frustration is to feel that nobody cares.

If Mother were more sensitive to Andrea's needs or better able to commit herself to them, she would be able to give Andrea the affection she craves.

Andrea: Momma, have you seen my teddy bear?

Mother: No, I haven't. Where have you looked?

Andrea: Everywhere.

Mother: Come here, dear. I haven't had a chance all day to hold you.

Andrea: I like being with you, Momma.

Mother: And there's nothing I like better than being with you. (*Holds Andrea for a few minutes.*) Now, here's my Special Bear Hug. (*Squeezes Andrea*)

Andrea: (*Delighted*) Ohhh.

Mother: You feel good to me. Now let's see if we can find your teddy.

The few words of interest and the hug make Andrea feel acceptable and lovable, valued and worthwhile. Mother loses a few minutes but she gains a grateful child.

How to Meet Your Child's Need for Affection

You are the prime source for your child's affection. Because you are so important, because you loom so significantly in his life, your affection is a magic talisman that banishes many a bad feeling.

Recognize and accept your child's enormous and apparently unending need for affection.

Show your affection. Genuine affection is a joy, not a chore. Have fun with your child as you hold him: squeeze him, tickle him, pat him on the shoulder, run your fingers through his hair. Show him that you want him near. Say, "I love you. You're great!" Express affection by spending time with him, listening to what he has to say, being considerate of his feelings and encouraging and praising his efforts to grow up. Don't be afraid of physical contact. Touching is good for your child and it will be good for you.

Give your child silent lap time. A simple, helpful way to show affection for a troubled child is just to hold him on your lap for five minutes or so, without comment. Nine times out of ten, this will calm an hysterical child. You can offer this comfort to any child up to 10 and sometimes to 12 years of age, or older. When the pained child calms down, you can discuss his problem with him.

R-6 Social Responsibility: "I've Got You in My Power"

Once upon a time, there was a village braggart who claimed to be the bravest man for miles around. Under the shade of his hut, he would regale anyone who would listen to his exploits. He would tell of the time he captured the Great Snake barehanded; of wrestling the King of Elephants to a draw before the Maharajah; and of his most-famous adventure of all—single-handedly capturing the dangerous Man-eater of Bengal, a tiger that had been preying upon the villages. The more he repeated these stories, the more he believed they were true. One day a tiger with glistening stripes strode into the village. Naturally, everyone was upset. They turned to the hero for help. He said grandly, "Be calm. I will handle the matter with dispatch." It was a glorious opportunity to prove his bravery once and for all, and to silence anyone who had snickered behind his back.

Before long, the hero had the tiger in hand. He had grabbed it by the tail and was holding on for dear life as the big cat bolted and snarled. He called out to the astonished villagers who had gathered to watch, "You see! I have captured the tiger! I have him by the tail!"

Just then, the village idiot spoke up, "Do you have the tiger, or does the tiger have you?" This so shocked the hero (who hadn't quite thought of it that way), he decided to let go. After all, discretion is said to be the better part of valor. Needless to say, he made an irreversible error. The tiger swallowed him in one gulp and bounded off to loll about in the jungle.

This tale illustrates the point that the apparent victim in a power relationship may have not-yet-realized power of his own. Every child feels helpless because of his small size, inabilities and inexperience. This is a normal feeling. Your child needs to realize his power is greater than he suspects. Even when he is very small, he has considerable power to make people feel good or bad. Ordinarily, your child will assume that he is a captive, subject to the will of others. Every day in one way or another he is reminded of his dependence and inferiority. At the same time, he is inexperienced at recognizing and coping with the feelings of new people he must deal with. As a result, he feels helpless and powerless, even when he is not.

Your role is to remove this conviction of helplessness by showing him the power he really has.

Tiger by the Tail

Scott, stoop-shouldered at seven, firmly believes himself incompetent and utterly helpless. Somewhat shy, rather sensitive and inclined not to fight, today he looks even more discouraged than usual.

Mother: What's wrong, Scott?

Scott: Nothing's wrong.

Mother: I can see you're in a bad mood.

Scott: You'd be in a bad mood, too, if you were me!

Mother: I think you'd better tell me what happened.

Scott: That smart guy, Peter Evans, was making fun of me.

Mother: At school?

Scott: Yeah, at recess. So I threw a rock at him.

Mother: And?

Scott: And he went and told the teacher and she got mad at me.

Mother: I don't blame her.

Scott: But he called me a weirdo!

Mother: You don't throw rocks just for name-calling.

Scott: Then what do I do? Everything I try is the wrong thing.

Mother: Just act like a gentleman and he'll leave you alone.

Scott: Oh no, he won't.

Scott, frustrated because of his inability to handle teasing schoolmates, is helpless to deal with their onslaughts against his ego. Under strong provocation, his response is violent. Mother's mistakes lie in making him feel he's done the wrong thing for the umpteenth time and in focusing only on the moral aspect of the incident. Scott still has no idea of how to deal with the underlying problem: how to protect his ego without getting into trouble.

Scott needs to know he too has ability to make others feel good or bad, that he can learn to get rid of his feelings of helplessness. Just now he believes himself on the receiving end of everything that can go wrong in a seven-year-old's world. The solution lies in realizing he has plenty of power potential. Someone need only show him how to master it:

Mother: I can see you're in a bad mood, son. What makes you feel so down?

Scott: That smart guy, Peter Evans, made fun of me! He called me a weirdo!

Mother: Then what?

Scott: So I threw a rock at him, and the teacher got mad at me.

Mother: So you really felt pretty bad, didn't you?

Scott: I felt rotten. I still do.

Mother: How did Peter Evans feel?

Scott: I don't know. Probably glad.

Mother: Did you ever think that maybe everyone has the power to make other people feel good or bad. Peter made you feel bad today. But you have power over how he feels, too.

Scott: I do?

Mother: Of course. You make me feel good, and then again sometimes you make me feel bad. You know that.

Scott: I do?

Mother: Just now, Peter thinks he's controlling you by making you feel bad. But you can affect him by making him feel the same way, and you don't have to throw a rock in order to do it.

Scott: How?

Mother: By not playing his game. When he calls you a weirdo, you could just laugh at him and say, "So what?" Or, "So what else is new?" And then ignore him. Go someplace else. That's one way to upset him.

Scott: Will it work?

Mother: Try and see. An even better way is to say to Peter, "Gee, that's too bad. I wanted to be your friend, Peter, but since you just want to make me feel bad, I'll find someone else. I don't want to spend time with somebody who goes around hurting people's feelings."

No results were apparent the first day, nor even the first week. But Scott's mother kept reminding him of the importance of persistence in the matter. Within a month, his provisional belief that youngsters would rather have friends than enemies paid off: Peter became Scott's friend.

Scott now knows of his power over others. Obviously he might misuse this power. As long as your child feels helpless, he will tend to be destructive, to resort to sabotage or social withdrawal. He may be negative ("I can't do that . . .") or he may be passive. But if he feels his power, he can take a chance on being constructive and positive.

How to Put the Tiger in His Tank
Make your child aware of his power:
"You're not as helpless as you think. You'd find out you're quite powerful, if you would think of what you can do. When you help me with the yard work, you make me feel good. When you fight with your brother, you make me feel awful. And you affect other people, too."
Emphasize the benefits to be gained from using this power in positive, constructive ways. Point out to him, "Power is a two-way street. When you make other people feel good, you have a right to expect they'll treat you in the same way. This is the basis of any healthy relationship. A person who gives good treatment to others is more likely to get good treatment."

R-7 Empathy: Yourself in Other People's Shoes

Every parent wonders, "When will my kid begin to show a little consideration to others and to me?" And every kid wonders, "How can I get people to be nice to me?" Kindness and consideration are valuable commodities in human relations, more so these days when our busy life-style makes them so much harder to come by. Consideration and kindness are basically the same thing. But consideration implies prior deliberation—a considerate person thinks beforehand about the consequences his actions will have upon the feelings of others.

Children usually are too embarrassed to request favors because to do so exposes them to possible refusal. They are reluctant to ask because they don't want to test their "worth." Your role is to help your child acquire both the language and the courage to request kindness and consideration from other people.

The Search for Kindness

Sara, nine, is strongly inclined to want and get her own way. She has been playing with her seven-year-old sister, Heidi. All went well until Sara wanted to monopolize the doll house Heidi had just received for her birthday. Heidi's refusal caused a pulling match. Sara slapped her little sister. Tears and screams have brought Mother to the scene:

Mother: (*Angrily*) Sara, why did you hit Heidi?

Sara: I didn't do anything.

Heidi: You did! You did!

Sara: Well, you started it.

Heidi: No, I didn't!

Sara: Oh yes, you did! I wanted to play with your doll house and you said no.

Heidi: It's my doll house!

Sara: I let you play with my things, Heidi. Mother, she was playing with my dolls but she wouldn't let me touch her doll house.

Mother: So you hit her?

Sara: She's a spoiled brat! She always takes my things but won't let me play with anything of hers.

Mother: You're off the point. I can't let you go around hitting your little sister.

Sara: She deserves it!

Mother: You'd better go to your room!

Sara: But it isn't fair! She's more to blame than me!

With punishment for misbehavior, this clash is treated in the conventional way. But the issue between the two sisters—the unkindness of one to the other—remains unsolved and will occur again, probably the next time they play. Sara was not completely innocent. But if she shares her dolls, she has a right to expect her sister to reciprocate. Were Mother aware of the more basic problem—the insufficiently developed considerateness of both sisters—she would have a more neutral approach and would teach Sara how to ask a favor from Heidi:

Mother: Sara, you know better than that! Why did you do it?

Sara: I wanted to play with Heidi's doll house and she wouldn't let me!

Mother: So you hit her?

Sara: She deserved it. She's a little brat. I let her play with my dolls and she won't let me play with her doll house.

Mother: Heidi, did Sara let you play with her dolls?

Heidi: Yes—until she hit me.

Mother: Sara, did you ask her to let you play with the doll house?

Sara: I don't remember.

Heidi: She didn't ask!

Mother: When you want a favor, you must ask, Sara. You could have said, "Please, may I play with your doll house?"

Sara: She still would have said no.

Mother: Maybe not, if you had asked nicely. And you, Heidi, must realize that when Sara does you a favor, she has a right to expect you to return the favor.

In this last example, Mother treats the more basic problem. Instead of pouncing on Sara, she tries to put the situation in better perspective for both girls, showing them a more constructive way to get their needs met.

How to Get and Give Kindness

Treat your child with kindness and consideration. As in every developmental process, your example is the most impressive model. When your child experiences your kindness on a regular basis or witnesses your kindness to others, he will be more inclined to act in the same way.

Make him aware of the kindness he gets and gives. Too often, a child doesn't appreciate what his parents do for him. Without sounding smug, remind your child of your efforts to feed, clothe, entertain and care for him. Also point out the kind things other people do for him: "Wasn't it nice of Mrs. Webb to give you that bone for the dog?" Or, "It was kind of your brother to lend you his ice skates, wasn't it?"

Provide your child with the language to ask for a favor or kind treatment. Use phrases like: "There's something I'd appreciate your doing for me. It's [name it]." "I wonder if you'd be kind enough to do me a favor . . .?" By your frequent repetition of this sort of language, your child gradually will acquire the pattern. You can also show him tactful ways to turn down requests. When he asks for something unreasonable or untimely, say, "I see how you feel and I'm sorry I can't do it for you right now. Perhaps I can do it later." Then tell him when. If you don't wish to do it later, tell the reason why.

R-8 Everybody Needs a Friend

Finding a friend is high on every child's agenda. It's natural to want the companionship and special affirmation which only a friend can provide. But the search for a friend confronts every child with a dilemma—a conflict between his loneliness and his fear. His loneliness tells him, "Go play with others." But his fear says, "They might not want to play with you." Part of the solution lies in his understanding how universal his conflict is. When your child is frightened about risking rejection, it is best to tell him that everyone has this fear. He may be surprised to learn he's not the only person with this problem. You'll make him feel much better about himself and encourage him to reach out for companionship.

Building a friendship involves two hurdles that every child needs to know about and contend with. Taking the risk of the first approach, making the first step to start a friendship is one hurdle. Another is coping with the bad feelings that inevitably develop between friends.

"I Can't Get Started with You"

Stuart, eight, a quiet boy, has grown up in a neighborhood where there are no other youngsters his age. He's severely shy, slow to start a conversation and prone to stand back from a group. It's not that he doesn't want companions—he wants them desperately. Today, Mother is searching for what lies behind his bad mood:

Mother: Why aren't you drinking your juice?

Stuart: Huh? Oh, O.K.

Mother: Something's wrong, isn't it?

Stuart: No.

Mother: Are you sure?

Stuart: (*A bit dubiously*) Yeah.

Mother: How'd things go at school today?

Stuart: (*Unconvincingly*) Aw right.

Mother: I don't believe you.

Stuart: I told you, everything was fine . . . except . . . well . . . except for recess.

Mother: What happened then?

Stuart: Well, I wanted to play basketball with the guys. But . . . They didn't pick me.

Mother: Did you ask if you could play?

Stuart: No.

Mother: What did you expect, then?

Stuart: I just thought they might ask. They needed another guy.

Mother: It doesn't make sense. I really don't understand you, Stuart Blaine. You mope around and expect people to know what you're thinking as if they were mind readers!

Stuart: You don't have to get mad and yell.

Mother: I'm not mad. I'm upset. I don't know what's the matter with you. You don't have sense enough to look out for yourself. Stuart, what *is* the matter?

Stuart: (*Retreating*) I don't know . . .

Mother: You're just afraid and you'll always be afraid. You're a coward.

Until she launched into a personal attack, Mother was on the verge of helping Stuart with his problem. He is inexperienced, lonely and afraid. Because his feelings are so severe, name-calling can only worsen his problem. Stuart needs advice and encouragement to make friends with other youngsters. Unless he receives the information he needs, Stuart will be like many other children who remain shy and alone because no one takes the time to show them how to make friends.

Perhaps Mother has been so much tuned in to Stuart's physical needs ("Have you had enough to eat?" "Are your clothes clean?" "Did I hear you cough?") that she is not oriented to his other needs.

Supposing Mother is more aware of every child's great need for compansionship:

Mother: What happened?

Stuart: I didn't get picked for basketball. Again.

Mother: Did you try?

Stuart: I just thought they might ask me.

Mother: That's what you *wish* they'd do. You'd probably have more luck if one of them was a friend who wanted to include you. Chances are those boys don't know you very well.

Stuart: They know me all right. They just won't choose me.

Mother: Are any of them your friends?

Stuart: Not exactly.

Mother: Is there one you like more than the others?

Stuart: Carlos is O.K. And I like Knute Olson, too.

Mother: Well, then, suppose tomorrow you invite one of them to come over after school. I'll have some cake and you can play basketball in the yard, the two of you. When he sees you're interested in him and how good you are at basketball, chances are he'll want you on his team next time.

Stuart: I bet he won't come.

Mother: If he can't come tomorrow, maybe he can come another time.

Stuart: Maybe he won't want to.

Mother: You won't know until you ask. There's a good chance he'll say yes. What have you got to lose? Right now, you're unhappy because you're lonely. If he says no, you won't be any worse off than you are now. But there's a chance he might say yes—maybe not tomorrow but some other day. Then, you'll feel a whole lot better. Isn't it worth a try?

In this case, Mother zeroes in on Stuart's loneliness and gives him supportive suggestions. Even if this attempt fails, she will continue to encourage Stuart's efforts to find a friend until he is successful. Mother understands how vital this is for her son's happiness. He still exhibits the uncertainty associated with loneliness. But with her gentle, persistent encouragement, he stands a good chance of finding friends.

How to Win Friends

There are a number of ways to help your child make new friends, but they require effort on your part. The rule is: Don't let him give up.

Encourage your child to risk possible rejection. Tell him, "I'd really be proud of you if you would take the initiative. After all, everyone feels the same way. Everyone is afraid of being turned down. It's a chance we all have to take. Besides, people especially like the person who takes the first step—he makes it safer for them."

Be available to comfort him when he is rejected. Not every attempt he makes will be successful. Some efforts at friendship simply don't work out. Say, "Not everybody you want for a friend is going to like you, any more than you're going to like everybody who wants you for a friend." Ask him about the children he knows, the ones he likes and the ones he doesn't. Ask how things are going in these relations.

You can serve as a bridge. Offer to bring your child together with a possible friend in some kind of activity. A visit to the zoo, a ball game, or an ice-cream parlor will often start off a friendship much more quickly than the hesitant, hit-or-miss, trial-and-error methods most children usually employ.

Prepare your child for mixed feelings in his friendships. Tell him it is inevitable that there will be times when he will feel upset with his friends. Emphasize that only relationships which have survived the test of bad feelings and disagreements are truly solid. This knowledge will prepare him for occasions when he and his friends disagree. It will enable him to understand that he doesn't have to lose a friend every time they don't see eye to eye.

If your child never asks for help in making friendships, you may assume that your offer of assistance would constitute an intrusion into his private territory. This is not the case. It isn't that your child doesn't want your help—he may not know how to ask for it. He'll be very gratified to find out that you know something about—and care enough to show him how to manage—such private feelings as his loneliness and fear.

R-9 Resisting Peer Pressure

Many parents fear the influence exercised over their child by other children. This concern about peer pressure is common. Is so-and-so teaching Will to smoke pot? What does he tell Will about sex? Is Barry a good influence or not? Does he use bad language? All these are legitimate concerns, even if they seem beyond parental control.

As a parent, you actually have considerable power to influence your child, the great pressure of his peers notwithstanding. That power lies in your relationship with him. If it's positive, if you give him the acceptance and affection he needs, he's unlikely to trade that asset for something less.

The usual peer problem involves manipulation. Sometimes your child finds himself in a situation where he is being controlled by a bossy—although inwardly fearful—"friend." To your child's dismay, he discovers himself doing most of the giving without getting much in return. A situation like this usually develops because your child is not fully aware of what is happening in the relationship. He probably feels uncomfortable but doesn't know why. He needs to understand that he's being manipulated unfairly to serve the other child's fear-based method of relating. Your child also needs to realize that the world contains many people who will manipulate him if they can.

Resisting Manipulation by Peers

Friendly Derek, eight, has been easygoing and goodnatured as long as his parents can remember. Not a colicky baby who cried all night, he took his bottle and contentedly dozed off.

But lately some of the easiness has gone. Now he seems down at the mouth. Something is bothering Derek:

Mother: What seems to be troubling you, Derek?

Derek: I don't know.

Mother: Something seems to be making you feel bad.

Derek: I'm mad at Will.

Mother: Why? What did he do?

Derek: Every time we play, it's always his way. He always makes all the rules up. And I always lose. I never can win.

Mother: You mean he changes the rules when he's losing?

Derek: Yeah.

Mother: How could you be so dumb? He's just using you. You shouldn't put up with it.

Mother's diagnosis is correct: Derek is being used. But her approach is counterproductive. There is no need to make Derek feel he is dumb. The cause of Derek's trouble is the manipulator who is taking advantage of the little boy's good nature. What Derek needs is advice and not a putdown:

Derek: Will always makes up all the rules. And I always lose. I never win.

Mother: He always wins because he is making the rules in his favor? Then, why do you play with him?

Derek: Will's the only one around. Besides I like him.

Mother: Would you care for my advice? Tell Will that, if he wants to play by his rules, you won't play. Tell him he has to agree on the rules in advance and that it isn't fair for him to try to change them in his favor. Ask him why he isn't fair. You see, you have the power to do something about the situation. And you can use it to get better treatment.

Here, Mother presents a practical suggestion that supports Derek's ego, instead of downgrading it. Derek, like other children, needs to know he has the power to negotiate. That power lies in Derek's option to withdraw his companionship from a friend who continues to be manipulative or coercive. First, however, Derek needs help to see what is happening to him. This awareness, coupled with his power to resist manipulation, will help him establish healthy relationships based upon a natural give-and-take, a mutual respect. Then he won't be subject to the emotional blackmail of coercive, one-way relationships.

For another look at the problem of undue influence, consider Mark, seven. His friends have introduced him to some new kinds of words—the sort all boys sooner or later discover and use to their parents' alarm. Mark has just shouted one of these choice four-letter words in the direction of his sister. Father now has Mark on the carpet:

Father: Don't let me hear you use language like that around this house.

Mark: I didn't say anything.

Father: I heard you, so don't make it worse by lying.

Mark: I didn't mean it.

Father: Then why did you say it?

Mark: I just got mad or something.

Father: What I want to know is where you picked up that kind of language. Not around here. Who teaches you this stuff?

Mark: I don't know.

Father: Come on. Which of the guys you hang around with? The Jamison boy? Or that other kid—what's his name—Magruder?

Mark: Well . . .

Father: If I catch you using words like that again, you're headed for trouble. *(Mark is silent.)*

Father: I don't want you associating with foul-mouthed kids. Understand? Find somebody else to play with.

Mark: Yeah.

Father: I'm not going to let some longhaired hippie ruin my kid with his dirty mouth. Get yourself some new friends!

Father's reaction is angry, moralistic and oblivious to the main point. He overestimates the power of Mark's peers and underestimates his own power to influence his son by means other than threats. Missing his father's attention, Mark has turned more and more to his peers, who are his only source of companionship. Because of his deep need for someone's attention, he has been compromised into paying a heavy price for "being one of the gang." Mark is behaving in ways he knows are wrong. Were Father more knowledgeable and supportive, he would realize that giving increased attention to Mark and building a firmer father-son relationship would make the youngster resistant to the influence of his peers. And his guidance would be more positive:

Father: I know how hard it is not to go along with something like that, son. But language like that just isn't attractive—people really won't respect you for using it.

Mark: If I don't, they won't think I'm one of the guys.

Father: It's better to be yourself. If people can't like you as you are, they're not really interested in you.

Instead of condemning Mark, Father uses his approval to influence the boy in a positive direction. He expresses his trust in his son by requesting cooperation instead of issuing a direct command. By focusing on the boy's conflict between his need for self-respect and his need to be liked, Father helps Mark see the possible consequences of his behavior. Father realizes he must give Mark more understanding, acceptance and personal interest on a regular basis. And, as a supportive, affectionate parent, Father will be too valuable a person for Mark to ignore.

How to Build Resistance Against Peer Pressure

Make your child aware of peer pressure when you observe him allowing himself to be coerced or bullied, or if he complains that he continually has to give in to the will of others. Children often do not consciously realize how they are being compromised or what to do about it. Say, "It's bad to give in all the time. You have your own values. Other people should respect this. And you're entitled to have some give-and-take in your relationship. Friends who won't accept your values are taking advantage and aren't true friends."

Help your child understand that, despite his doubts, he has power to deal with the situation. Advise your child how to resist pressure and ask for fairness. If he is refused, tell him to inform the other child, "I'm sorry, then. I wanted to be your friend but you don't want to treat me fairly. So—see you later."

Show your child how to distinguish between valid and invalid social pressure. Valid pressure is the kind a parent exerts to keep children from exposing themselves to danger because of their impulsiveness or inexperience. This is the kind of coercion that protects. Invalid social pressure is the kind exerted by people who feel they must dominate others. This involves an unhealthy and neurotic relationship which operates for the sole benefit of the manipulator. The victimized child is coerced or imposed upon to serve the neurotic needs of a domineering one.

Ask your child about the pressure he's getting from peers: "Do you have any problems with the kids these days? Are they tempting you with things that can get you into trouble? How are you handling it?"

Listen and advise without criticism. As he tells you the pressures, don't moralize. Criticism will close him up and reduce your power to influence him. Instead, calmly discuss the implications of knuckling under to the pressure, and how it will harm him if he pays too high a price for the illusion of acceptance.

Reduce the threat of peer pressure by spending more one-to-one time with your child; notice and praise his good behavior; show an interest in him and his feelings; ask him every day what went well or badly; show your affection.

By using these strong, supportive approaches, you can insulate your child against negative peer pressure.

R-10 Painful But Loving Confrontation

To many parents, confrontation has a harsh sound. It implies a fight or argument with a disrespectful, mouthy kid. For many parents, confrontation is always a painful, ego-bruising battle, a contest of wills. This is because many parents don't confront their child's behavior until they've become hysterical about it. The result, for the moment, is total war. Hysterics, cross-accusations, tears, shouting and curses fill the air.

But confrontation can be much more reasonable and play a very constructive role in your child's development. This means confronting your child daily in a calm, supportive way. Let him know in a loving way what kind of feelings he is producing in you.

Your child also needs to learn how to confront you in a positive way. He needs your help and encouragement to become brave enough to tell you how you make him feel. This is the part of confrontation that many parents fail. They are afraid, often unrealistically, that their child will inevitably become disrespectful if he is allowed to be candid. Nothing could be farther from the truth. The more he is allowed to tell how you make him feel, the more he will grow to trust and respect you. Daily confrontation clears the air of resentment and establishes an honest relationship based on your shared feelings. Then you can work together on resolving your conflicts.

Eyeball to Eyeball

Rick and Rae, eight-year-old twins, incline to be boisterous and competitive. Rick has been reasonably content building a model airplane. Rae is miffed at Rick's neglect and is jealous of the attention he is giving to the model. Since she can't make him notice her directly, she attempts other means:

Rae: What's this called?

Rick: It's the tail, the elevator.

Rae: It doesn't seem very strong. Look how it's bending.

Rick: Hey, cut that out. You'll break it.

Rae: No, I won't. See?

Rick: (*Grabbing for it*) Gimme that. It's mine!

Rae: No! (*Rick grabs for it but Rae won't let go and the elevator is smashed.*)

Rick: Now see what you did?

Rae: I didn't either.

Rick: Yes, you did, you dummy! (*He pummels her with his fists as she starts screaming as loudly as she can.*)

Mother: What's all this noise? Rick, stop that this minute! (*She has to separate them physically.*)

Rick: Rae broke my plane, on purpose!

Mother: I don't want to hear about that.

Don't you dare lay a hand on her! She's your sister!

Rick: She's a brat! You're not fair! You always take her side!! You both make me sick!!!

Mother: I don't like your attitude. Go to your room till you can show some respect.

Ostensibly, Mother is in control. She scolds Rick and punishes him by sending him to his room. In reality, the confrontation is a failure. Like most parents, Mother overly personalizes Rick's back talk. She takes as a personal affront his accusation of unfair treatment, instead of as a fact-as-Rick-sees-it. Even worse, she cuts off deeper expressions of his true feelings as well as any further discussion.

Rick withdraws from the scene of battle with deep resentments against his mother and his sister. His undischarged bitterness over being treated unfairly will fester in his subconscious and eventually surface as some negative behavior directed against them. By failing to listen and thus exhaust his negative feelings, Mother merely has kept the gun loaded for the next time.

How could she have better managed the situation? The manner of confrontation is critical.

Here is an example of a supportive confrontation, without moralizing or scolding:

(Mother has just separated the children, physically.)

Rick: Rae broke my airplane, on purpose!

Mother: Now just a minute!

Rick: You're gonna take her side! You always do!!

Mother: Maybe not. Tell me exactly what happened.

Rick: She broke my plane, on purpose. She bent the tail and it broke.

Mother: Just the same, I don't want you beating up your sister. When she bothers you, you come and tell me about it, instead. Is there anything else you want to say?

Rick: Yeah. When are you going to get after Rae like you get after me?

Mother: Rick, sometimes I haven't liked things you've done, but that doesn't mean I'm against you. I'm always interested in you and any legitimate complaint you have.

Rick: Oh, sure. You always blame me even if it's Rae's fault.

Mother: Maybe I've made some mistakes. But if Rae just broke your elevator, that's a legitimate complaint and I'll see to it that she understands she mustn't tamper with your things.

Here, Mother invites a full expression of Rick's feelings. Without criticism or scolding, she listens to his resentment at her intervention. She accepts his complaint as valid and worthy of consideration. Finally, she shows a commitment to protect his rights.

Giving Support
Positive confrontation goes hand in hand with support. If you strive to support your child with attention, acceptance, approval and affection, he will be able to mature and grow into a more rewarding and loving relationship with you. The amount of this support, measured in concrete actions or time spent with him, is critical. This is the Law of Support: By a wide margin, it should exceed the total of your demands, criticisms and confrontations.

How to Encourage Constructive Confrontation

Confront your child every day with the things he has done to upset you. If you don't do this regularly, your accumulated resentments will later erupt in anger or hysterics. Regular confrontation reduces these negative feelings. The style of confrontation is important. Sit down with your child calmly, listen without comment to his explanation and then ask, "Is there some way you can get your needs met without causing trouble? What do you suggest?" Through your example, you can help your child develop the power to confront. It is not enough for you to express your negative feelings; he must have a chance to express his.

Accept his confrontation as his way of seeing things. Don't regard it as a personal

attack. Most of us tend to personalize criticism and lash back at the accuser. Candid confrontation need not be seen as a threat to you nor to your authority. It is a factual report on his feelings which it is important for you, as a parent, to know. He may be a mile off but it's better to know his way of seeing things. If you accept your child's feelings in regular confrontations, he will be much less apt to try to either challenge or sabotage your authority.

Help your child develop tact in confronting others. If you are diplomatic with your child, chances are he will learn some diplomacy from your example. It's a matter of style and consideration; it comes from an awareness of the pain present in confrontation and criticism. You can help your child develop this awareness of others' sensitivity to criticism by telling him: "I do not mean to cut you down but I want you to know what you're doing. I want you to be aware of how you affect other people's feelings so you won't make enemies or have people dislike you. If you're aware of what you're doing, you'll do better in life. I don't want you to grow up hurting others without even knowing it." Also, point out the basic principle of tact—to cause the least amount of pain to resolve a difference. Make your child aware that every confrontation involves pain, which is inevitable, but that the tactful person tries to minimize the pain involved.

When your child confronts you with strong feelings, allow him to get it all off his chest. When verbalizing his negative feelings, he is effectively reducing them. Ask him, "Do you have anything else you want to tell me? Do you have any other feelings about this?" You are his testing ground, his sparring partner, and his trainer. What he learns in his confrontations with you is what he will be willing and able to use with others.

R-11 Mutual Support: the Tie That Binds

Every parent wants his child to get along with others. The answer lies in reciprocity and cooperation, two social skills that are the foundation of interpersonal harmony. Give-and-take, the essence of every good relationship, means, "You meet my needs, I'll meet your." Good relationships exist on mutual support—two people helping each other. Without it, no relationship lasts very long.

Doing Things for Each Other

Lance, nine and decidedly lazy, expects his mother to wait on him hand and foot. He is well on his way to becoming a male chauvinist. Big Lance is the same way, so it's not likely he ever will see anything unusual in his son's behavior. Mother is the family martyr who suffers in silence as chief cook, chauffeur and housemaid. But she finds herself becoming more nervous and angry these days and is determined not to be walked over.

Mother stands in the middle of Lance's room, which looks as if a small cyclone had hit. It makes Mother weary just to see it.

Lance: Mom, can I go to the movies with Kiko this afternoon?

Mother: Lance, what about your messy room?

Lance: It's not too bad.

Mother: You've got to be kidding.

Lance: It looks okay to me.

Mother: I'd appreciate it if just once you'd bend down and pick up a few things. It really would help.

Lance: I'm busy right now. Maybe later.

Mother: But that's all you ever say, Lance.

Lance: Kiko's waiting for me now. I'll do my room later. Honest.

Mother: That's your story. I'm sick and tired of that line and this mess. You're going to clean up your room before you go anywhere.

Lance: It's not my job. It's your job!

Mother: I have news for you. It's your job from now on.

Lance: Whaddya mean by that?

Mother: Lance, there's something you've

got to face. Every day I do plenty of things to make you comfortable and happy. I get your meals, drive you around to your friends, buy your clothes and toys, do your laundry. I break my back for you. What do you ever do for me?

Lance: Well . . .

Mother: Nothing! You never do anything. You're no help. And you never even say thanks.

Lance: (Weakly) Sure I do.

Mother: Do you think it's fair for me to do so much for you, and for you to do nothing for me?

Lance: *(Again, weakly)* I suppose not.

Mother: You bet it isn't. Never has been and never will be. As long as I continue to do these things for you, I expect you to do some things for me. If you don't, I'll be less interested in doing things for you. Understand?

Lance: I guess so.

Mother: Good! And you can start right now. If you'll cooperate and help me clean this room, I'll consider taking you and Kiko to the movie. You have my commitment and I want yours.

In this example, Mother confronts Lance with his lack of consideration and appreciation. When a child doesn't realize how much his parents are doing for him, he takes it all for granted. The danger is that he becomes passive, a consumer who receives but doesn't give. Because he's not productive, he begins to accumulate feelings of guilt and unworthiness. This is self-destructive. Sooner or later, his failure to recognize and appreciate what others do for him will boomerang and he will suffer the rejection that inevitably comes to the ungrateful. Mother's technique though brusque, is simple and effective. The Romans had a phrase for it, *quid pro quo* (something for something). This is the basis of reciprocity, the first law of any good human relationship. Each person must contribute something useful and beneficial to the other. Mother realizes the time is overdue for Lance to start contributing to their relationship.

The sooner your child is aware and able to reciprocate by helping you, the deeper and more lasting your friendship will become. Starting at age three is not too soon.

How to Make Contracts

Point out to your child how you and he and various people he knows are meeting one another's needs in some way. He especially needs to know exactly what you do for him. Be specific about the reciprocal treatment you expect from your child. Establish contracts with him: "Here is something you can do for me. Now, what can I do for you?" Be sure that your child follows through with his commitments.

R-12 Decision-making: Sharing the Power

Lord Acton, the English historian, once wrote, "All power corrupts, and absolute power corrupts absolutely." Had he been a child psychologist, he might have added, "Absolute power exercised by parents over children corrupts and destroys their relationship. It is an open invitation to indifference and rebellion." The tragedy about parental power is that some parents try to control a child arbitrarily, on the basis that they are wise enough to make all decisions without consulting him. The result is a psychological disaster for both parent and child. Not allowed to function or decide things for himself, the child feels put down. In response, he becomes resentful and uncooperative, experiencing his parents as unreasonable jailors.

In exercising your power, you need to take into account your child's natural urge to grow up and to function independently. Along with acceptance and affection, the sharing of your decision-making power is an essential ingredient for building and strengthening your relationship. The reason this sharing is so powerful is that it demonstrates to your child that he merits your fundamental respect and consideration and that his thoughts and feelings are important. At the same time, it gives him a stake in his own life: the freedom and elbow room he needs to practice and develop as a competent person. The extent to which he participates in making a decision will be the extent to which he also is committed to meeting the agreed-upon responsibilities. Having a share in the decision makes it his game, too. And he'll be more likely to play it responsibly. Sharing your power to make decisions does not mean giving your child complete control over his own affairs. It does not mean letting him do whatever he wants to do. Rather, it is a chance to participate, to have an input in matters affecting him. Here is how this sounds in actual practice:

Telling	*Sharing in Deciding*
"I'm going to paint your room blue."	"What color would you like your room painted?"
"You're going to have oatmeal for breakfast."	"What cereal would you like this morning? We have oatmeal or cornflakes."
"For vacation we're going to go on a camping trip [whether you like it or not]."	"We have a vacation coming up. What would you like to do?"

Your child's power to make wise decisions will increase as he matures. Then, you can give him a larger share in decision-making. Gradually, he will become better able to function well independently.

By slowly allowing him more power to decide things as he proves his responsibility, you give your child the best of two worlds. He has the benefit of your protection when he needs it, along with your judgment and experience. At the same time, he is able to decide and do those things he can do well for himself.

Making Decisions: The Roadblocks

Mother has had a hard day. So has Father. They're both tired and somewhat down. When Father returned home from work, Mother said, "Let's take the kids out to eat tonight. I'm not in the mood to cook and then clean up the mess that goes with it." They routed Dolores and Tim from their play, and all packed into the car. As they drive along, Dolores, nine, asks:

Dolores: Where are we going?

Mother: To Harry's Hamburgers.

Dolores: I don't want to go there. The hamburgers are terrible—too little and dried up. I hate them. I want to go to Gino's for pizza.

Mother: We're going to Harry's, you're going to get a hamburger and you're going to like it.

Dolores: I won't eat it.

Mother: Oh, yes you will. You'll eat it and like it. Don't tell me what you will or won't do!

Next morning, Dolores is just out of bed and fishing around for some clothes to wear. Mother arrives with a jumper and blouse that she thinks make Dolores look cute. They're clean and they're ready.

Mother: Here, put on this jumper with your blue blouse.

Dolores: I don't want to. They're ugly.

Mother: What's ugly about them?

Dolores: I don't know. They just don't go together.

Mother: They look fine and I want you to wear them.

Dolores: They look rotten together. Besides, I don't like blue any more.

Mother: I'm not about to argue any longer. This is what you'll wear today. And that's final.

Mother is not allowing Dolores to make enough decisions for herself. If the girl's ability to decide is constantly restricted by parental muscle, either of two things will happen: She will openly rebel or she will become indifferent and apathetic. "What do I care?" may become her motto, along with, "Nothing I do or say will change things." Depending upon her inherited temperament, she either will despair or openly become very angry. The feeling she gets from putdowns is that she's helpless and no-account. Sooner or later, she will begin to live these roles because they are the only ones she knows. For her part, Mother doesn't want to take the time to ask Dolores for an opinion. Mother's assumption, like that of many parents, is that she always knows best. But this attitude overlooks Dolores' need to exercise power over her own destiny. If she doesn't make any decisions for herself, she never will really grow up; she will not become responsible. Responsibility entails facing the consequences of one's own decisions. Mother needs to know this and to permit Dolores to learn from these important experiences.

A better approach would have been to ask Dolores and Tim what they would like to eat:

Mother: We're all going out to eat tonight. Any ideas on what you'd like?

Dolores: I'd like to go to Gino's for pizza.

Tim: I want to go to Harry's.

Dolores: I don't want a hamburger.

Father: I do.

Mother: So do I.

Dolores: That makes three for Harry's. So I guess I'm left out tonight. But we can go to Gino's next time, can't we?

Mother: Fair enough.

Dolores shares in the decision-making process knowing her wish will be fulfilled next time. The decision pleases three people instead of one, and Dolores can live with this until the next time the family eats out. She feels that she was heard and is sharing the power.

How to Share the Power in Making Decisions

Learn your child's desires. Consult your child on his preferences in matters that affect him. Obviously, when he is very young, some choices will have to be made for him. But the more often you ask for his input, the better he will feel about the way you share your power and control.

Let his growing wisdom and responsibility be your guide. It's not advisable that your child have a full, adult share in decision-making. But it's important that he be able to express his view for your consideration. Whenever his view is reasonable, it should prevail or modify your decision. There then is a greater likelihood that he will meet the commitments which shared decisions imply.

R-13 Promises! Promises!

One of the primary ways we express our commitments to one another is by the promises we make. When we keep them, we demonstrate our good will, and invariably are liked and respected in return. When we fail to keep our promises, we become suspect and disliked. A kept promise says, "I respect myself and I respect you." The broken promise says, "I don't mind letting you down, and I don't respect you either." Children need to be taught why they should keep the promises they make: "It is the decent, considerate thing to do. It demonstrates your character. A promise is a commitment. And the considerate person keeps his promises. Doing so also shows your respect for the other person and his feelings. Meeting the promises you make is how you show that you care. To the extent that you keep your promises, people will have reason to regard you as reliable and considerate." You start your child on the road to keeping his promises by first keeping your own. At the same time, encourage him to keep the ones he makes, praise him when he does and remind him when he doesn't.

Broken Promises

Seth, eight, visited a friend after school today. Permission was granted on the premise that Seth would be home at five, well before dinner. It's now six, and he still hasn't arrived. A phone call to his friend discloses that Seth left home a short while before. Mother is worried because darkness is falling.

Seth: (*Walking in nonchalantly*) Hi! What's to eat?

Mother: Dinner is over. Where have you been?

Seth: It's over?

Mother: We ate a half-hour ago. Where were you?

Seth: At David's house.

Mother: But I told you to be home at five.

Seth: We were having so much fun, I just forgot about the time.

Mother: Seth, you promised me that, if I let you go to David's, you would be back at five.

Seth: Well, I'm here now.

Mother: An hour late. I suppose you'll expect me to fix you something to eat?

Seth: Yeah, well, I'm hungry.

Mother: Do you realize I've been worried stiff? How was I to know what happened to you? You didn't call, and David's line was busy for a long while. For all I knew you could have been hit by a car, or kidnapped.

Seth: I guess you can see now that I wasn't kidnapped.

Mother: Don't try to be funny. I was nearly sick with worry and now I'm damn mad.

Seth: Well, I'm sorry.

Mother: It's not that easy, Seth. The reason I'm mad is that you broke your word.

Seth: But I was just a little late . . .

Mother: You were a whole hour late! But that's not the point. When you made the promise you made a commitment, a contract to do something. And you didn't do it. That's serious. You broke your word and made me worry needlessly. You knew that you were all right. But we didn't. What do you suppose I'll think the next time you make a promise?

Seth: You won't believe me?

Mother: Exactly.

Mother confronts Seth about breaking promises before it can become a bad habit. Probably this is not the first time she's had to bring up the matter, nor will it be the last. Seth will need to be told many times before he fully absorbs the message. But notice how Mother connects the broken promise to her bad feelings, thereby teaching Seth at the feeling level, where it counts.

If the boy had arrived on time, Mother should have told him, "Seth, thank you for being prompt. It means a lot to me when you keep your word." Such reinforcement goes a long way toward encouraging him to keep his next promise.

How to Foster the Keeping of Promises

Keep the promises you make to your child. This is the single most impressive way to encourage him to honor his own promises. It shows him your good will and delivers a powerful message: "I care enough about you to make an effort to keep my word to you. I want you to know that I care. Therefore I keep my promises." But it's not going to be easy. At times you'll be severely tempted to give in to your child just to get him off your back. Resist the urge to promise him something merely to shut off his insistent demands. The cardinal rule is: Never promise your child anything you do not fully intend to deliver. If there is a delay, let your child know why and when he can expect you to keep your commitment. At issue here is your good will as well as your character.

Remind him when you fulfill your promises. Normally, he won't notice when you do. It will be necessary to say, "I'm keeping my word. How about you?"

Praise him when he keeps his promises. It is vital to show him your approval and tell him, "I think it's great that you kept your promise. It shows me that you're growing up, that you keep your commitments. We both can be happy, knowing that you're becoming a responsible person."

Challenge your child whenever he breaks a promise. Don't overlook, condone or ignore his broken promises. This is a serious issue, however innocuous the promise itself may seem to be.

R-14 Fighting

There probably is nothing more aggravating and exhausting for the parent than children's fighting. What is behind it? What are the different kinds of fighting? Most of all, how do you cope with it? Contrary to popular belief that such behavior is "normal," fighting almost always is the tip of an iceberg, proclaiming a larger problem beneath. Without provocation there could

118

be little fighting. It's better to look for causes than to throw up your hands in despair and resignation and say, "What's the use? All kids fight."

You will make it easier for yourself if you first decide just what sort of fighting is going on. For example, if your eight-year-old son roughly shoves his six-year-old sister and she hits back, her self-defense is a healthy response. In a way, this is a good kind of fighting. Insistence on respectful treatment, even if demanded in an immature way, at least shows striving in a healthy and constructive direction. You should encourage your children to stand up for their rights.

You can show your child that one better way to guarantee his rights is to ask you to protect him against a larger sibling. Bringing in a wiser and more powerful person to help find a mature way of solving the problem can teach your children how to resolve arguments more effectively.

Try at once to learn the reason behind any fighting. If your daughter caused the dispute in the first place by breaking one of her brother's toys, then she will have to be taught about respecting his property. As she learns this lesson, this type of fighting will stop. On the other hand, if her big brother instigated the fight, then possible causes must be sought. If there is one sure thing, it's that the most effective treatment is going to result from accurate, on-the-spot determination of the basic issue.

What are the most frequent causes of fighting, other than children adaptively standing up for respectful treatment? There are Issue-oriented Fighting and Boredom-based fighting. When dealing with Issue-based Fighting, you should follow the routine of listening to the feelings, the complaints and accusations, the history, the wants and needs, and what each person will settle for. Here the true problem is some interpersonal conflict. You can and should be wise King Solomon.

But the problem-solving just does not apply and will not work if the fighting is boredom-based. In family after family, time after time, the parent will find himself caught up in a game which might be called "courtroom."

The precise purpose of this game, often clear to the child but escaping the awareness of the parent, is to get attention. What you need to know is that the disagreement is not a true issue but window-dressing to "legitimately" capture and keep your attention. The primary goal is not conflict-resolution. In fact, the purpose is just the opposite—never to resolve the situation but to continue to be the center of attention for as long as possible. When you finally stop to realize what actually is going on, you can refuse to play. You will recognize that you're being enmeshed in a situation overwhelmingly directed by what is perhaps the most immature way of getting attention: fighting.

Before you proceed to look for other causes, you should be aware of the most basic of them all, the plight of the child who has been displaced by the birth of a younger sibling. It will be very difficult for the older child to share the love he has had from you. He resents the competition, cannot find anything good about it and feels the fury of any dispossessed rival. Like the slow-motion grinding out of a Greek tragedy, this situation will go on and on, year in and year out, changing only in the sense of its surface appearance. As a parent, caught up in daily chores and routines, you can very easily lose sight of the underlying resentment. In your own heart you know that you love both children, and you will tend to discount just how powerful childish jealousies are. But your children never are quite sure that you really can and do love both. Therefore they are going to lead you astray continually, causing you to think the real problem now is who can wear whose sweater, who gets to control the TV or who receives homework help first. Once you realize the real issue is rivalry and not fighting, you are far ahead in terms of finding a solution. Then use the guidance given in the next section, R-15, Rivalry Means Insecurity [pages 120-124].

The Issue-based War

Leif, 12, has arrived home after playing a Little League game. His team has lost and he's in a snit because he struck out twice. After dinner, in the den where younger brother Martin is watching a cherished TV program, Leif marches over to the set and switches the channel to a show he wants:

Martin: Hey! What are you doing? I was here first.

Leif: Tough luck! Now I'm here.

Martin: I'm first. I get to have my program. I was already here. *(He gets up and moves toward TV set.)*

Leif: Let it alone.

Martin: I will not! *(He switches program back to his channel.)*

Leif: *(Hitting his brother)* I told you to leave it alone! I'm gonna watch what I want to watch.

Martin: *(Hitting back)* You leave me alone! I was here first!

Father: What's going on? Stop it! At once!

Martin: I was here first and he came in and changed the TV show I was watching. Then he hit me because I switched it back.

Leif: It was a rotten program anyway. Mine was better.

Father: Did you ask Martin if you could change it?

Martin: No, he didn't. He thinks he's so big!

Father: You can't do that, Leif. You can't just come barging into a room and switch TV stations without asking the person who's watching. That's inconsiderate!

Leif: Martin does it to me!

Father: Then let me know when he does. In the meantime, just so you both understand, we're going to have a house rule. No one is to switch the station on any program someone else is watching. If you don't like the show that's playing, you can choose the next one that comes on. But you have to wait until the other person has seen his show.

Leif: I will if he will.

Father: Fine. If anyone breaks this rule, he has to spend the evening in his room without TV. I'm not going to have you two being inconsiderate of each other.

As fairly as he can, Father intervenes here to deal with the issue that caused the fight. But this incident, or a similar one, is likely to recur. That is not to say that Father has failed. He actually is laying the ground rules for future incidents by defining the issue and establishing the consequences for violation. The more times Father defines the rule and applies the solution, the more chances Leif will have to learn how to be considerate in this one situation. Unless there is a severe rivalry with Martin, Leif will eventually gain the necessary understanding to be considerate toward his younger brother.

How to Reduce Issue-oriented Fighting

First, stop the physical fighting. Then try to determine what the basic issue is. As soon as you know enough facts, define this basic issue so that everyone can agree what the conflict is about. Next, establish a fair rule which will settle the conflict for the time being and also will apply to future incidents. If necessary, write the rule out and post it where it can be seen. Then tell your children what the consequences will be if this rule is broken. It is very important that you consistently enforce the rule. If you ignore violations, you will lose your credibility and your effectiveness.

The War Between the Wills

As your child matures out of the toddler stage, he is going to develop more of a mind of his own and entertain ideas different from yours. In his mind, he's going to be right; in your mind, you will. Your child is striving toward the healthy goal of self-determination. But you have all of the responsibilities, at least in the earliest years, and naturally feel that your authority should be recognized and respected. Yet it will often seem that, the more you give and sacrifice, the less gratitude and respect you receive. As a parent you may often ask yourself, "Why does he fight me so much? Is he threatening my sense of adequacy or importance? Is he making me feel helpless or unappreciated? In front of other people, is he exposing my self-doubts as a parent? Try to determine where your vulnerability lies. If your child is asserting his drive for self-determination and goes about it in a reasonable way, there is no good reason to fight with him. Instead, he should be supported. As you identify various needs and help your child meet them, you will become more effective and will therefore be more adequate and less easily threatened.

If you realize that you are feeling unappreciated, you might sit down and list for yourself five or six things that you do for your child. Read them to him and ask if he likes what you do for him. Then ask if he would do you a favor and tell you some of the things he does for you. Often this will get the point across that he's only at the receiving end; his sense of fair play may encourage him to become more helpful and appreciative.

If public embarrassment in stores is a problem with your young child it may be that he becomes tired, hungry or overstimulated. It is not wise to try to override his need because you have a more pressing one. Instead, when you go shopping, count on a few hours of peace and fun by arranging in advance for a babysitter.

Boredom-based Fighting

Boredom-based fighting is a very different thing from issued-based fighting. As such, it requires an entirely different approach. Fighting caused by boredom, excess energy or restlessness represents no true conflict between two people. The real cause is to be found elsewhere, in your child's lack of development. Children who have active interests in sports and constructive hobbies are happily occupied. When a fight arises on the baseball field, it is due not to boredom but to some true if minor issue, and is quickly resolved and as soon forgotten. To combat boredom, develop your child's active and constructive interests. If you don't, the inevitable will happen. He may see a sibling as a very handy, easy-to-provoke human toy that can be teased or tormented until some interesting response results. This form of

"entertainment" must be considered one of the least mature ways to fill time. You can help your child do better.

How to Reduce Boredom-based Fighting

Break up the monotonous routine of being in the house all day. Sometimes it can be helpful to take your children for a 10- or 20-minute walk or a brief visit to some neighborhood attraction.
Stop the physical fighting or verbal feuding. Give the rule that in your house fighting is not allowed. Tell your children you are arbitrary in this one way, and that's that.
Separate the children into different rooms so the fighting cannot be continued.
Individually explain to each child that in your opinion he is fighting because he is bored. Offer to help him find some constructive outlet—a way to express his energies without bickering and chaos, a more grown-up way to have fun.
Be sure that your children are exposed to a wide variety of athletic, cultural and nature interests. A visit to a well-stocked hobby store or craft shop will often help your child find an activity to command his interest. There also are many stimulating, worthwhile games to fill empty hours; encourage your child to call a friend to join him. The most developmental activities are genuinely useful chores for which your children can earn a reward and also gain a sense of importance, contribution and recognition.

R-15 Rivalry Means Insecurity

The basic issue in sibling rivalry is insecurity. It often surfaces when you're giving attention to one child, and another comes along to demand equal time. The second child wants to be included or insists that you stop what you're doing and play with him. If you don't, there are the usual accusations of, "You like him better than you do me. You always do things for him. But you never do anything for me."

You can survive these situations if you accept some rivalry as an unavoidable, immutable fact of life and use it as a growth experience.

Say, "Yes, I know that you'd both like to have me play with you now. But I can give my attention to only one of you at a time. Whoever goes first this time will go second the next."

The jealous child—the one who feels he should be getting whatever his sibling has—is insecure. This usually means that he isn't getting enough approval and affection. He needs more positive feedback from you in order to make him feel worthy.

How to Deal with Insecurity

You cannot rely on words alone to reassure your child that he is a worthy and capable person. Of chief importance are the many little things you can do every day to affirm his acceptability:

Listen to him.

Focus on his feelings.

Convey your understanding of how he feels.

Give him plenty of one-to-one time.

Encourage him to take the initiative in making friends from whom he can get additional attention.

Give him responsibility and

Praise him for his effort and accomplishment.

Competition

Life is competitive in many ways. Competing for the attention, acceptance, approval and affection of one's parents is no different from competing for other good things. So expect competition between children; a certain degree of it is one of the normal ways your child tests his acceptability.

How to Deal with Undue Competition

The competitive aspect of jealousy can be dealt with by telling your children, "My heart is big enough to love you both, and also to love your father—and even the dog." This will help them understand they're not trapped in an either/or situation in which one must be a loser. They will know they both can have your love.

Your child needs some point of reference to see how well he's doing in the departments of worthiness and capability. Invariably, the nearest sibling to him becomes the comparative measure of his self-image. But a problem can arise out of such comparison. Often the child is highly subjective and tends to downgrade his brother or sister in order to feel better about his own self-image. Or he may be unduly inclined to upgrade the other child as having the better deal or basking in favoritism.

You can deal with exaggerated comparisons by emphasizing to your children that each of them is special, each is different and therefore unique in his own way. No one is inherently better than the other, except to the extent that one is more experienced or developed. Each one has his good and bad points. If one wants to discuss the other's weak points, he should be ready to discuss his own limitations as well.

Peer Rivalry: The Fight Next Door

The feeling underlying peer rivalry is one of power-striving. The kid up the street is attempting to prove his social effectiveness when he says to your child, "I can beat you up." Part of what he really is saying is, "I can prove I'm better than you."

Peer rivalries take many shapes and forms. If your child appears to be self-sacrificing in a relationship or paying too heavy a price by taking abuse, the relationship should be discouraged. But if there is only the normal amount of antagonism that occurs between children, your child should be encouraged to work out the problem.

How to Deal with Peer Rivalry

Listen to your child carefully and seriously; allow him to exhaust his feelings verbally. Hear him out till most of the emotion and anger subside. Then ask for his solution to the problem. If he doesn't have one, invite a solution from a sibling. Frequently, the sibling will notice something that's been missed entirely:

Pat: Damon's mean to me all the time.

Mike: Yeah, but remember the day you hit him?

Pat: Oh, I forgot about that.

Mike: Maybe that's why he's mean.

Encourage your child to confront his peer with a positive solution, one they can work out together. And encourage your child to show attention and acceptance, to be considerate of others' feelings while protective of his own, and to be willing to reciprocate what others do for him. Explain that in this way he'll be drawn into fewer fights. His peers will like and respect him; not many will want to risk losing the friendship of such a supportive companion.

Bully: The Ogre Next Door

How does your child cope with a bully? The truth of the matter is that usually he can't. Generally, the bully has greater physical power. If the power ratio is close (say, 52% to 48%), some day your child may summon enough confidence to confront the bully and put him down. In most situations, however, this does not apply. The bully—hostile, insecure and, underneath it all, cowardly—will prevail by virtue of his physical advantage.

Your best solution, apart from confronting the bully and his parents yourself, is a developmental one. It is to build up your child's sense of power, confidence and self-worth. With this inner strength, he can stand up to many situations and learn to avoid the others. Building inner emotional strengths is the only long-term answer, too, if your child is the bully. The dynamic of a bully is that he yearns for more self-confidence and a better self-image. As he begins to feel more effective, he won't need to overcompensate for his feelings of inadequacy. Punishment definitely isn't the solution. It merely heightens the bully's feeling of inadequacy. Give him plenty of attention, acceptance, approval and affection.

Superiority: The Snob's Appeal.

Sooner or later, your child is going to meet someone who will tell him, "I'm better than you are. You're not so much." If this doesn't happen with a playmate, it will occur at school or on the playing fields. This is a more sophisticated form of fighting—superiority or snobbishness. Its basis also is insecurity. The child who practices it is saying in effect, "I will build myself up by tearing you down. I can inflate my ego at your expense."

This way of relating is always an act, even though the child doing it is often unconscious of his reason. Underneath he feels, "I'm basically inadequate or unacceptable to others. What I need to do is to impress people. By pushing them around and putting them down, I can feel powerful at least temporarily and they will pay attention to me." This child has a Napoleonic complex. He tries to build a momentary sense of adequacy by projecting his inadequacies onto others. Such a child needs large doses of confidence and self-worth. And he needs consistent support, praise and recognition so that he can feel more adequate.

To a child, the pain of a put-down lasts a long while if it isn't put into proper perspective. You can provide one for your child by telling him, "You are not inferior! You're just dealing with a person who feels inadequate, a person who doesn't have much self-confidence. That's why he tries to put you down—so he can feel better. It has nothing to do with whether you are adequate or smart or a better person. He acts the way he does because he lacks confidence about his acceptability and is trying to strike back by cutting you down. For this reason, you should be very cautious about believing anything he says." It is vital to make it clear to your child that his tormentor has feet of clay that tend to invalidate his ability to make a fair estimate of your child's worth. Otherwise your child, because of his inexperience, may accept the tormentor's estimate of his inferiority as valid.

How to Deal with Snobbish Superiority

If he is the target of a snobbish child, you

can help your child's perspective by telling him that what his tormentor says is caused by that child's doubt about his own self-worth. Armed with this knowledge, your child will be less prone to see credibility in such an attack.

Triangles Are Trouble

The triangle with its two-against-one relationship has been a perennial conflict portrayed in literature for centuries. The same agonies visited upon people in adult triangles also affect children in their three-way relationships. As a parent, it's important to know where the difficulties lie in order to help your child deal with this inevitable challenge.

In every three-way relationship among children, one child frequently feels left out. The remaining two form an alliance, often temporary, that meets each other's need for attention but simultaneously closes out the third person. As John gives attention to Bill, he's not giving attention to Charlie. This usually is not malicious; it is difficult to give two people attention at the same time. To complicate matters, Charlie's sense of being left out is heightened by the fact that someone else is getting the attention he craves. He suffers a double pain, as it were: the pain of not receiving the attention he wants and of seeing it go to somebody else. The problem is a trying one for most children. Very few are experienced enough to reassure or attend to two other children in a considerate way at the same time. You can make your child aware of where the problems lie, what they mean and how best to deal with a triangular relationship.

Father has been playing checkers with Skip, six, when Bart, eight, arrives. Bart's nose now is out of joint because his father is playing with younger brother Skip.

Bart: Hurry up, Skip. Finish the game so I can play.

Skip: Leave us alone.

Bart: Dad, he's cheating. He's taking too much time.

Father: Leave Skip alone. Give him time to think.

Bart: I want to watch. Can I have an apple?

Father: Later.

Bart: No, I want an apple now.

Father: Now, just a minute. What is it you really want?

Bart: I want an apple.

Father: I think you just want me to stop playing checkers with your brother. Right?

Bart: Well, sure, you know I like to play checkers with you.

Father: I think you're jealous, and that's why you keep interrupting. Are you worried that, because I'm playing checkers with Skip, I like him and not you? Are you feeling left out?

Bart: Maybe. It seems like you play checkers with him more than with me.

Father: Bart, who was out playing ball with you this morning? Did that mean I liked you more than Skip before lunch?

What Father does here is to make Bart's resentment explicit by giving it words: "Are you worried that . . . I like him and not you?" This very well may be the reason behind Bart's interruptions. Being a child, he is feeling less important, less desirable and less cared for because the attention directed toward brother Skip is a threat to his security. In his narrow self-centeredness, Bart finds it hard to conceive that his father can still care for him while caring for Skip. Bart's afraid there won't be any affection left for him. For this reason, Father allays Bart's fear of exclusion and deals with his central fear: that Father's affection belongs solely to younger brother Skip. Father confronts Bart with this fear and the resentment it has generated.

The value of this kind of experience is that it openly and clearly defines the problem for Bart. In the process, he will gradually learn that he still is loved and cared for, even if he isn't always the center of attention. This will give him a better feeling of security in other triangular relationships.

How to Set Triangles Straight

Prepare your child for the problems that triangles will pose. Tell him it is almost always difficult for young children to know how to give equal attention to two of their friends at the same time. Help him to see that their lack of experience doesn't necessarily mean that he is being deliberately left out. And point out he isn't helpless to deal with the problems of three-way relations.

Let your child know there may be times when he will be deliberately excluded. Say, "When this happens, it's because the other children are trying to prove some point. For example, they might be trying to convince themselves that they are more desired because someone else was excluded." Help him to realize that other children are also inexperienced at handling people. Remind him that when he likes one child he also is apt to ignore others himself. Especially tell him about the importance of trying to give equal attention to two other people in a triangle. Say, "Try to include both of them in your talk or play. And don't gang up to exclude someone or make another kid feel bad or inferior." Be sure to remind him that all children get left out at some time, as the search for friendship shifts from day to day.

Ask your child to include and give attention to others: "This is how you get and keep friends and how you make sure that you will get the attention you need." When your child gives attention to others and you know about it, show your approval.

Urge your child to deal forthrightly with triangles. "If some of your friends try to exclude you, simply ask to be included. Maybe they just forgot. If you're sure they didn't forget, let them know how you feel. They may show you more interest. If they don't, then you'll have to look to some other kids for friendship. Not everybody can be interested in everybody else."

R-16 Becoming Likable

The issue of being liked was put succinctly by the poet who wrote, "Human love needs human meriting. How hast thou merited . . .?" Most of us have asked ourselves this question, and all of us have worried about the answer. The desire to be liked is fundamental to all of us; it's also one of the ways we measure our self-worth.

Children especially worry about how they can make themselves likable. And they need to know the answer: human meriting. It's a fact about human relationships that people tend to like you for what you do for them. Being kind, helpful or supportive, taking the time to offer a lonely person companionship or sympathy—these are the things that make a person liked. Your child needs to know these facts.

Laurie, 10, is in search of a friend.

Laurie: Nobody likes me!

Father: It can't be true. Things can't be that bad.

Laurie: They are. I don't have a friend in the world. I wish I had just one.

Father: What do you do to make people like you, Laurie?

Laurie: What are you supposed to do?

Father: The best way to have someone like you is to do something for them. What have you done to make someone feel good in the last day or two?

Laurie: I wouldn't know what to do for anybody.

Father: I see. Well let's discuss someone you'd like for a friend. And let's see if we can find something you can do for her.

Laurie: I'd like to know Mavis Simmons better. But she's got everything already.

Father: I find that hard to believe. For the next few days, you watch her closely at school. Ask yourself, "Does Mavis need anything?"

A few days later:

Father: Have you noticed anything about Mavis yet?

Laurie: At first I couldn't see anything she needed. But then I found out she was having trouble in arithmetic. So I asked her if I could help and she said yes. So I've been helping her. And now we play together during recess and she wants me to come to her birthday party.

Father helps Laurie by directing her attention to the basic principle of being liked: doing something considerate or useful for the other person. Laurie can now be sure there is nothing wrong with her, that the issue of not having friends lies only in her lack of meaningful action. Her lack of friends is a situation she can do something about, not a fixed defect she carries around with her.

You can relieve your child of some very painful anxieties by teaching him the issues involved in becoming likable and by showing him how to overcome his feelings of unacceptability. The information and encouragement you provide will help your child find his niche among his contemporaries.

How to Help Your Child Become More Likable

Show your child how he can become popular. Point out the basic rule: "Always accept and include others. Take the initiative to make friends, to help others feel less lonely, and you'll always have plenty of friends."

Suggest your child do something for others. Tell him it's not enough to know what the other fellow needs or would like. "You have to do it." Tell him to try this and to see what happens.

Remind him to keep trying. Occasionally ask him about his acquaintances and friends: "How are things going?" "Do you have any problems you'd like to talk about?" In this way, you can open him to a discussion of any problems he may have but probably would not have brought out into the open on his own.

Periodically discuss his likability, in order to increase it: "If you ever want some ideas on becoming more likable, let me know and I'll try to give you some help." Ordinarily, the child will not be ready to admit he needs help. But if he is approached about it (the earlier, the better), he will be more open and direct and less defensive about the subject of being liked. Age four or five is not too soon.

R-17 "I Have Mixed Feelings toward My Friend": Ambivalence

Mixed feelings perplex a child in his relationships, just as they do adults. A child isn't quite sure how to react. On the one hand, he feels angry at his friend and wants to vent his bad feelings. But he fears losing the relationship. This universal quandary causes great frustration.

The important thing for your child to know is that mixed feelings are part of every human relationship. Sooner or later, a friend will say or do something that will cause pain. Your child will be better off if he's prepared for this. Otherwise, the shock of being hurt by a friend may disappoint more than it should and set off a backlash that makes any reconciliation impossible. Knowing that fights and disagreements with his friends are inevitable, he can begin to learn how to take on such situations as they arise and keep his friends instead of losing them.

Forgiving Cleans the Slate

Sandy, 10, is upset, angry, ready for trouble.

Mother: What's the matter, son?

Sandy: Absolutely nothing!

Mother: Come on. That's not true and you know it.

Sandy: O.K. I'm mad. That's all.

Mother: What happened?

Sandy: Woodie Johnson, that's what happened.

Mother: Woodie? But he's your best friend.

Sandy: Not any more! I hate him!

Mother: But he stayed overnight here only two nights ago. And you two seemed to have loads of fun together.

Sandy: He's been blabbing a secret to everybody.

Mother: Secret?

Sandy: Yeah. What he promised not to tell. You know . . .

Mother: Oh, you mean about wetting the bed? He's been telling people about that?

Sandy: I hate him!

Mother: That was an accident that could have happened to anybody.

Sandy: Just the same, he's been telling everybody.

Mother: So you're not friends any more? That's too bad. You had a lot of nice times together. And you feel pretty broken up about what's happened, don't you, Sandy?

Sandy: Oh, Mom! Why did he go and tell?

Mother: Because he's not perfect. He still has some growing up to do, just like you. He's acting like any 10-year-old. Oh, I don't approve of what he's been doing. But it just proves that he needs to learn the importance of being considerate of your feelings.

Sandy: He sure does.

Mother: Do you really want to lose him as a friend?

Sandy: I don't know. I'm mad at him. But I wish it could be like before when we were friends.

Mother: You'd like to keep him as a friend if he'd stop and not do it any more?

Sandy: Maybe. I guess so.

Mother: Why, then, talk to him about it, Sandy. Tell him you don't like what he's saying. Ask him to stop. Ask him to promise he won't do it again. Let him know that otherwise you can't be his friend any more.

Sandy: I don't know . . .

Mother: It's up to you. You can try to keep him for a friend or you can lose him as a friend and feel sorry for yourself.

Sandy: I'd like to punch him in the mouth.

Mother: That's not necessary. Maybe he doesn't realize just how bad it makes you feel or that's he's close to losing your friendship. Tell him. Give him a chance. And give yourself a chance, too.

Sandy: Well . . .

Mother: The thing to remember is that your friendship will be stronger because you had a disagreement and got over it without breaking up. The strongest friendships are those that have been tested and have survived.

Mother tries to help Sandy realize that, whatever his friend did, it is forgivable if only because the friend is after all a child himself and therefore likely to make mistakes. If Sandy can forgive his friend, their relationship has a good chance to survive. This is important for children to understand: Friendships also include mistakes and disagreements.

What happens too often is that many children cut off their friendships at the first unpleasantness. This may leave them with few friends and a wholly unrealistic view about finding the "perfect" friend. Since no such person exists, the result is prolonged loneliness. Your child can avoid this outcome by turning his ambivalence into a problem-solving opportunity, instead of the end of a friendship.

How to Live with Mixed Feelings

Your child needs to be informed and encouraged to deal constructively with mixed feelings that occur in his relationships. Your role is to supply the basic facts about what those feelings mean and how to cope with them and the dilemmas they present.

Let your child know that he should expect to have a mixture of good and bad feelings toward his friends from time to time. Tell him this is inevitable and that he should not be shocked when it occurs: "It happens to all of us. Try not to lose friends over one disagreement. Work out your differences."

R-18 The Opposite Sex: a Never-ending Interest

Ask any 10-year-old boy if he likes girls and the odds are he'll make a wry face and say, "No way! No way!" Ask any 10-year-old girl if she likes boys and you can expect the same negative response. Does this mean that 10-year-old boys are not interested in girls and vice versa? No way! The opposite sex is always interesting at any age. But children often mask that interest because they're afraid of being rejected. To fend off such a possibility, they deny their interest and, using reversal formation, overtly harass the opposite sex in order to get the attention they want. They tease and torment, put down and call one another names. Behind a pretense of contempt and antagonism, they hide their real interest and fear of not being liked.

The interest here is not sexual. The principal concern is one of being accepted by someone of a different sex. Your child will want to play a fail-safe game: He seeks an involvement that will be safe and not test his acceptability. That safe game appears on the surface as teasing, taunting and name-calling. Girls, equally anxious about their acceptability to boys, suffer serious qualms about their attractiveness as people. As they see it, the stakes are high—a life bright with companionship or of frequent loneliness. Your child needs considerable help and encouragement to deal with these anxieties and concerns. Point out the main solution—that being considerate to the opposite sex is the surest way to gain eventual acceptance. You also want to point out to your child that, although physical attractiveness is an undeniable asset, the way a person treats others has more lasting value and is therefore a greater asset. Looks do matter but what you really are matters more.

Dealing with the Opposite Sex

Craig is a typical robust 12-year-old. He plays baseball, is a good student and usually is even-tempered. But today Craig has a problem:

Mother: Now tell me why in the world you don't want to go to Gupper's party.

Craig: Because it's going to be a dumb party.

Mother: But he's your friend, isn't he?

Craig: Sure. But I just don't want to go to this party.

Mother: You always like parties. Why not this one?

Craig: He's goin' to have a bunch of girls come, too.

Mother: Oh. And you don't like that?

Craig: No. Girls make me sick.

Mother: You don't like any girls at all?

Craig: Who needs them?

Mother: You know, sometimes when somebody makes a big deal of claiming not to like someone, it means that maybe he really does like that person after all.

Craig: Not me. I don't like any girls. They're all pests, always buggin' you.

Mother: Do you bug them?

Craig: I just tell them what I think of them.

Mother: And that is?

Craig: You know, that they're pests.

Mother: Does any one girl bother you more than the others?

Craig: Well . . . the worst one is Melissa Shafer.

Mother: I know her. She's a cute girl.

Craig: She's gross. Whenever she's a pest, I just tell her to bug off.

Mother: Craig, that's no way to behave. You'll hurt her feelings.

Craig: Yeah, well you ought to hear the things she says about me.

Mother: I think the two of you are kidding yourselves. You both probably like each other a little already, and would like to be friends. But you and she both are too scared to take the chance.

Craig: That's stupid.

Mother: You can kid yourself, Craig, but you can't kid me. You'd like to know Melissa a little better, if you could be sure that she wouldn't make fun of you.

Craig: Maybe . . . if she wasn't such a pest.

Mother: Did it ever occur to you that she's being a pest because she wants your attention? And she's probably afraid you'll make fun of her if she lets you know she really likes you. She feels the same way you do. It's silly for the two of you to make each other feel bad because each is afraid of the other.

Craig: (Flattered) You really think she likes me?

Mother: What's so unusual about that?

I like you, sometimes. It's natural for girls to like boys and for boys to like girls.

Craig: Well, maybe Melissa's O.K. But she'll make fun of me if I tell her so. I know her.

Mother: You don't have to go overboard. Just treat her decently; instead of hurting her feelings, be nice once in a while. Then she'll be confident enough to trust you. You'll never know unless you give it a try. It's hard to go wrong when you treat someone decently.

What Mother does here is to unmask the denial-and-reversal formation that keep Craig from being friendly with a girl. As long as he operates with the fail-safe game of involvement through teasing, he will suffer the vexation and anxiety that come from denying his real interest.

The key to Craig's behavior is his fear of being rejected. He's known from an early age that he's destined for involvement with the opposite sex. Being inexperienced in dealing with them, he's scared and inarticulate. The best strategy, he decides, is to hide his feelings until he is more sure of what to do. Without Mother's counsel, Craig could become locked into his own private obsessions. Children are beset with so many doubts: "What can I do?" "How can I talk with them?" Craig is lucky to have someone sympathetic to explain these natural feelings. When was the last time you talked to your child about the problems of and ways to get along with the opposite sex? If your child is eight or nine or ten and has not yet verbalized such a question, it's safe to assume he has a growing concern about this matter. Your taking the initiative in opening up the subject can make all the difference.

How to Reduce the Mystery of the Opposite Sex

Let your child know that *liking the opposite sex is natural and normal.* Say, "When you're young, you'll tend to worry whether they'll accept you, whether they'll include you. And you'll be inclined to get involved in a lot of silly, self-protective games. Once you gain a little confidence, though, you'll stop the games and begin to get to know and like each other."

Question negative behavior toward the opposite sex. As you notice or learn of your child's teasing, name-calling or ganging up, say, "This is part of your natural protective instinct. This bad treatment shows that you're afraid of putting your acceptability on the line with the opposite sex. As they find you likable, you'll become less defensive and have less reason to act this way."

Stress the importance of offering decent treatment to the opposite sex: "There's nothing to be that much afraid of or angry about. As you treat them well, they'll begin to respond with the reassurance you need. But, like all kids, you are unsure because you just haven't had enough experience. You'll get more and more proof that other people like you, and gradually you'll feel confident and accepted. Then all this behavior will end. This is just a fearful stage right now. You'll get over it. It won't always be this way for you."

Encourage your child to treat the opposite sex in an open, direct way. Matter-of-factly suggest that he take the first step in making friendly contact with a member of the opposite sex: "If you take the first risk, they'll really appreciate you. The same thing will happen if you treat other kids nicely, whether they're boys or girls. So try the best you can to show kindly interest. There's no need to be afraid that they won't like you. They're just waiting to be shown that 'you like them first.'"

VI   Competence
How to Have Capable and Self-Confident Children

Effectiveness is the Key to Survival

All parents want their child to do well in life—first, by becoming self-reliant in dressing himself and attending to his own toilet needs; later, by adapting to school and by learning to fix things when they don't work. Ultimately, you want him to have the training and education required for a rewarding job that offers high pay and personal satisfaction. In short, you want your child to become competent.

You wish for your child more than just money, success or material well-being. Instinctively you know that the real issue is personal happiness. Life can be an exciting, pleasurable experience or a chronically miserable one. A person who can do things and do them well, who is capable and confident, has a much better chance for a happy, satisfying life than someone who is unskilled, insecure and underdeveloped. Competence means developing capability and genuine self-confidence.

The latter is especially important. Too often, we see highly trained people who are capable of excellent performance but somehow utterly devoid of self-confidence. Even though they produce for society and themselves, they just can't seem to relax and feel secure about their abilities. They chronically expect to fail, be rejected or face sudden disaster at every turn; rarely are they happy or content with themselves. To be competent, your child needs both ability and a strong belief in himself.

Competence enables your child to obtain many benefits. The most obvious one is sheer survival. None of his needs can be met unless he develops his abilities. Competent functioning also opens the door to fulfillment. As your child develops his inherent talents and capabilities, he will fulfill his potential. If he can function at the upper reaches of that potential, he will lead a more effective and satisfying life.

Becoming competent plays a vital role in forming your child's self-concept. As we already have seen, your child measures his self-worth by two yardsticks: the way he gets along with others and how productive he is. In order to like and respect himself, your child must be productive. Inadequate people never have a good self-image.

As THE PARENT BOOK has repeatedly stressed, one of your child's main feelings is that of helplessness. The antidote for this is competence. Through having real abilities, recognized accomplishments and a genuine sense of self-confidence, your child will be and will experience himself as that competent person he can become.

Most children are extremely underdeveloped; they come nowhere near realizing their potential. Food and water are attention enough for ordinary physical development. But this is not the case with the development of a child's abilities. Competence requires hard work, plenty of practice, and challenges that are mastered over and over again. The inner satisfactions of work and social recognition reinforce and complete the process.

How can you be sure all this happens for your child? The answer lies in knowing and fostering the basic traits of competence. You

TABLE IV

Competence Issues of Emotional Development

C-1   Energy and Effort

C-2   Knowledge and Skills

C-3   Planfulness: Thinking Ahead

C-4   Initiative: Getting Started

C-5   Creativity: Keeping Your Child Adaptable and Inventive

C-6   Realistic Expectations: Myths of Our Time

C-7   Self-sufficiency: "I Did It By Myself"

C-8   The Courage of Assertiveness: Willingness for Challenge

C-9   Caution: Real Danger vs. the Magic Mantle

C-10 Self-confidence: Belief in Self

C-11 Responsibility: No Reminding Needed

C-12 Ambition: Interest in Success

C-13 Goals: "I Know Where I'm Going"

C-14 High Standards: The Key to Quality work

C-15 Cooperation: Pooling Talents

C-16 Flexibility: Bending Without Breaking

C-17 Developing One's Own Interests

C-18 Problem-solving: Where It All Comes Together

can do this as you encourage such fundamental competencies as the willingness to apply effort, self-discipline, courage and initiative, and the ability to distinguish what is realistic from what is not. Your child must do the work and supply the effort. But he needs your encouragement and guidance. Don't expect too much at first from either your child or yourself. After all, just as he needs time to develop his skills and abilities, you too need time to learn how to help him more effectively. None of this will be easy or come about without effort, risk-taking and frequent failure. So be patient with your child and yourself.

C-1 Energy and Effort

Young children have vast amounts of physical energy which they invest in everything they do. From dawn to dusk, this raw power propels your child from one thing to another in constant, unflagging motion. He never seems to stop. If he does, it's only to change direction. He literally is a machine, transforming food, water and oxygen into energy that is vigorous, lively and seemingly inexhaustible.

In the beginning all of this energy and power is pretty much unchanneled and undirected. It's often destructive or wasted. Nevertheless, your child's energy is normal, healthy and adaptive. Directed to objectives, it is indispensable to competence. His energy fuels the work and effort necessary for his development. A child who is energetic and active gets things done. One who is sluggish does not.

Many parents stifle the child's energy at a very early age and later wonder why he is incompetent and lazy. What typically happens is that parents comment on their child's energy only when it causes them annoyance—when it's noisy, inconvenient or destructive. The child hears his more-energetic activities continually referred to as "bad." Seldom if ever do parents notice and praise their child's energy when it's positive and productive. Instead, they constantly bombard him with "don't do this" and "don't do that." The common theme of all

these admonitions is "Movement is bad. Don't move." The child is growing and needs muscle activity and experience exploring but may assume there's something "bad" or "wrong" with himself every time he has an urge to move.

To build your child's competence, you need to teach him that energy is useful and good. This doesn't mean that you can't or shouldn't comment on disruptive or destructive behavior. But it does mean that positive expressions of energy are deserving of more notice and comment. It is good for your child to realize that being active—running, playing ball and so on—is good for him. And he can learn this from hearing you tell him how glad you are that he's lively and energetic.

Sean, four, is neither listless nor hyperkinetic. He's reached the age when his physical development has made it possible to deal with his energy in a more reasonable way. When he was younger, the only way to keep him from tearing the house apart was to curtail his activities because he couldn't be communicated with in any significant way. Now his brain is more developed. Sean is ready to deal with his energies through verbal understanding. Unfortunately his mother is not.

The difficulty lies in Mother's orientation. An active, goal-directed person, she thinks of herself more as a housekeeper than as the developer of her young child's personality. She rarely sees herself as a protector and guide for this vivacious little stranger she brought into the world; consequently, she plans no activities to direct or channel Sean's energies.

The day has been an ordinary one for Sean, roving about from room to room, playing with the cat, turning the TV dial, watching Mother. Suddenly, the afternoon tedium has been broken by the delivery of an intriguing carton containing a new swag lamp.

Sean: (*Tugging at box, which has been placed on coffee table while Mother lets the delivery man out*) What's this?

Mother: Sean, get away from that box. There's something inside that could break.

Sean: I want to see.

Mother: You don't have to get into everything. You'll see soon enough. *(Works with screwdriver to remove staples from box lid.)* Now just keep away while I open this box.

Sean: *(Chugging around the room)* I'm a delivery truck! *(As Mother triumphantly opens box, Sean runs up to her side.)* Got a package for you, lady . . . Oh, what are those little white things?

Mother: Styrofoam peanuts, used for packing.

Sean: Do I get to keep them to play with?

Mother: They just litter up everything. You don't need them. You have plenty of toys.

Sean: Then can I keep the box, Momma? Huh?

Mother: We'll see. First, I have to put these lamp parts together.

Sean: Can I help?

Mother: I'm in too much of a hurry to be "helped." I want to have this lamp hung and surprise Daddy when he gets home. Isn't it cartoon-time on TV? Why don't you go watch television and leave Mother alone. *(Phone rings.)* Of all times! Sean, don't you touch a thing until I get back!

(After Mother leaves, Sean peers into box, enticed by "peanuts." He removes as many as he can. Box falls on its side with a thud offset by the four-o'clock traffic noise. Mother returns, sees styrofoam stacked on floor by Sean, whose feet have pulverized some of pieces.)

Sean: See my snow pile.

Mother: You naughty boy. I told you not to touch anything. Can't you ever be still for a · minute? *(Notices tipped-over box.)* Good grief! My lamp!

Mother misses one opportunity after another to give Sean a little notice, praise him for his curiosity or suggest any alternate activity that would be an outlet for his normal, healthy expression of energy. This kind of treatment eventually will teach Sean that activity is "bad" and indolence is safer. Since your child's energy will continually propel him into the proximity of danger, you need a basic formula for handling the situation. Each time your child approaches some possible danger, slight or considerable, even while you restrain him, be sure to make some positive remarks about his interest. Then divert him to some other, safer activity.

How to Deal with Your Child's Energy

Keep in mind that, at the outset, he's not particularly interested in the constructive or destructive implications of his actions. His first interest is to feel and understand his power and to test its possibilities: "Can I reach the cookie jar?" "How high can I jump?" "How fast can I run?" You may perceive any of these as destructive or disobedient. But your child sees them as a test of his power.

To help him begin to feel capable and powerful, stress the following: Look upon your child's energetic activity as an expression of his developing powers. In the beginning, expect random, aimless activity. Instead of criticizing him for "getting into everything," provide him with safe and interesting play things that are suitable to his developmental level.

When you see your child engaged in some activity, however simple it may be—walking, running, playing a game—tell him you are pleased he's doing it. Say, "It gives me a thrill to see you ride your bike so well."

Effort: The Willingness to Expend Energy

Some children are eager beavers, ready to do anything at the drop of a hat. Others have a more sluggish temperament. A normal child will fall somewhere between these two extremes. To know the kind of temperament you're dealing with, as early as possible it is wise for you to assess his innate willingness to apply effort.

Children, like the rest of us, prefer quick and easy results. Magic always seems preferable to effort. The technology of modern society surrounds your child with an abundance of

labor-saving machines to make things easy, seducing him into thinking everything is or ought to be effortless. He tends to become a passive consumer who expects all things to come quickly and easily without any effort or sweat on his part.

You know better. You know a goal cannot be reached without effort. Most of your child's competence will come from the step-by-step efforts of pursuing a specific goal. Sometimes he will succeed, sometimes not. But his effort will never really be wasted.

Jamie, six, is idly filling time. He has watched TV and eaten some cookies—all passive, consumer-type activities. Now he is gazing out the window and still not expending any effort in a productive way. His mother has had some training in child-rearing. Instead of waiting until he has slipped deeper into his passivity, she takes the initiative by approaching him with a challenge:

Mother: Jamie, I'm going to cook some fresh peas for supper. They have to be shelled first. Would you like to help me?

Jamie: O.K. That sounds like fun.

Aware that Jamie's environment encourages children to be passive, Mother knows that, if she failed to make some very deliberate efforts, she would be allowing Jamie to pass up all kinds of interesting and productive opportunities.

Assume that Jamie refused his mother's offer to participate in some useful activity:

Jamie: Naw, I don't want to shell peas.

Mother: Jamie, are you telling me you wouldn't like to shell peas? Or you just don't want to do any work?

Jamie: Both. I'd rather watch cartoons on TV.

Mother: You've already seen plenty of those. How can you know you wouldn't like shelling peas with me? You've never done it before. You might find you like it. Besides, you'd be helping me to make a good dinner.

Jamie: I'll give it a try.

Later, to his own pleasant surprise, Jamie discovers that helping his mother with some of her work is a satisfying experience. Had not Jamie's mother taken the initiative and even applied some mild pressure, nothing positive would have happened. As a parent, you need to be aware of the long-term consequences of your child's escapism and each time confront his tendency to avoid work and effort.

Emotional maturation does not come from being fed, clothed and bedded down. It results from meeting demands and challenges with a vigorous, willing effort. As a loving parent, you are going to have to do those things to ensure it will occur.

How to Encourage Effort

First, make some estimate of his innate energy level: accept him at his energy level. You can then suggest specific activities to your child, telling him how proud and pleased you would be if he made an effort to do them.

Your child will not always cooperate. *Invariably he'll want to take the easy way.* If you give him the chance, he will. You'll need to confront his inertia by proposing interesting things to do.

In a number of ways, you can help your child develop his willingness to expend effort:

Accept the fact that, for most children, laziness is easier than effort. Be encouraged that—no matter what his disposition—your child always will expend effort when something truly interests him.

Tell your child that, despite his distaste for effort, it is the only way to get the results he wants. Explain that it's the same for you. Without effort, you don't get anything you want, either.

Point out that magic doesn't work but effort does.

C-2 Knowledge and Skills

In our society, children are required to assimilate more different and more complex kinds of knowledge than ever before; consequently, education starts early in preschools and often continues on into postgraduate studies. Obviously, your immediate concern is not the mysteries of

136

calculus or whether your child will earn a master's degree in political science. Your foremost job with a young child is to teach him on a daily basis the things he needs to know.

The same is true of the development of skills. You want your child to love doing and making things, to find pleasure in working with his hands. Whether it is sewing or sawing, planting a garden or playing a bass viol, skills are essential for his development. In addition to helping him survive and earn his way, they pay your child some very important emotional dividends. Having skills enables him to gain the approval of others, to experience his self-worth and to overcome his basic feeling of helplessness. And all this is also personally satisfying.

As a parent, you may be inclined to worry needlessly about teaching your child and overlook that Nature has provided you with two powerful aids—your child's curiosity and his instinct for imitation.

You needn't worry about how long it takes him to learn. Unless he suffers from a learning disability, there is plenty of time. When highly motivated, children can often learn one year's course of a school subject within a few weeks. Schools concentrate so heavily upon teaching academic skills, they usually fail to recognize that the child's self-concept, especially his self-confidence, is of far greater importance than what he learns. Almost every skill is acquired gradually. Little by little, your child learns to do some things moderately well, finally becoming skilled after much experience. The cost is persistence, practice and the pain of failing. You can relieve your child of his need for immediate success. If he worries about succeeding on the first try in everything he does, he could become immobilized by the fear of failure. Help him understand that he's not expected to do things perfectly the very first time out.

Ultimately, your child is his own best teacher. But he needs your help and guidance when he is young. The kind of teacher you are is crucial to his attitude about learning. There are two kinds of teaching. The first employs a more traditional and arbitrary method. It relies on commands and strict adherence to authority. Its principal method is to dispense information which the child must accept and repeat whether he understands it or not. The disadvantage for the child is that he becomes a passive receptor of information, learning only at a superficial "know-about-it" level. What he "learns" he soon forgets or resists applying.

The second kind of teaching is more effective. The teacher is a guide and resource and takes into account the child's active role as his own teacher. This method concentrates upon the process rather than the content of learning. You provide the materials, the books, experience and guidance; your child provides the act of learning. He profits in two ways: He acquires information and, most of all, he learns how to think.

Cora, five, is forever asking questions. Her mother, like most of us, needs time to herself. She is wrapped up in her own problems and regards questions as a nuisance:

Cora: Momma, why does Muttsie bark at the plumber?

Mother: *(Her mind elsewhere)* Because Muttsie is a dog.

Cora: But Muttsie doesn't bark when Daddy comes home. Why is that?

Mother: Because Muttsie knows Daddy.

Cora: How does Muttsie know so soon? The plumber has the same kind of car Daddy has.

Mother: You're beginning to sound like a broken record.

The underlying emotional message undermines Cora's relationship with her mother and her attitude toward learning. The message about learning is, "I don't care if you learn or not." And the interpersonal one (which Cora will use to measure how much she truly is wanted) is, "You're a bother to me and I wish you weren't around." Neither message is going to foster a positive attitude toward learning. Feeling emotionally deserted Cora will tend to slip into indifference and lethargy.

Cora's mother would do well to take a few moments to answer her little girl thoughtfully. She might say, "Dogs are bred for their ability to smell the difference between strangers and the family, just like race horses are bred to run fast." This takes less than a minute but carries a completely different set of underlying messages:

"I approve of your interest in gaining more knowledge."

"I am interested in whatever you're curious about."

"I want you to know what I know."

"Keep on asking questions because I will answer them."

"I like having you around."

With such messages, Cora can develop a positive attitude about gaining new knowledge. She will continue wanting to learn and be disposed to regard school as a great opportunity rather than a form of incarceration.

The same implications apply to skill development. Later, Cora may show interest in how to load her mother's washing machine. Of course, Mother can do this five times faster than her little girl. But to teach Cora this little chore would also reinforce a yet more positive attitude about learning. In a few short minutes, Mother can show her how to help with the loading, put in the soap and—most impressive of all—to press the "Start" button.

How to Promote Learning

To help your child learn effectively, you have to accept and trust his innate abilities and the likelihood that, given the proper guidance, they will emerge. Relax, while you set about giving him the positive outlook he needs:

Set the stage for learning. Create an environment in which your child's natural interests and skills will flourish. Provide him with a variety of new experiences, materials to work with and people to meet. Access to tools, art materials and simple household tasks will give him a chance to develop a variety of skills.

Plan the day. Discuss with your child the next day's activities. Let him join in making a pleasant, workable plan. It will save you countless frustrations and annoyances. And it will relieve much of the anxiety you may have over the conflict between the things you want and need to do and his need for attention.

Be alert to your child's natural drive to acquire knowledge and skills. Signs that he really wants to learn something can easily escape your notice. When he asks you a question or expresses a wish to do something, he is naturally primed for learning. This is the best time to teach him. He is emotionally ready. With recognition and praise, encourage his efforts to learn: "I'm glad you're willing to learn how to play the guitar."

Keep the answers simple. Without telling him a great deal more than he asked, tell your child what he wants to know. Your child usually will stop listening as soon as he hears what he wanted to know. If your reply is long and elaborate, chances are you may find that you are talking to yourself.

When you don't know the answer, say so. In these days of exploding knowledge, there is certainly nothing wrong with not knowing everything. Admitting that you don't know will help him understand that nobody can know everything. In addition, you keep your credibility intact by being honest. When you grow weary of marathon questioning, say, "I'm sorry, but I sure feel tired just now. Would you mind saving the rest of your questions for later? I would appreciate it. Thank you."

Direct him to the source. When your child can read, make it a practice to refer him to available sources of information such as the dictionary, encyclopedia and yearly almanacs. Tell him, "That's something you can look up. I'll tell you where to look." Make yourself available to help him understand anything that's difficult. You'll increase his self-sufficiency as well as his knowledge.

Let him do it his way. Once you've given him your advice or instruction, he should be on his own. Don't criticize. Be patient with his often-bumbling, trial-and-error methods. This is how he learns.

Accept the need for repetition. Parents often

find it aggravating to repeat advice, instruction or guidance in the face of their child's continual failure to live up to their high expectations. It may become easy to think that the child is contrary or personally opposed to you. Chances are, however, that your teaching has not yet penetrated deeply, even if it has reached his surface level of understanding. You can save yourself considerable pain by realizing the necessity for repeating many things literally hundreds of times before he learns or accepts them. Trying to force his learning will only be counterproductive.

Readiness: A Special Note

In an almost-forgotten experiment done more than 50 years ago, a pioneering psychologist studied timing's role in learning. Using identical twins, he gave one of them daily experience in climbing stairs while denying this experience to the other. The first twin developed his stair-climbing ability very slowly. Just about the time he was beginning to perform well, the second twin was given a short period of training and caught up completely. This classic research illustrates the principle of readiness for learning. Readiness is the optimal time or age for any particular child to develop a skill quickly and easily. If training is provided too early, much time and effort will be wasted. If your child is experiencing considerable frustration and confusion, it may be wise to set aside his training for a time until he shows a better degree of readiness.

There also is a corollary: If the optimal time for training is missed, the skill is progressively more difficult to acquire. This clearly can be seen when one considers how much more easily a child learns to ride a bicycle than an adult.

C-3 Planfulness: Thinking Ahead

Meg, a typical five-year-old, can never find anything she looks for. She's constantly misplacing her slippers, toothbrush, even her favorite toys, because she drops them where she finishes with them and then can't remember where they are. When she needs something, there usually are tears before it can be found. Meg just isn't planful. Her parents haven't taught her to be.

It's 7:30 a.m. As usual, Meg can't find her toothbrush. Frantic, she seeks help from Mother, who is preparing breakfast:

Meg: Mom, where's my toothbrush?

Mother: How should I know? I'm fixing your eggs. Where did you leave it the last time you used it?

Meg: I don't know. I put it someplace.

Mother: Try to remember.

Meg: I've tried and tried but I can't.

Since she herself fostered some of the problem by failing to teach Meg to plan ahead, Mother might at least have suggested a place where the toothbrush could be kept so in the future it could be found more handily. The same is true of Meg's other possessions. Having failed to teach this basic lesson, Mother now must deal with havoc, disorder and Meg's daily tantrums every time the little girl can't find what she wants. Ironically, Mother would never think of going to the supermarket without a list or plan enabling her to shop in 20 minutes for everything she needs. Without it, she might spend an hour and still come away without something she wanted.

Children need the skills of planning, too. If your child plans what he's going to do after school, he can make arrangements with a friend to play. If he waits until the last minute, the friend may not be available. Planning makes it more likely your child will get what he wants.

Most children operate on the spur of the moment and rarely plan anything. They function randomly, act haphazardly and waste considerable effort. Planning reduces this aimlessness. It gives your child's activity meaning and purpose, besides providing self-discipline, orderliness and the focused effort he needs to function effectively.

Unless you tell your child about the importance of planning and how to go about it, he's not likely to learn from his own random activity. He needs to be shown, to be given a road map to more-effective functioning. It is best to start this as soon as possible after he becomes three or four. Gently suggest to your child that he can do things more effectively by planning. Then show him how. You can do this with simple activities, planning with him what he needs for playing at the beach, painting a picture or visiting a friend. Your own example as a planner and organizer is, of course, extremely important. As he compares the chaotic outcome of his haphazard activity with the better results from a little planning, he'll be happy to take the few minutes it requires.

In the total picture, there are other considerations: A great deal of planning will be done for your child in school. This tends to deprive him of the experience of making his own plans. Don't lose sight of his need to have free time to express and explore his own spontaneous urges. Too much planned activity can be as bad as too little.

How to Encourage Planfulness

Tell your child that there is such a thing as planning, and explain why it can be valuable to him. In the beginning, you will frequently have to remind him to plan his activities. Say that he will become better at planning by trying, and you'll be proud of him. Have him select an activity; then guide him through the planning process in order to give him a chance to see how it works.

Point out the advantages of planning. When he plans for things that go well, mention how planning has made it possible. Otherwise, he's not likely to make the connection. Conversely, when he acts randomly and gets poor results, gently suggest how planning might have helped him.

C-4 Initiative: Getting Started

Many children tend to become passive unless they are encouraged to be assertive. Initiative—the willingness to start activities, particularly new ones—is an essential ingredient in your child's competence.

Initiative means being a self-starter, breaking new ground, accepting the risk of failure, putting an idea into action and being hopeful about the outcome. As such, initiative is highly adaptive. It shows the courage that is the beginning of self-reliance and independence; without initiative, nothing gets done.

One reason children aren't self-starters is because they dread failure. The child's philosophy can become excessively security-oriented: "Nothing ventured, nothing lost." This attitude shields him from possible failure and having to say, "I am incompetent." You may need to encourage initiative in your child. If it's insufficient, he may slip into a passive, self-protective pattern and not develop the active orientation essential for getting his needs met.

Your main task is to notice expressions of initiative, comment on them and praise your child for this kind of adaptive behavior. Otherwise, to protect himself from failure, he could end by living a dull, unrewarding life lopsidedly influenced by other people. He would not be without company, for passivity is now the most pervading neurosis in our society. Initiative, however, is a sign that your child will become self-reliant, his own person. It is the mark of all those who lead the most satisfying, interesting and exciting lives.

Silas, an enterprising six-year-old, is building an airplane out of scrap lumber in the garage. He approaches his task with optimism, even though what he is building barely resembles anything that flies.

Silas' father, a computer programmer, trained to be precise and factual, has just come into the garage to fix the water heater and encounters Silas at work:

Father: What are you trying to do, Si?

Silas: I'm making an airplane.

Father: (Noticing only the result and not the value of Silas' initiative) It doesn't look like any airplane I've ever seen.

Silas: I'm gonna fly it when I get finished.

Father: Don't be too surprised if it doesn't get off the ground.

140

Silas: *(Feeling put-down and defensive)* I knew you wouldn't think it was any good.

Father: *(Still missing the point)* Never mind. Go on playing. But don't come around the water heater while I'm fixing it. I don't want you in the way.

Given his product-effectiveness orientation, Father completely misses all the underlying implications. First, he fails to notice or commend Silas' initiative. Next, Father's expectations are unrealistic. The boy has no training in building an exact replica of an airplane. Silas is merely exploring his ideas and capabilities, breaking into new territory on his own and, in a sense, putting himself on the line. From Silas' point of view, the whole enterprise might fail, or at the very least not turn out as well as he would like. But he nevertheless moved ahead. His father's perception that Silas is "just playing" is a typical parental error. "Playing," so-called, is not mere entertainment but an important way children learn and develop.

Were Silas' father better tuned in to the elements of his son's emerging initiative, here's what might happen:

Father: What are you doing, Si?

Silas: I'm making an airplane.

Father: It looks interesting.

Silas: Do you think it'll fly?

Father: *(Realistic but now focused on the main issue)* I'm not sure it will fly. Whether it does or not, it shows me that you have initiative, Si. And that makes me proud of you.

Silas: Can I show it to you when I'm finished?

Father: You bet. By the way, I'm going to be fixing the water heater. If I need your help, can you spare me a few minutes?

Silas: *(Flattered)* Sure.

Here, Silas' father shows that he recognizes and values his son's initiative. Father understands that this is more critical than the quality of Si's finished product. Father also does something he didn't do in the earlier encounter version: He rewards Si's initiative by inviting him to help with the water heater. Father knows that this kind of recognition will build Si's initiative.

How to Encourage Initiative

Be alert to spontaneous expressions of initiative.

Try to provide an environment with interesting and appropriate materials to challenge your child. Notice and praise him for his initiative. Whenever you see your child undertaking a new challenge, let him know that you realize what he is doing and that it pleases you. This recognition can give him the emotional boost he needs to persist in the face of possible failure.

C-5 Creativity: Keeping Your Child Adaptable and Inventive

Because your child is a unique person, his creative potential is thoroughly his own. Like his personality and genetic signature, it's entirely different from anyone else's. When he puts crayon to paper, he is bound to express perceptions that are as singular as his personality. Whether it's a childish scrawl or a masterpiece, the result will bear an imprint distinctly his own.

As we saw earlier, children often look upon their uniqueness as a liability [pages 76-78]. They are not alone. Some parents are frightened by original expression. A boy who wants to play the harp instead of football may be considered deviate or strange. When a child wants to express himself in novel ways, some parents feel this originality will reflect poorly on them. They either damn it with faint praise or deliberately set about to discourage it. They ridicule the child's creativity with statements like, "It looks queer." "It won't work." "Normalizing" the child by forcing him to conform, they preserve appearances and their own shaky self-image. In the process, they stifle the child's creativity and deny him the chance to be himself.

Similar conforming goes on in school where standardization too often is the rule—albeit sometimes necessary because of crowded classrooms. Too much conformity can be a threat to your child's creativity. He's surrounded by sameness: desks, blackboards, paper, room arrangements and even books that are much the same. More significantly, teaching and testing procedures are almost identical for all 30 or 40 children in each classroom, even though each pupil has a completely different personality. To make conformity even more general, all the children compete for the approval of the same teacher. Teachers worry because they realize their limited time restricts the amount of effort that can be devoted to each child's one-of-a-kind learning capacity or creative potential. The pitfall is that your child may come to believe his self-interest lies more in conforming than in striving to be his own original self.

Although a certain amount of conformity is essential for good adjustment, the child pays a price for it. He gives up some of his own creative opportunities. Instead of following his own creative urges, he makes an effort to appear more "normal," wears the same kind of clothes and looks like everyone else. But no one may know what's going on inside his heart and mind. He may become an alien to the world around him, giving an artificial appearance of sameness to gain an artificial "acceptance."

Your child should be made to feel that it's all right, even desirable, to be creative and original. Allow him to express his own inner prompting. If your daughter wants to play the drums or your son wants to learn needlepoint, why not? Some measure of originality makes everyone more interesting. There's no way to know in advance where your child's creativity will lead. Many far-reaching discoveries have been made while a researcher was looking for one thing and, because he was open and inventive, discovered another. In this way, Sir Thomas Fleming, reacting creatively, discovered penicillin while looking for something else. Creativity always has been indispensable to human progress. And creativity is not just a matter of drawing pictures or playing the violin. Scientists, inventors and even politicians need to be as creative as artists and composers. They use their own individual talent—that singular combination of intelligence, experience and imagination—to do and make things useful and beneficial for mankind.

Creativity also has a personal dimension. Nothing is as soul-satisfying to a child as his own invention. His creation also gains him approval from others, approval that is genuine in contrast to the "acceptance" he gets for most of his conforming. Being creative also gives your child invaluable experience in making decisions and meeting challenges. No one can create a song, a scientific hypothesis or a statue without making a decision.

Perhaps most of all, creativity enables your child to see that his uniqueness is an asset, that his search for his true self is valid and worthwhile.

Not everything your child produces will be worthwhile or successful. He's likely to make a lot of mistakes and produce his share of clinkers. But the main thing is to keep him actively using his creativity.

Focus your encouragement on his creative effort, his activity, rather than the merits of his finished product. On the other hand, don't overdo your enthusiasm. You will lose your credibility if he is overpraised. He will feel embarrassed and inadequate. Your objective is to keep him busy so he can gain enough creative experience and skill to recognize and seize the inspirational moment when it comes. In that way, he may produce something useful or beautiful for all of us.

Merry, seven, has just returned home from school. She likes it but finds there's something missing—a chance to try out her own original ideas. Now she's alone in the kitchen while Mother is busy with the baby. Unable to find any cookies to go with her milk, Merry suddenly came up with the exciting idea of baking her first cookies. The cookie sheet, flour, eggs, shortening and milk are out. The oven is set. An egg has just fallen on the floor as Mother enters:

Mother: What in the world are you up to? This place looks like a cyclone hit. (*It does too—just as it does when Mother makes cookies.*)

142

Merry: We ran out of cookies so I'm baking some.

Mother: This morning I spent an hour cleaning up this kitchen. Now look at it!

Merry: *(Less terrified than most seven-year-olds)* I'll clean it up when I'm finished.

Mother: Then start cleaning. You're finished right now!

Again, it's a matter of a parent missing the more basic issue. By her hasty reaction, Mother unwittingly is degrading her daughter's movement toward Emotional Maturity. A list of the damaging messages to Merry include:

Don't start things on your own or you'll get into big trouble.
The appearance of this house is more important to me than your development as a creative person.
I don't really know or understand you.
In this life, it's better to play things safe and do only what you're told, when and how you're told to do it.
Mother makes the common mistake of seeing the "mess" instead of the message that Merry is engaged in the creative process. Without thinking, Mother writes off Merry's creativity as irresponsible play. How might Mother have dealt with these creative tendencies had she been able to recognize them for what they are?

Mother: What's happening here?

Merry: I'm making some cookies. I never made them before but I've watched you a lot. I sure hope they turn out O.K.

Mother: What kind of cookies are you going to bake?

Merry: Oatmeal-raisin.

Mother: Sounds yummy. Mind if I sit here and watch?

Merry: Would you?
I may have to ask you some questions. But first, I've got to clean up this egg.

In this exchange, Mother expresses her surprise as neutral, nonjudgmental curiosity. She reserves possible harsh and premature judgment about what actually may be taking place in all the chaos. Now her messages are entirely different and infinitely better:

I think you're an O.K. person.
I believe you're capable of having good, serious ideas.
I see this unpleasant mess but it's less important than recognizing and rewarding your creative efforts.

How to Foster Creativity

Recognize early, approve and bless your child's inborn creative potentials. Watch for creative signs in what at first blush may appear to be ordinary play. Besides having a good time, your child may be testing his ability to put two or more ideas into some new combination. Occasionally ask him what he's doing. His reply will give you an insight into his thinking so that you can make more-accurate observations about his activities. Instead of telling you he's building with blocks, he's more likely to say he's constructing an airport or a city. Here your response is crucial. If you tell him he's "cute," he may sense it as a putdown. If you show serious interest in his project, he'll appreciate and learn that his creativity impresses you.
Steer your child away from television.
Omnipresent, seductive and insidious, the TV medium—despite its many advantages—literally robs your child of his own creative potentials. It coerces him into being a passive observer, giving him quick and easy entertainment without any effort or creativity on his part. As a better recreation, show him your creativity in house or garden. Even at work, if possible. Let your child know the pleasure it gives to create things. Make sure that each day he engages in some productive activity, preferably of his own choosing.

C-6 Realistic Expectations: Myths of Our Time

One of your child's most difficult problems will be to come to terms with his own limitations. Luckily, this is one of those areas where you can help him a lot. Remember, what you are and do provides the model on which he forms his expectations for himself. If he thinks you're perfect and almighty, then he feels he has to be. If he knows you're fallible and make mistakes, he can feel more comfortable about his own. Much of his pain and misery will come from believing that you're perfect and he's not, particularly since he automatically concludes from his mistakes that something is "wrong" with him.

If you look closely, you will notice your child tends to have unrealistic expectations in four major areas. First, about time. He often expects things to happen right now, even sooner. Second, he is unrealistic about his performance. He expects to give a superior performance with little training, effort or experience. Third, he compares himself unrealistically with others. And, finally, he believes that fallibility and failure are unique to him, that only he makes mistakes. He doesn't realize that it's always easier to imagine and wish for success than to achieve it.

You won't be able to dispel all his grand hopes or illusions nor protect him from every disappointment. But you can give him a more realistic perspective about himself and others.

Realistic expectations will protect your child against the inevitable disappointment and lowered self-esteem that come from mistakes and failure. Being realistic means accepting one's own fallibility. It also means believing in *Murphy's Law: Anything that can go wrong will.* All of this may seem pessimistic. Actually it is not. Accepting his limitations puts your child's mistakes into perspective, teaching him that his failures and mistakes are an inescapable part of being a fallible human being.

A child has a disconcerting way of connecting his failures to his total self-image. He tends to look upon his minor mistakes as major flaws. Moreover, he is more impressed with his failures than with his successes; consequently, each success means less to him than it should.

He feels this way partly because of the false perception he has of others. He believes firmly that no one else makes mistakes. In our culture, many people work very hard at giving the impression that they know exactly what they're doing. And your child is easily taken in. Comparing his feelings with the poise many other people project, he thinks he comes up short. You owe it to your child to teach him otherwise—that other people often are not nearly as competent or self-assured as they may appear.

Another false expectation is that he should be able to do things well, immediately, without effort. Here, your child is victimized by his own inexperience. He simply hasn't learned the value of practice and hard work. Television feeds this illusion. All he sees on the tube are champions and accomplished performers in action. He doesn't see through to the grueling work, the hours of practice, the effort and the failures along the way. He expects instant success. When he fails to get it, he assigns the reason to some innate personal defect rather than the fact that he hasn't practiced or worked hard enough. You owe it to your child to teach him that no one does anything well until he first works hard at it. Unless you point this out frequently, he can wind up with an inferiority complex. From the very beginning, his insecurity and helplessness feed this tendency. As he becomes frustrated trying to perform to perfection, his sense of inferiority becomes confirmed.

Unrealistic Expectations about Time

The child leaps from wish to result. He wants things to happen fast. When they don't, he becomes impatient. Todd, four, is no exception. Father has brought home a big jigsaw puzzle for him. Containing 18 pieces and marked for ages four to six, it represents a moderate challenge to Todd's capabilities. Father notices Todd gives up the challenge after about two minutes:

Father: Having problems, Todd?

Todd: (Saving face) I don't like this puzzle. It's no good.

Father: Would you like it better if you had more luck with it?

Todd: It's too hard.

Father: It's not hard—it just takes time. *(Todd is silent, hoping to slip away.)* You're not being fair to yourself, Todd. Puzzles always take time to do. You can't expect to solve one in a few minutes.

Todd: I can't do it.

Father: Son, I'll bet you can. Do me a favor and try again. And I'll give you a hint: Find all the border pieces that go together—the ones with the straight edge—like this.

Todd: O.K. but . . .

Father: *(Reinforcing Todd's tentative assent)* I'm glad to see you're willing to try.

Todd: *(A few minutes later, finding success)* Look, Daddy, look. I put these two pieces together. Now I got it started.

Father: Todd, I knew you could do it if you gave yourself the time.

Father confronts Todd's unrealistic expectation and exposes it as an obstacle to his progress. Father is gentle but persistent. He knows that Todd has a very good chance for success, once he gets over his unrealistic expectations.

Unrealistic Expectations about the Quality of Performance

Skills are developed through dedicated effort and, often, only after many failures. But your child has no way of knowing this. In our pre-packaged society, the finished automobile, doll or musical group is regarded as an instant, overnight success. Children especially have little opportunity to observe the shaping of an expert craftsman or performer by trial-and-error and tedious, demanding work.

Roderick, 11, having watched a lot of championship tennis during the recent TV season, has persuaded Father to take him to a court to play. But Rod isn't doing too well:

Rod: Dad, I don't want to play any more. Let's pack it in and go home.

Father: Hey. What is it with you? We just got here, Rod. We've only been playing for 10 minutes.

Rod: Yeah, and I've only hit three balls. I've had it.

Father: Not so fast, Rod. When's the last time you played tennis?

Rod: A couple of years ago. But I wasn't any good then, either.

Father: How long did you think it was going to take for you to play well?

Rod: I don't know. But I should play a whole lot better than I do.

Father: You expect to play well without any practice or experience?

Rod: Yeah, why not? Other people can.

Father: That's not true. And that's your problem. You think you should be able to play like a champion the minute you step on the court. Every time you miss a shot, you think you're no good. You can't tell yet if you're good or not. You haven't tried hard enough to know.

Rod: I just don't think I can make it even if I try.

Father: Tell me one thing that you think you or anyone else can do really well without first trying hard and making some mistakes.

Rod: . . . I can't think of anything, I guess.

Father: Because there isn't anything. Even champions have to go on practicing. Hours and hours every day. So let's get back to the court.

Here, Father confronts Rod's unrealistic expectations about performance. Father takes the time to explain that it isn't tennis that Rod dislikes but himself for failing. Then Father shows his son why this attitude is unreasonable and unrealistic. Whenever your child is engaged in a relatively new activity, be prepared. You will need to remind him over and over that practice and work are necessary to achieve excellence.

Unrealistic Comparisons with Other People

A child, as we've noted, magnifies his failings

and unfairly downgrades his capabilities. This is especially true when he compares himself with other people. Your child will be overly impressed by what others can do. He will be least impressed by himself, even when he does well. But if he loses, he will think of little else.

Tina, 10, has been in 4-H only four months. Today she has just exhibited her lamb at the County Fair for the first time. Now Tina is back home and crying because she received no recognition for her lamb:

Mother: What is it, Tina? Can you tell me about it? *(Tina doesn't reply.)* I can't help you unless I know what's wrong.

Tina: It wouldn't do any good, anyway.

Mother: Perhaps it might. But you'll have to tell me what it's all about so I can be sure. I can't guess.

Tina: Gretchen won first prize.

Mother: And that's why you're crying?

Tina: Yes, Wouldn't you?

Mother: No, I wouldn't. There's nothing wrong with Gretchen winning a prize, is there?

Tina: But I didn't even get second or third prize for my lamb. And I took care of it four months.

Mother: And you think that, because Gretchen took first place, you're no good?

Tina: I never do anything good enough.

Mother: Did you feel certain you'd win a prize?

Tina: Yes.

Mother: And now you think you're a failure, a loser?

Tina: Well, I didn't win anything, did I?

Mother: You didn't win *this time*. That's a big difference. In my book, you're not a loser. You tried hard and I'm proud of how well you've taken care of your lamb. Gretchen is a year older than you and has had more experience. Besides, her father raises lambs—that's another advantage she has going for her.

Tina: But I worked real hard.

Mother: And that's why I think you can be a winner, too. All the hard work you did this time will help you next time.

Mother zeroes in on the unrealistic notion that, because someone else has won a prize, Tina must be a loser. Mother takes the time to learn the facts, to draw Tina out, and then attacks the false comparison. She then explains why Tina shouldn't look on herself as a loser so early in the game just because somebody else won. And Tina understands her unrealistic conclusion a little better.

Unrealistic Expectations about Making Mistakes

Your child will tend to believe in the delusion of his own uniqueness, the misconception that only he makes mistakes. You can dispel that notion: Tell your child that everyone makes mistakes. You will have to tell him this repeatedly before he will believe you. Point out that many people hide their mistakes in order to avoid feeling inadequate and embarrassed—and that those who do the most hiding are the most insecure.

Without degrading anybody, cite some mistakes made by people your child knows. But be careful not to overemphasize mistakes. Your object is to show him how others err and not to give him an excuse for sloppy performance.

Don't hide your mistakes from your child. Don't give him an impossible model to follow.

Let your child know that his mistakes mean only that he has more to learn. Failure is essential for learning. As we gain more experience, we tend to make fewer and fewer mistakes. But none of us reaches the point of absolute perfection.

How to Develop Realistic Expectations

Gently but firmly tell your child when his expectations are unrealistic. Tell him they cannot happen for him or anyone else. Point out that such expectations are common. Explain that every child has unrealistic expectations and that this is normal. Children simply lack the experience to know how slowly or quickly success can come. Also let him know that everyone who has fantastic, unreal expectations ends by feeling disappointed.

When your child is disappointed that his expectations didn't materialize or succeed, confront his feeling of failure. Ask him to tell you what some of your weaknesses and limitations are. Then invite him to tell you how these limits could prove that you are "no good."

Protect his self-image. Show how wrong he is about his idea of being "no good" because of his inability to attain unrealistic expectations. Assure him he is, in fact, quite normal and more capable than he thinks. Remind him that, if he wants to do better, there is no substitute for hard work and practice.

C-7 Self-sufficiency: "I Did it by Myself"

You'll know your child is growing up the moment he starts relying on his own resourcefulness. This will impress and delight you because it will relieve you of chores you've had to perform on his behalf. Nevertheless, there are some parents who are actually afraid of their child's self-reliant behavior. They feel somewhat left out, less needed, as their child demonstrates his ability to dress himself, get his own food or turn on the TV. To relieve their fears, they often continue to do things for him that he can easily do for himself. Don't be surprised if this happens to you. After all, as a parent you derive a sense of importance, a feeling of being needed, when you do things for your child. It's a feeling we all enjoy. Unless you are the most secure parent in town, expect to respond with mixed feelings to your child's increasing self-reliance.

This talk of the self-reliant child does not refer to the socially withdrawn child who is often mislabeled "independent." Many parents express concern about their child's "independence" when they actually mean his "isolation" from others. This is social withdrawal or detachment. Such children avoid closeness because they are extremely sensitive to criticism and rejection. By avoiding contact with others, the child seeks to protect himself from feeling anxious, afraid or depressed. The problem is that he also cuts himself off from the affection and social contact he needs to make him feel worthy. This is self-destructive and emotionally unhealthy.

Here instead we are discussing the self-reliant child who can get his needs met without being unduly dependent on others. This self-reliance, the ability to do things for oneself, is important and valuable because it promotes both survival and a good self-image. Your child will feel best about himself when he finds that he's powerful enough to do things for himself; self-sufficiency serves his ego as well as his survival. Your function is to help him build a track record of self-reliant experiences that will confirm his ability to look after his needs. Don't yield too much to your desire to keep things running smoothly and to get sure results. This could deprive your child of needed opportunity to do things on his own.

If you want a self-reliant child, the cardinal rule is: Never do anything for your child that he can do for himself. Tying his shoelaces to save a minute, when he is capable of doing it himself, damages his self-esteem and self-confidence. It tells him that you really think he's incompetent or that you'd rather not have him become self-reliant. Once you give him such a message, he will readily comply. Why should he take the responsibility or make the effort if he knows you're more than willing to assume it all yourself?

Christie, eight, is having trouble with homework in third-grade arithmetic. Her father is a concerned and devoted parent, but he sees the situation as a problem in learning rather than a question of self-reliance. Learning is of course important; but in the long term it matters more to be a self-reliant person:

Father: Having trouble with your math, Chris?

Chris: Yeah. It's really hard. I don't understand it at all.

Father: Here, let me show you how to do it.

Father: What you're telling me, then, is that you don't want to take the chance of putting yourself on the line because you'll feel bad if somebody turns you down. In other words, you don't want to be rejected. Right?

Kyle: Yeah, I think so. Why should I take a chance like that?

Father: Yet you still want the bike?

Kyle: Sure, I do.

Father: Well, then, if you don't take that chance and ask people if they need something done for them, you'll never get that bike. Some people may say no, but some people may say yes. You won't know till you take the risk of asking them, will you?

Kyle's concern is about his personal acceptability. He's afraid to put it on the line because he wants to avoid the pain of possible rejection. In his view, being turned down doesn't mean that his neighbors simply don't need any chores done, but that he is worthless. Therefore he doesn't want to put it to a test.

The basic issue here is that there are a lot of things Kyle wants and needs but won't get unless he takes the risk involved.

Father understands Kyle's reluctance and tries to make his son aware of the underlying fear and the dilemma the boy is left with: He can get the bike only by exposing himself to possible rejection. Father knows that the payoff for Kyle's risk-taking and work isn't just the bike. The real payoff is the feeling that "I took a chance and it worked out."

How to Help Your Child Become More Assertive

The more you encourage him and the more success he has, the more your child will take on new risks. But he needs a start, and your encouragement is where it all begins.

Urge your child to take the initiative. *Challenge him to stick out his neck a little from time to time.* You will have to be there to pick up the pieces when he fails, and be there with your praise when he succeeds.

Say, "We're all afraid of having someone tell us they don't want whatever we're offering. But there's nothing worth getting that doesn't involve a certain amount of risk. So

give it a try. If you need my help, I'll be glad to supply what advice I can."

Tell your child some of your experiences in regard to taking risks. This might be one of your successful experiences or one in which you failed or were rejected. When he does fail, show him he still can go on, that the pain is something he can survive. After all, you survived similar experiences and he can, too.

If you have an exceptionally passive child, ask yourself if you're too protective: "Am I doing what I can to raise an independent, assertive child—or am I smothering him by giving him too much? Should I do a little less for him and encourage him to do a little more for himself?"

C-9 Caution: Real Danger Versus the Magic Mantle

In your child's development, fantasy will come before logical thinking and a firm grasp on reality. His fantasies will play an active part in his life. But there is one fantasy to beware—the dangerous myth of the Magic Mantle. This is the belief of almost every child that he is invulnerable to harm mainly because he doesn't want harm to befall him. When he darts into the street after a lost ball, he imprudently relies on this magic mantle to protect him. He believes his wishes are reality: "It can't happen to me because my wish is so strong." He'll swing from tree branches and ride his bike through stop signs—while you blanch in terror.

The magic-mantle fantasy is a triumph of wish-over-reality. It is reinforced by those animated cartoons children adore—the ones in which fanciful characters beat up and even blow up but miraculously never get maimed. Your child's own skinned knees, bruises and broken bones will always come as a surprise to him, although chances are you've warned him all along. If he is to mature (and, in some cases, if he is to survive), he gradually must relinquish this unrealistic notion so he can deal with reality as it is.

Your child needs to develop a sense of caution, an awareness of the true dangers in his environment. Sadly, this is best learned by experience, not by admonition nor command. As someone has said, "Experience is the best teacher but the tuition is awfully high." Most of us try to avoid pain but in one sense it can be beneficial. A small amount of pain can instill an important lesson in your child to keep him from more serious harm later.

To teach your child to be more realistic about danger, let him experience small doses of pain in situations where the physical danger is mild. Understandably this may be difficult for you to do. But it is not cruel. Indeed, it well may be a substantial cruelty to overprotect your young child so that he never experiences any pain or his vulnerability to it. Better to learn about collisions on a tricycle in his backyard than in a car on the freeway. The sooner he understands the painful consequences of his rash behavior, the less likely he is to suffer serious injury.

The guiding principle is to calibrate the amount of pain so that it is instructive without being really harmful. Let your child experience pain only in situations where you can foresee the consequence and are satisfied there is no serious threat. Jumping off a hassock or the living-room sofa is not likely to be as damaging or painful as jumping off the roof. But the small amount of pain suffered will go a long way toward teaching the dangers of self-induced free falls.

Instead of actual exploits, help your child experiment with a dry run of some potential peril. Suppose your seven-year-old likes to rock back and forth on a kitchen chair. He easily could fall back and smack his head on the wall. You can demonstrate the danger by tilting the chair backwards, yet not letting him fall. The sensation of falling and the fear that you might let go will impress him with the dangerous dimensions of his own action. In a similar way, he can learn about the dangers of baseball bats from the whack of a plastic bat. The object is for you to protect him from real harm but nevertheless let your child experience a mild preview of the pain associated with the danger. A child who does not know any pain can't know

reality. He is merely being set up for a serious, traumatic downfall. This is why the Magic Mantle is so treacherous and why it must be dissolved.

How to Dissolve the Magic Mantle— gently

Assume your child has a magic mantle. Innately cautious children are in the minority. It's wise to assume that your child has a reckless wish to believe that "Nothing really bad can happen to me." Whenever possible, be alert to his interests and plans for any possible risks and dangers. *Remember Murphy's Law.* Assume that dangerous things not only might occur but are likely to. This is not being overprotective.

Question the danger. You owe it to yourself and your child to anticipate possible harm. Ask your child to tell you what dangerous things might possibly happen as a consequence of his actions. If he shows a healthy, realistic appreciation for possible dangers, say that you agree and then ask how he proposes to overcome them. But if he doesn't convince you that he is keenly aware of dangers, spell out for him what they are. Do not allow him to proceed afterward with his questionable plans—he might hurt himself or someone else. Let him down gently. Assure him that you will let him do what he wishes once he demonstrates that he is responsible and cautious enough to recognize the possible perils involved.

C-10 Self-confidence: Belief in Self

"Am I a winner or a loser?" "Am I good enough?" "Can I do this? Will I succeed or fail?" These are the self-doubts that resound through the recesses of your child's mind. They're most active and apparent at ball games and at school, where the challenge to perform is direct and immediate. At home they are less obvious; nevertheless, your child always is measuring how well he can perform.

At first glance, the answer to his self-doubts seems obvious: To develop his skills and abilities, to become effective and do things consistently well, should allay a child's uncertainties. Ironically, this is not the whole answer.

All of us know people widely regarded as competent and effective who on close acquaintance reveal themselves to be riddled with self-doubts. Thus, you have the judge who is privately unsure of his decisions, the surgeon who secretly doubts his procedures and the respected politician who feels himself inadequate to lead. Despite their ability and effectiveness, these people suffer inwardly from an old-fashioned inferiority complex. They feel "no good," incompetent and even fraudulent although they obviously possess great knowledge and skill. Something is wrong. There's a split between being and feeling competent.

Ability alone is not enough. Your child must not only be competent, he also must possess belief in the abilities he really has. It is absolutely vital to his emotional well-being. With confidence, he can honestly and proudly say, "I can do things. I am an adequate person." Without confidence, even with an impressive record of accomplishments, all he can say and feel is, "I can't do things. I'm a failure. I'm inadequate." Capitalize on this concern for success by giving your child simple but challenging responsibilities. As you do, adjust the challenge to his capability so he can be assured of success with a little extra effort.

The formula for confidence is performance socially reinforced—or, more plainly, success plus parental praise. Just being able to do something well will not make your child feel competent. His accomplishments have to be coupled with social recognition. And that recognition has to come from you, his parent. You are the most significant adult he knows. What you think matters.

Your child needs your tributes to his accomplishments to offset his tendency to exaggerate his failures. Children have very fragile egos. With your recognition and praise, balance your child's lopsided impressions of failure and success.

Your child wants and needs to succeed. No matter what he does—constructing a model, completing homework, fixing his bike—he may be more deeply concerned with whether he'll succeed than with the task itself.

Giving him these repsonsibilities is a vote of confidence. He reads it as a message that says, "I believe in you." And so he believes in himself a little more. For you, the bonus is that he will like and respect you even more for giving him your praise. For him, it's an ebullient feeling of confidence that can come only from performance coupled with your recognition.

Slim, nine years old and bright, performs at or near the head of his class at school. He felt pleased yesterday when he brought home his report card of four "A" subjects and one "B." But his perfectionist mother said she was disappointed that Slim didn't have a straight-"A" card and that she expected her son to do better. Father was more blunt: "I don't want you goofing off in school! Get rid of that 'B'. Understood?"

Slim understood that as well as all the latent messages between the lines. Today he's at school feeling miserable when he meets his friend Brad, an average student:

Brad: Hi, Slim! Did I tell you what happened? My parents liked my report card so much, they took me to a hockey game.

Slim: They did? What were your grades?

Brad: Mostly "C." But I got one "B" and one "A."

Slim: And you got to see hockey for that?

Brad: Yeah. My parents said they were real pleased about that "A." How'd you do?

Slim: O.K., I guess.

Brad: What'd you get?

Slim: I would've had a straight-"A" card, except for one "B."

Brad: Wow! What did your parents do for you?

Slim: They yelled at me because of the one "B." That was all they could talk about.

Slim feels let down, and well he should. He delivered a good report card. But his parents chose to dwell on the least successful part of the report and ignore his very apparent accomplishments. As a result he doesn't feel competent, even though he's done very well. He's on his way toward becoming an adult who's effective but unable to believe in himself, and therefore always anxious about his ability.

Slim's parents, like many others, don't understand either the importance of confidence or the absolute need for praise. They commit the common mistake of thinking that the best way to spur their child to greater feats is to attack his weaknesses. All they actually do is rob him of his confidence and make him fearful.

The best way to encourage your child to do better lies in the opposite direction: Praise his strengths. Build on something positive. The more he believes in himself, because he knows you believe in him, the more likely he is to do better.

How to Increase Your Child's Self-confidence

Recognize and praise your child's accomplishments—it's the single most important thing you can do to make him self-confident. He may recognize that he's competent or has done something well but he needs to know that you know and approve.

Systematically challenge him to do things within his grasp—or just beyond. Confidence is too important to be permitted to develop haphazardly. Plan so your child can make steady progress in feeling successful and confident. When he succeeds, reinforce his confidence with your praise.

Be sure his challenges lie within his sphere of interest. Make available a variety of materials to challenge his interests and skills. Include him in your activities in such a way that he can share in the results and receive recognition for his role. Remember, if he isn't interested at the start, he is likely not to finish. That's one of the reasons some children do poorly at school: There, they have to learn what interests someone else rather than what naturally excites them.

Adjust the challenges to your child's level of competence. Make sure the level of difficulty doesn't overawe him. You can follow the rule of thumb that your child is likely to take on a challenge if he sees at least a 90% chance of succeeding. As he gradually builds up a good record of success, you will see him more and more willing to take the risk of putting his ability on the line.

Praise both the accomplishment and his willingness to try. Place the emphasis on his willing and brave spirit, letting him know that nobody can be assured in advance that success will result.

Keep your credibility high. Many parents make the mistake of praising dubious or insignificant accomplishments as if these were meaningful. In the process, their obvious insincerity convinces the child he is incompetent, even though their words say otherwise. Be sure to praise only real accomplishment. It doesn't have to be something big. Magnitude isn't what counts. It's the reality of what he's done that matters—and your credibility when you praise him.

C-11 Responsibility: No Reminding Needed

When your child washes his hands, does his homework or feeds the dog without having to be reminded, you'll know he's becoming responsible. Responsibility means making and—most especially—keeping commitments without having to be urged. Self-motivation is the essence of responsibility.

You must deliberately foster your child's responsibility. It seldom develops naturally. But parents often assume it can. They believe that a child will automatically become more responsible as he grows older. But getting older or bigger has little to do with it. Your child will not become responsible unless you expect and demand it of him. He will need your continual challenge and support.

To build responsibility, your demands have to be specific. It's not enough just to say, "I want you to be responsible." You need to give him small, explicit challenges he can understand and fulfill.

If you expect too much too soon, he'll rebel. But if you ask for too little, he'll probably do nothing at all. The tasks you set him to do must be not only moderate and manageable, they must also require application.

All of this will be hard-won territory. Resistive to hard work and wanting to be taken care of, children will dodge attempts to make them face and meet obligations. It's very hard for your child to become responsible on his own. He needs to be challenged. That means you must be persistent in repeating the basic formula of challenge and reward. Before your child becomes responsible, there will be many years and countless episodes in which—in a supportive way—you demand real performance. As you make your demands, keep in mind that he needs considerable support. If your child feels loved, accepted, listened to and respected, he'll respond. If he doesn't feel supported, your demands will be thwarted by escapist tactics.

Every challenge that is met should have a reward, even if it's only notice. Your approval is, after all, the most powerful reward. Focus your praise on the fact that the commitment was met without a reminder. This emphasis on his self-motivation is the crucial element in developing his responsibility.

Dori, nine, is having trouble with homework which she's now being given for the first time on a regular basis. A note finally has arrived from the school:

Mother: Dori, do you have your homework tonight?

Dori: I guess so.

Mother: When do you plan to do it?

Dori: I forgot about it. But I'll do it after dinner.

Mother: Would you have done it if I hadn't reminded you?

Dori: Yeah . . . sure, I would.

Mother: I'm glad to hear that because today I received a note from your teacher, saying you don't hand in your homework.

Dori: I do, too!

Mother: She said you've missed about half the assignments.

Dori: Well, I forget sometimes. Nobody reminds me.

Mother: Do you have to remind me to do your laundry or cook your meals?

Dori: You're supposed to do those things. You're the mother.

Mother: Just like you're supposed to do your homework because you're the pupil.

Dori: It'd be easier if you reminded me.

Mother: Oh, I know. It would be easier for me, too, if somebody reminded me. But nobody does. You have to take responsibility for your own obligations, Dori. Otherwise you won't really grow up. You'll only get bigger.

For several days, Dori obliges her mother but, predictably, soon begins to slip back and forget. Mother, fortunately, is a realist. She reiterates her demands for Dori's becoming more responsible. Eventually, after dozens of such gentle confrontations, Dori will comply. But it will take a lot of grit and determination on Mother's part. In one way, Dori doesn't want to grow up, an attitude virtually universal in children.

How to Increase Responsible Behavior

The Formula: Specific demands plus gentle confrontation (to see that he meets those demands), together with praise when he obliges and lots of support and persistence. All elements here are necessary but two things stand out: support and praise. Your child will accept the challenges you demand of him only if he has ample amounts of loving support. Then, praise him when he acts responsibly.

Make it easy for your child to get started. Keep your demands simple and clear. Be realistic in your expectations. Constantly insisting upon superior performance will discourage your child from ever being able to please you, and he'll stop trying.

Tell your child that his doing a chore without having to be reminded or constantly kept after is what will impress you most of all.

C-12 Ambition: Interest in Success

Today many people hold ambition in contempt on the grounds that it's destructive and self-serving. But they see only half the picture. There are two kinds of ambition: One kind, sometimes described as ambition, is actually overcompensation, an excessive drive for success and power. This drive, rooted in fear mixed with anger, is a severe kind of neurotic functioning which often borders on paranoia and fanaticism.

The other kind is genuine ambition, a natural and normal drive to be productive, to do and make things. This kind of ambition is not an ego trip. It springs from your child's basic energy, his intellectual curiosity and his natural desire to be useful.

When your child is young, he will often demonstrate his ambition spontaneously. Instinctively, he realizes that his survival and development depend upon his becoming a productive person. Watch for early manifestations of his ambition and verbally reinforce them. Say, "I like what you're doing. I really appreciate your being so useful."

You also can stimulate his ambition by giving him useful tasks to perform around the house. It must be necessary work and it must have meaning. Your child will recognize make-work and will balk. Opportunities for useful work are not as prevalent in the urban environment where most of us live as they are on a farm where every set of hands is busy. Nor do children's games and athletics offer much chance for productivity. However, with a little forethought and ingenuity you still will find suitable things for your child to do.

In amount of ambition, every child is different. If yours is a self-starter by temperament, he will need only minimal support and encouragement. But you'll have to meet him more than halfway if he seems sluggish by nature. Then he'll need a wider selection of choices in things to make and do. And he'll require an extra measure of challenge, notice and praise.

There is no need to become frantic about your child's productivity. Children who are continually pressured to perform will build up an inner anger, which they and their parents pay for sooner or later. Be firm but flexible and tread a moderate course.

The emotional opposite of low ambition is overcompensation, an excessive drive to do things to "prove" one's adequacy and self-worth. The overcompensating person feels acutely inadequate. He's afraid that others will reject him and hurt his feelings. Consequently, he denies his fears and anxiety about his inadequacy and strives to gain so much power that no one can dare hurt him. This drive for great power, deeply neurotic, is always motivated by fear and anger toward other people.

Overcompensation is unconscious. People who overcompensate really are unaware of what they are doing and what they truly need. The person buries his fears and anxieties deep inside himself, below the level of consciousness. The denied feelings spur him to acquire greater increments of power and success.

In the process, those who overcompensate lose sight of their need for human involvement. They feel unloved. The tragedy is that they don't know what they really need. At the conscious level, they do not see their need for human acceptance. Without psychotherapy, this problem never will be uncovered and resolved.

Moreover, when the power-hungry person finally "succeeds" and gains great power, he is never satisfied with it. The reason is simple: He never really wanted or needed it in the first place. What he needed then and needs now is to feel loved. In between, the excitement and intoxication of acquiring vast amounts of power delude him into thinking he's getting what he wants. Actually, he still holds himself in low esteem and needs to be busy all the time to bolster his weak inner image.

What can you do about it? How can you properly socialize these strivings?

Lars, an overcompensating child, now is 12. Always precocious, he walked and talked early and by age three had begun to try to dominate every person he came in contact with. This urge to dominate, just like his superior intelligence, is largely a genetic component of his personality. For nine years, his parents literally have been at war with the boy because of their clash of wills against his inborn urge to prevail. Lars has never had the love and reassurance he so badly needs; his parents gave up too soon.

His presence is inescapable and impressive, and his brightness intertwined with insistence, perseverance and raw tenacity. It's four o'clock on a Saturday afternoon. Lars approaches his father. Clearly, Lars is used to having what he wants, the way being made easy by his forceful intelligence and the sheer awesomeness of his personality:

Lars: Dad, you have to drive me to pick up an M-23 transistor.

Father: Can't you see I'm busy right now paying the bills?

Lars: Yes, I see, but this is terribly important. I'm making a model computer to keep my Junior Achievement records. The store closes in half an hour. If you don't hurry, we won't have enough time to get there. Then I won't have my project ready on time. You can always do the bills later. Be a pal.

Father: (*Wanting to avoid a fight*) O.K., if it's that important to you. Hop in the car and I'll take you over.

Once again, Lars' father is giving up without firing a shot as Lars pressures him, threatens him and finally seduces him. By submitting to this young bully, Father conveys several latent messages to his son that eventually will lead to disastrous consequences:

Even though you're younger and less experienced than I am, you can push me around.

You can get the things you want with pressure tactics and flattery and by using emotional blackmail (as in implying what a bad person I would be if I said no).

People (myself as an example) do not stand up and demand respectful treatment.

Your egocentric behavior is a successful way to function. It will get you what you want.

It's not important to be considerate of other people.

And yet what can Father do? Suppose he is not about to be terrorized or bullied. Instead, he makes Lars see himself as the boy really is:

Lars: Dad, you have to drive me to pick up an M-23 transistor.

Father: Are you asking or demanding? It

sounds to me as if I have no choice. Supposing I said no?

Lars: It's too important for you to say no—unless you want to ruin my Junior Achievement project.

Father: I've no intention of wrecking a project. But I'm more concerned about your personality, your chance to become a considerate person.

Lars: Dad, I don't have time for a lecture. The store is about to close. Are you going to take me or not? If you won't, I'll call Berndt's father. He'll take me.

Father: The answer is no. I'm busy doing something important. And I think it's inconsiderate of you to come in here and demand I take you at the last minute.

Lars: Then I'll call Berndt's—

Father: No, you won't. I'm not going to let you threaten me with Berndt's father or let you try to use him at the last minute the way you've tried to use me.

Lars: What are you trying to pull? I came in here to ask a very simple thing and you're giving me a bad time.

Father: You're the one who's giving the bad time. I was busy and you came in here demanding and pressuring me to drop everything for what you want.

Lars: You're missing the point. I desperately need that part.

Father: YOU'RE missing the point: You're inconsiderate and demanding, and you don't even realize it. That's the problem, and that's what I want you to see.

Lars: O.K. O.K. I see. Now will you take me?

Father: Lars, you're not even listening to me. You want me to be considerate and to support your interests. But you're never willing to consider my feelings and needs.

Lars: All that can wait till later. Right now, the store won't wait. If it closes before I can get there, it's going to be your fault.

Father: Oh, no, it won't. You're trying to blame me, make me look bad. That's intimidation, do you realize that? Well, it won't work. If I let you get your way, you'll continue behaving like a dictator. If you keep on with these tactics, the people you want for friends won't like or respect you.

Lars: I don't see what any of this has to do with going to the store.

Father: Now you've got the point. We're not talking about going to the store. We're talking about your appalling lack of consideration. What's at issue is the demands you make—your intimidating behavior.

Lars: Hey, now just a minute. You're the one who's got your back up for no good reason and won't take me to the store. And you're trying to make me into the bad guy.

Father: Lars, I want to help you with your project. But I won't be forced or pressured. It's too late to go today. But I'll be glad to take you Monday.

Lars: You know that's too late. I've explained why I have to go now.

Father: Sorry. The answer is no. And I'm even sorrier that you persist in being so inconsiderate. You'll never get the love you need from other people till you begin to understand their needs and treat them with a little consideration.

Lars: I can't believe I'm hearing all this. It's unreal! All I want is a ride to the store. Is that such a big deal?

Father: It is, as long as you keep putting your projects and plans before the feelings of other people, as long as you keep manipulating people to get what you want. You must feel very helpless inside to crave so much power. And I'm sorry for that most of all.

Lars: If you really were sorry or cared at all, you'd simply take me over to the store.

Father: Lars, it's because I really do care that I won't.

Rather than reject Lars' inconsiderate demands out of hand, Father uses the encounter to raise his son's awareness of what the boy is doing. Remember, because overcompensating is unconscious, Lars is not at all aware—he's protecting himself from his innermost fears and feelings of helplessness. This confrontation is going to leave Lars deeply frustrated. The only way healthy maturation can be assured is by a steady program of one-to-one time, for longer periods than the usual 10 minutes daily. Lars' fear is so strong that his one-to-one time will need at least a half-day each week. Lars will require this diet of rich support for many months, perhaps even a year or more. And chances are that Lars' problem already may be too serious to be helped by his parents alone. He may need professional help—the most effective and dedicated psychotherapist his parents can find. If Lars receives insufficient help now, not only will he be damaged, but in time he will damage the lives of others who associate with him.

How to Deal with Overcompensation

Prevent it from happening, if at all possible, by noticing and dealing with the symptoms early. If your child is especially anxious about succeeding or seems almost too industrious, he may be feeling extremely insecure about himself. (Ironically, this type of child often is very talented and productive.) Assure him that he is wanted and worthwhile, that he is an adequate and useful person. As he comes to believe you, he will grow more secure and the overcompensation will lessen.

When you are pressured by a child who is overcompensating:

Resist his demands. Tell him they are unreasonable and inconsiderate. Point out his attempts at manipulation.

Point out his power-urge. Tell him it makes you sad because to be so power-oriented means to feel very inadequate and helpless within.

Resist his pressure. Say you will not be intimidated by it.

Give him more one-to-one time. It is the surest means of reducing his overcompensatory strivings and will provide needed support to sustain your confrontations.

How to Encourage Healthy Ambition

The most effective way to develop your child's ambition is to give him the feeling of being productive. Without it, your child will flounder through life.

Find useful things your child can do around the house and challenge him to do them. Fit the task to his level of competence and to his interest. Vary the tasks you give him so he won't become bored.

Give him fun things to make. Provide inexpensive do-it-yourself kits plus the necessary tools and a place to work. Cooking projects and household repairs can also be fun. Find out what classes for hobbies are available in your community. Look into the after-school program of your city-school system, check with the YMCA, with the Park and Recreation department, and with churches, responsible private clubs and even fraternal organizations that may schedule special programs for children.

Offer your help, but only when needed. Without diminishing your child's self-sufficiency, tell him you're on an "available-when-you-need-me" basis. Be careful not to imply or suggest—particularly by your vocal tone—that you doubt his ability to do something on his own. When your child completes a task, praise his effort and accomplishment.

C-13 Goals: "I Know Where I'm Going"

Without challenges and demands for performance, most children tend to become aimless. This is a fact of life, especially in families in which both parents work. When children—particularly adolescents—are left to fend for themselves, they often slip into a lazy, purposeless existence. They don't know what to do with themselves and may express this meaninglessness by mischief or more-serious trouble.

Your child needs to be primed to seek out and attain goals. Goal-directedness means that one organizes activities in terms of goals and then pursues them. Goals themselves, however, are often less significant than the process of trying to realize them. It's this habit you want your child to form: to work toward the goals he sets. In the process, his life will be more interesting and rewarding. To cultivate goal-directedness in your child, expose him early to many different

experiences and activities. That word—activities—is the key. TV-watching, although it shows your child many things he otherwise might never know or see, is static; it makes children passive. Your child needs activity, movement, interesting projects that he follows through from beginning to end. You'll easily find many likely activities around you; research others. Fishing, swimming, craft work, camping, sailing, backpacking, folk dancing, rock-hunting, bird-watching, sleight-of-hand magic, gymnastics to music, acrobatics, playing a musical instrument, junior golf programs, racing pigeons, skiing—expose your child to as many activities as possible to give him a chance to find the few that will genuinely interest him. Then he can develop more-meaningful goals by doing something he wants, not just what you suggest.

You haven't enough money to afford such activities? Instead, provide your child with priceless information. These days, there are very few sizeable cities in which fine recreational opportunities are not going begging. Once you have analyzed likely avenues of expression for your child, all you need is the telephone. After you have checked on all the free or nearly free city- and county-sponsored park-and-recreation schedules for youngsters, query the individual schools about their leisure-time programs. Don't forget the YMCA and YWCA nor overlook your city's cultural institutions. The latter often put together imaginative participatory programs for the very young. Try your chamber of commerce for suggestions—those packets sent to tourists sometimes contain surprises for residents. Many private clubs encourage participation by juniors. Camera clubs, for instance, often have a junior division. Even seemingly exclusive yacht clubs have been known to make free sailing lessons available for kids. Once your child's interest and bent become known, adults who share the same enthusiasm will be very apt to give him a boost along the way.

Once your child shows a marked interest, support his efforts to become deeply involved in it. If his interest is photography, provide him with an inexpensive camera, film, light meters and other accessories. These things do not have to be given to him. He can earn them and will appreciate them even more if he does. He can "pay" by performing tasks around the home, babysitting, mowing lawns and so on. Although you may suggest goals, he must make the final decision. If he yearns to play the guitar, it's not advisable to tell him to learn the piano first. He is apt to lose interest in both. One of the worst things you can say is, "Find something to do," without giving specific suggestions.

As your child sets his goal, he'll become interested in the intermediary steps by which to reach it. He'll be more amenable to listening to your guidance and even will seek it out. He'll be more realistic and knowledgeable about what has to be done to obtain results. And he'll feel less apprehensive about facing future challenges. Pursuing goals will help integrate his personality; he will become a very "together" person through bringing all his abilities into working harmony. Also, pursuing definite goals broadens perspective by sharpening the concept of past, present and future. Your child will gain a sense of passion and purpose and a taste of the excitement of life.

Roger, 11, does almost nothing but eat and watch television. Except for school, he has no active involvement with anything remotely goal-oriented or productive. To make matters worse, he's not a scholar. For him the most exciting thing about school is ditching classes or smoking with his "friends"—cigarettes or pot. At home, he's alone. He has no brothers or sisters.

His working parents have become more aware of his aimlessness over the past few months. But they haven't really understood the problem and have done little but scold him and ask why he never does anything productive. Finally, on the advice of friends, they obtained the help of a psychologist. Tests showed Roger to have better-than-average intelligence, lower-than-average drive and less-than-average curiosity. The psychologist suggested enrolling Roger in some goal-oriented activities with the Boy Scouts. Roger has agreed to try scouting for a three-month period. His parents have pledged to support his efforts. Further, Roger's father committed himself to working with Rog on a joint project at least two hours every Saturday. The family also resolved to listen better to one another and to communicate at the feeling level. This effort was needed to end the isolation and loneliness of family members who, while living in the same apartment, often functioned like strangers.

As they drive home after Roger's first Boy Scout meeting, Father asks him about the new program:

Father: Have you decided on what you're going to do? There are over 120 badges you can go for.

Roger: Nah. I don't think it's gonna work out.

Father: You can't expect overnight results. It takes time.

Roger: It's too much of a hassle.

Father: Roger, you can't be happy unless you find some real interest. You owe it to yourself to try.

Roger: I don't like anything they showed me.

Father: Then you're going to have to do a little experimenting. You have to expect that some things won't interest you. But there's sure to be something that will.

Roger: You sound just like our shrink.

Father: It doesn't take any effort to blow pot. But it won't get you anywhere in real life. I hope you're going to see this thing through without making us feel as if we're putting you through some kind of torture. I know I'm learning something from all this and I know you can too, if you try.

Despite this shaky start, after two months of regular attendance, Roger grew interested in a number of Scouting activities. He went deeply into Boy Scouts and began to feel a sense of fulfillment. At the same time, he started a part-time job so he could earn money to pursue some of his new interests. As a result, he's living with more depth, more purpose and satisfaction.

How to Foster Goal-directedness

Your child cannot be happy nor capable nor can he feel worthy unless he has goals and actively strives to realize them. Goal-directedness develops your child but aimlessness does not. Living without goals arrests his development.

Be your own good example. If he sees that you are goal-oriented, he is likely to follow your way. Give him your encouragement and guidance to set a few goals for himself, a chance to develop his own interests, and your support to pursue them in depth.

Watch for symptoms of aimlessness. One clue to be tuned in to especially is the brevity of time or effort he's putting in on his own behalf. Aimless children go for the short and easy satisfactions. They do a lot of ''hanging around,'' a lot of passive consuming. Goal-directed children usually have a general plan, are willing to put forth effort and persevere for results.

Praise your child's goal-directedness. Say how pleased you are to see him using his time well to pursue something of worthwhile interest.

Confront his aimlessness. Tell him of the great satisfactions he's missing by not having some kind of goal. Tell him what you do to reach the goals you set for yourself. Explain that the major consideration isn't really how things turn out; it's the fun of going after something, and the sense of involvement and purpose he will enjoy along the way.

After he finishes something, tell him how pleased you are. Gradually encourage him to undertake more-complex, longer-term projects. Assure him of your support for this deeper involvement. Even though he may tend to complain that you're prodding him, later he'll be grateful that you did.

C-14 High Standards: The Key to Quality Work

It's both natural and advisable for you to want your child to have high standards of performance. His self-concept depends on them. The better he performs, the more he will like and respect himself. And the more others will like and respect him, too. High standards also have a practical value in terms of survival. They are the ticket to getting and keeping a good job and, with it, the many advantages that make for a good and rewarding life.

High standards of performance do not mean trying to be perfect, but trying consistently to do one's best in any given situation. As a general rule of thumb, this means ''B+,'' not ''A+.'' Don't compare your child to anyone else to determine what he ''should'' be doing. He should be judged only by his own capacity. If you expect too high a level of performance from him, he will feel inadequate and resentful. Lacking experience and confidence, he may be crushed by your demands and tell himself, ''I'm not good enough because nothing I do pleases anybody.'' On the other hand, your child is not likely to develop high standards of performance unless you make that demand upon him. Without this challenge, he'll do what other children typically do—try to get by with the least amount of time, effort and application.

You will need to demand performance but you should be aware that too intense or great a demand may undermine your child. You can offset this danger by making it a habit to praise him for the good standards he adheres to. Another way to protect his sense of adequacy is to ask him, ''Do you think I'm asking too much of you? How do you feel about it? Does it seem like I'm cutting you down?'' If you are, he'll tell you, especially if he knows you're willing to discuss it without accusations and recriminations.

Developing your child's standards of performance will require a long time. It's critical that he first acquire the earlier competence skills already discussed in this chapter.

Dale, 10, friendly and easygoing, has amiable parents who have neglected his standards of performance—both at school, where he is mostly a ''C'' and ''D'' student, and at home, where his work is on the same level.

Today, however, Dale was given a chance to earn a weekly dollar by washing the family car every Saturday. Dale accepted eagerly.

He has just finished. Father views the poor result with close attention because the car is new:

Father: Are you finished?

Dale: Yeah. Can I have my dollar now?

Father: Not yet. You didn't wash this car. Look at it. All you did was push the dirt around.

Dale feels shot down, betrayed. Father doesn't deal with the basic issue—Dale's low standards—in a constructive way. That's because Father's own upset feelings are obscuring the issue. Obviously he wants his child to do a good job—any parent would. But the way lies in appealing to the child's personal pride and his respect for the wishes of others:

Dale: Can I get my dollar now?

Father: In a minute. First, I'd like to get your opinion on something. How good a job do you think you did?

Dale: Well, it's washed.

Father: I know. But that's not answering my question.

Dale: At least it's cleaner than it was.

Father: How would you grade it—from "A" to "F?"

Dale: About a "C." Maybe even a "B."

Father: You're far too generous. How has your bike been doing? Have you had any trouble with it since I fixed it last week?

Dale: (Puzzled) No.

Father: How would you rate the job I did on it?

Dale: Why all the questions? Are you trying to get out of paying me?

Father: No. I'm trying to help you realize the importance of doing things right. If you don't put enough of yourself into your work but still expect other people to work hard for you, you're not being fair. People don't respect a person who turns out sloppy work. Today, I'm going to pay you the dollar as I agreed. But I'm not sure I want to continue our arrangement. If you're going to do this kind of work, I'll find somebody else who does a better job, somebody who'll give me my money's worth.

Dale: I guess I have to do better.

After this encounter, Dale will go back to redo his sloppy job. He now responds to three messages received from his father:
If you expect good work from others, it's only fair to do good work for them.
If you want the high regard of others, you have to turn out high-quality performance.
If you want to remain employed, you have to do a good job.

How to Encourage Better Standards of Performance

You need to demand good performance but, as with any demands you make of your child, you must give plenty of support—in this case, recognition and praise for what he does well.

Most children need to be challenged to perform well. A few children try to gain acceptance by super performance but they usually are compulsive achievers who are driven by fear and anxiety rather than inherent standards of excellence. The typical child tries to just squeak by. If little is demanded, very little will result.

Expect resistance. Your child will not give up his lax ways without a struggle. Expect a lot of static—he's discharging some of the frustration associated with his really digging in to do a better job. Try to take this goodnaturedly. What is important is that he learns to value good work and the importance of a job well done. Society wants people who can do good work. Your child needs to know this.

Question your child's lack of performance. When he doesn't do at least "B" work, tell him he's not doing as well as he could. (His innate intellectual and temperamental potentials must be the standards of your judgment.) Point out he's not building the habits needed to get what he wants out of life. Tell him most people will not tolerate poor performance.

Ask him if he wants you to tell him he's great when in fact he's not. Usually he will say no.

Ask him to strive for a better standard of performance, one that's both realistic and better than his present level. Get your child to make a commitment to these higher standards. Each time he lives up to his commitment, tell him how proud it makes you feel. If he doesn't live up to it, repeat this process of confronting and challenging his low standards.

C-15 Cooperation: Pooling Talents

There are many things we need that we can't do or accomplish alone. One person can't play a symphony, build an airport or run a city. These activities require cooperation with others to get the job done. Given the interdependence and complexities of our society, cooperation is required for survival. Cooperation means pooling one's talents and effort with someone else to produce something that otherwise could not be done. Invariably, the end product has a better quality or greater magnitude than one person possibly could produce. Cooperation, then, implies the ability to work with others; a division of labor; and even the surrender of a certain amount of independence and autonomy to achieve a common goal.

Many parents, however, misconstrue cooperation. To them, it means absolute and unquestioning obedience to parental commands—submission and knuckling under to whatever they tell their children to do. This attitude cannot produce anything remotely resembling the ability to work constructively with others. It simply incurs both hidden and open displays of resentment because it is so basically disrespectful of the child. In adolescence, these children literally go to war with their parents to gain independence. They're not able to cooperate with their parents because their parents have never taught them how.

Although you probably can do many of your daily tasks more easily if you do them alone, invite your child to help you. Without this kind of experience, your child cannot learn cooperation. If he is only four or five and shows some interest as you set about to repair a door hinge, invite him to hold the screws or tools that always seem out of reach. If he's seven or eight, he might help tighten the screws. The secret is to offer your child participation at his level of ability in areas where his talents and interests lie. You will also find this is one of the best ways to build rapport between you and your child.

As though by magic, your child will become more amenable, friendly and positive. This development comes from receiving the powerful underlying messages implicit in your invitation to work together, messages like, "I believe you have something to offer," and, "I like to do things with you."

Ivy, 11, can do things fairly well by herself although she has had very little experience in learning how to cooperate with others. Her family has never shown much interest in cooperation; each person operates largely on his own in relative isolation from the rest. Today, Ivy's mother is making a slipcover. Mother sews well but has never been very good at cutting out patterns. Vaguely, she's aware that Ivy has fine eye-to-hand coordination and uses scissors quite well. Mother sees this as an opportunity to develop cooperation:

Mother: Ivy, I'm getting ready to slipcover a chair. Would you like to help? I've noticed that you're very good at cutting things out and I'm really not.

Ivy: You want me to help cut?

Mother: Would you, please? It would be fun to work together. You cut and I'll sew. Then, when we finish, we can make something for your room.

Ivy: Sounds like fun.

Mother: You know, there's more to this idea than just sewing.

Ivy: What do you mean?

Mother: Just that it's good for you and me to do things together. In the first place, I'm sure I'll do a better job with your help. It gives me a chance to see how good you are at things and to teach you what I know. And it's so much more pleasant not to work alone.

Here, all the right messages are present—the trust and approval, the need for help and the confidence in Ivy's capability.

How to Develop Cooperation

The principal way to develop the spirit of cooperation is through actual participation rather than the usual lecturing and moralizing. As in all things the model you set is the one that will be followed: Be alert to your child's special interests and abilities. See if your child can make a special contribution to any chore or project you may be engaged in.

Tell your child his talents are needed to do your job better.

Praise him for his help and skill and especially for his willingness to lend a hand. Be sure to remind your child how two people working together can do a better job because they have pooled their talents.

Make him aware of your real pleasure in a joint effort—this will serve as added reinforcement.

C-16 Flexibility: Bending Without Breaking

Lawrence Kubie, a highly respected psychiatrist who did psychotherapy for over 40 years, once wrote that, although there is room for opinion on some aspects of neurosis, there is one aspect no one would seriously dispute. That point is the fact that a neurotic person always is rigid in at least one major aspect of his functioning: He's not able to change in the face of new challenges or circumstances. The normal person is flexible. He's open-minded and ready, willing and able to listen.

Flexibility is the single best sign of mental health. It means being adaptable and, as such, is essential for survival. Flexibility is the ability—under changed conditions—to modify your approach to an objective. For your child, it means being open to change and being able to cope with obstacles and new demands.

As your child's guide, clarify in your mind the sometimes fine distinction between flexibility and not having any commitment at all. "Hanging loose" is not flexibility; it is simply not being involved or goal-directed. Neither is being sloppy or too casual a form of flexibility. That's merely a case of low standards.

Being flexible does not mean you have to surrender your principles or give up your personal ideals to suit the times. If anything, flexibility is a way to pursue your objectives in an imperfect and unpredictable world by adjusting to the available means to gain your objective.

Children need the skill of being flexible. Because they are basically insecure, they cling to routine and set ways. When something out of the ordinary happens, they frequently don't know what to do and become upset or frustrated.

As with many other things, your child learns far more about flexibility from observing you than he does from what you say. Therefore it's necessary for you to become more aware of how flexible you actually are. Then strive to be more so. Chances for improvement and for illustrating flexibility to your child exist around you every day, since every day brings a crisis of some kind.

April is 12. For some time, she has been planning a slumber party for five friends. All eagerly are looking forward to staying overnight at her house on Friday. On Wednesday, April's mother learns that Grandmother and Grandfather will be

coming to town Friday and will expect to stay with the family that night.
April's plans have now been superceded. She's taking it rather hard, even though she'd like to see her grandparents:

April: It's just not fair. They've ruined everything. Couldn't they come some other time?

Mother: It was the only day your grandfather could get away. I'm sorry about what this does to your party.

April: What good does your being sorry do?

Mother: Don't be so rigid. It's not the end of the world. Things have changed—we change with them.

April: I don't want to change. Besides, what will the girls think? They'll probably hate me.

Mother: Don't be so dramatic.

April: Just tell Grandma and Grandpa they can't come. I've got other plans.

Mother: I wouldn't think of doing that. They haven't been able to visit us for over a year. We'll simply have to find another solution for you.

April: But it's all set. There's no other way.

Mother: You're being very inflexible, do you realize that?

April: You just don't care about me and my friends.

Mother: That's not true. I do care. But there are plenty of possibilities. The most obvious one is to have the party another time, or to plan something else with your friends Friday. Or you might even be able to hold the party at someone else's house. Now there are three different ways you might solve your problem. I'll help you any way I can. But, if you can't bend a little, there's not much anyone can do for you.

April: I suppose we could have it next week. But what will I tell all the girls?

Mother: Tell them exactly what happened. They'll understand. Things like this happen to everybody.

The girls may or may not understand. But at least their disappointment will be tempered by the knowledge the party isn't completely off.

For April, the most important lesson is acquiring greater flexibility. Mother guides her to understand that there are other alternatives available in the situation, that everything is not lost. By the 10th, 20th or 50th time they have been through this kind of conflict, April will be working out her own solutions without being immobilized by bitterness and despair into a rigid way of functioning.

How to Improve Flexibility

Observe your child's approach to problems— is it basically flexible or rigid?
Praise your child for his flexibility. Point out how being flexible makes life easier and more enjoyable.
Challenge your child's rigidity. Tell him he's not being adaptable. Explain that he is likely to fare poorly in life unless he learns to loosen up and use imagination to find alternate ways to get what he wants. Give specific examples of how you've had to be flexible to solve problems. Preferably mention incidents in which he either has participated or been an observer. Offer your help by suggesting options for reaching a thwarted goal. Be prepared to use this same approach over and over again.

C-17 Developing One's Own Interests

Psychotherapy over the years has revealed some interesting insights into what people think about their jobs and how the work they do affects their happiness. Surprisingly, those with the least-demanding jobs often are the most unhappy. Invariably they have felt unfulfilled because they were doing something which did not interest them. In contrast, the people happiest in their work were pursuing strong interests. Or they were small-businessmen who in effect ran their own show. They worked long hours and seldom complained; even salary or income did not seem to be a primary consideration. Their chief concern was that they were doing what interested and excited them. They were doing their own thing; despite other problems, they were content with their work.

You can help your child avoid the boredom of work he dislikes by encouraging him to do his own thing. Nothing will make him better satisfied. Of course, first he must discover his thing. Ordinarily, most children don't receive a wide-enough exposure to determine their true interests and abilities. Exposure and participation will make the difference. One hour of skin-diving is worth more than watching a dozen films about it

It also is important to read on many subjects. This will provide a wide range of exposure your child can obtain in no other way.

You will not want to expose your child to some experiences when he is too young to appreciate them. Because his interests will alter after early childhood, you should re-expose him periodically—every two or three years—to some of his earlier experiences. Different ages will see the same thing in a different light.

In addition to your child's age, three other factors will influence his preferences and suitability for certain kinds of work: his intellectual capacity, his temperament and aptitudes. Intellectual ability determines the range of his interests and how effectively he can realize them. If your child has a modest but normal I.Q. of 95, it's not likely he'll ever become a biochemist or a nuclear physicist. Probably he wouldn't want to and it's advisable he not try. And a gifted child won't feel fulfilled by a job with routine demands.

Certain jobs require a distinct personality for optimum success. Check to be sure your child's temperament suits his expressed interests. If he's poorly coordinated, he won't be a good surgeon. If he's careless with details, he won't succeed as an engineer. If he doesn't like to listen to people, he won't like being a psychologist.

A century ago in his famous studies of genius, Francis Galton found that aptitudes tend to run in families. This doesn't mean that every son of a successful businessman is going to want to be a businessman or is guaranteed success. But it does mean that your child's life is not determined solely by his environment. Inborn aptitudes wield a hidden influence.

At times your child will want to do something for which he is not suited. Be ready for this situation. His best interests are not served by trying to prolong an inappropriate or unsuitable pursuit. As it falls apart of its own weight, move in to help your child find something else more appropriate. Help him to understand we all have to find our aptitudes in order to get the most out of life.

Patrick never was meant to be a scholar although his I.Q. is over 120. Like many bright children, he has little interest in scholastic challenges. Also, he suffers from dyslexia, a reading disability. Failures he experienced before diagnosis of his problem had led him to think he was a "failure." A stint in a private school gave him one-to-one attention. It also showed him that success was possible for him in subjects other than reading. At the same time, he began to exhibit a lot of interest in working with his hands. By age 10, he had staked out the garage as his territory. There he tinkered with anything mechanical he could lay hands on. He had a natural feeling for making or fixing things, as if he had a mechanic's or an engineer's genes.

Soon he became interested in surfing; with a little help from his parents, he was able to buy a used board. Not long afterward, he was in the garage repairing the "dings," first on his own board and almost immediately for those of his friends. By the time he was 13, he was turning out surfboards. The first was no masterpiece but, because he was fascinated with his work and derived so much pleasure from it, he quickly became a proficient surfboard manufacturer, his boards well-known, respected and sought-after.

Patrick may not be making surfboards all his life. But at this time it definitely is his thing and will remain so till he finds something more exciting and as well suited to his range of aptitudes and level of intelligence.

Too many children never have such an experience. Patrick's brother Rusty is one of them. He had better luck in school but whatever challenges he's undertaken haven't really turned him on. Now 18 and in college, he is exposing himself at the same time to new experiences through various odd jobs. But he is a little apprehensive and often talks to his father about it:

Rusty: I'm never going to find anything I really want to do. Nothing I try works out. I haven't found anything that excites me like Patrick with his surfboards.

Father: I know it's frustrating for you. But don't worry too much. First, be realistic about what you can do well and what you can't. Then keep looking to see what's available that you can enjoy and learn to do well. Just keep looking. Sooner or later, you'll find something that turns you on.

How to Help Your Child Find and Do His Own Thing

Take note of what he does well and of what his natural interests are. Then encourage and support these activities. The depth of the involvement will be one issue, the variety of interests another. Exposure is important. Praise is good but less necessary here because of the intrinsic feeling of satisfaction your child will experience when he becomes truly involved.

Get to know your child. In his early years, observe him carefully so you can judge his aptitudes well enough to help him find suitable interests. *Never try to select his thing for him; the choice must be his.* Some parents pressure their children subtly or directly to follow a certain pursuit, vocational or otherwise. Such attempts almost always backfire. Either the child fails or rebels.

Expose him to different experiences. Choose activities with either a hobby or occupational potential.

Promote more than one interest. In our culture, there are many more young people interested in art and music, for example, than society is ready to support. To earn a living and yet be fulfilled, these young talents will need a second and even a third string to their bow. Gently but insistently point out this reality to your child.

Have patience—and ask him to have patience too. Some children turn on, occupationally speaking, earlier than others. If by his late teens he still hasn't found anything that really attracts him, he might benefit from psychological or vocational counseling. Often his first fulltime job will serve as a catalyst for crystallizing his latent interests.

C-18 Problem-solving: Where It All Comes Together

Problem-solving is the essence of life. It is a requirement that is inescapable and never-ending, since life itself is one problem after another. In discussing the hierarchy of human needs, Abraham Maslow has clearly shown that, when we solve one problem, another one automatically surfaces. William Glasser has described this process from another viewpoint, saying that the business of life is getting our needs met.

As a skill, problem-solving is the pinnacle of competence. It will involve all of your child's abilities. To solve a problem, he has to have willingness to apply effort, initiative, creativity, self-reliance, flexibility and other traits of competence. The more competent he is, of course, the better problem-solver he is likely to be. The less developed he is and the fewer his inner resources, the more he will suffer failure.

To be effective, your child needs to develop a method of approaching problems. He'll need your guidance and lots of practice. Whenever you do see him wrestling with a problem, the worst thing you can do is what you'll be most sorely tempted to do—solve it for him. It's true that in our culture the overriding consideration is to solve a problem and dispose of it, rather than to upgrade the individual's problem-solving skill. But you have to bear in mind that, each time you intervene, you undermine your child's chance to develop this crucial capability for himself. Remind yourself that the most important part of almost every problem your child contends with is his willingness and ability to take it on and work it out.

Kim, 15, though she is intelligent, never has done very well at school, primarily because she never could understand how studying would do her much good. Heretofore she has coasted, daydreamed and played her way among "C" and "D" averages. Since she's not at war with her parents, we know the problem is not severe. She has just been passively resisting school.

While vacationing last week, Kim met a 15-year-old boy who was extremely high on politics, science, economics and the problems of the world. They liked each other but Kim was distressed because all she could do was listen to what he had to say. She felt stupid and desperately wished she could make an interesting contribution.

At last it has occurred to Kim that school might be of some use after all. She is acutely aware of how far behind she has fallen and takes the problem to her mother:

Kim: Mom, you know how dumb I am in social studies and practically everything else?

Mother: Dumb, no. Uninformed, yes.

Kim: Well, I'm finding I really don't like being the way I am.

Mother: I'm glad to hear that. You've been sort of indifferent.

Kim: Whatever am I going to do about it?

Mother: It will take hard work if you want to catch up.

Kim: What can I do?

Mother: Solve the problem.

Kim: I don't know how.

Mother: All I can do is tell you what I do when I have a problem. First, I either tell myself what I want to do or I write it down. Then I talk to a few people to get an idea of what other people think would be an intelligent way to proceed. I try to gather all the information I can.

Kim: Suppose different people tell you different things?

Mother: Happens all the time. I just listen to everybody. Finally, when I feel right about taking one approach or another, I start with that. But you can't expect the best solution the first time out. I rarely solve any problem without changing my tack and doing a considerable amount of trying.

Kim: Sounds too complicated for me.

Mother: Maybe I can put it more simply: Never completely discard an idea because it sounds strange—just keep your mind open while you're gathering your input. Have a reasonable attitude about things not working out at the very first try. And keep trying.

Kim: Mom, I really want to know more and be a more interesting person.

Mother: That's the very first step. You've defined the problem.

Over the next few weeks Mother remains available to help Kim accumulate necessary information. Kim runs into one hitch after another. To hire a tutor, she has to earn money babysitting. The first two tutors prove unreliable. But she keeps on, untangling each problem as it comes up. Hard as it is, Kim remains determined and hopeful about solving her problem. In the process, of course, she's on her way toward becoming a first-rate problem-solver.

How to Improve Problem-Solving Ability

Again, avoid the temptation to intervene in your child's problem. (But neither should you let him break his neck, just to make your point.) There is a wide range of problems he certainly can shoulder alone if you first *teach him the steps:*

Define the problem. Write it down if necessary.

Collect all the information you can about the situation and your possible options.

Ask other people for their opinion.

Develop a plan: don't expect it to be foolproof; be prepared to alter it.

Never stop trying.

VII   Integrity

How to Have Children with Self-respect and the Respect of Others

Building and Maintaining Self-respect

Every child needs to value himself. This is an emotional necessity. But true self-love does not materialize out of thin air. It can come only from self-respect, from knowing one behaves decently. If your child is honest and sincere, he will like himself; his self-image as a lovable, worthy person will grow.

The growth of your child's self-respect is a gradual process. Before age four or five, he has little sense of morality. Between five and seven, he still will be uncertain about your rules for decent behavior, especially the finer points, because he's relatively inexperienced. After age eight, there will be much less doubt in his mind. He will have enough experience to know the difference between behavior that is decent and considerate, and that which is not. From that point on, he will judge himself according to his own need to be a self-respecting person.

All of us judge others by the way they treat us. If a person is fair and honest with us, we value him. If he lies to us and is unfair, we dislike him and may grow to hate him. Children instinctively judge others by this standard, categorizing people as "good" or "bad." When we judge ourselves, this same standard is inescapable. Ultimately we judge ourselves by the way we treat others.

Like all of us, your child will be tempted to adopt a double standard: a loose, tolerant one for himself, and a strict, unremitting one for others. Yet, no matter how he rationalizes or excuses his own dishonest behavior, he never really fools himself.

He can easily absorb a few missteps and still live with his subconscious. But steady behavior of this kind will overload his capacity to deny. The feelings of guilt and unworthiness will provoke him into even more-blatant misbehaviors. He literally will seek out punishment to purge his guilt. Integrity refers to all those skills your child needs to build and maintain his self-respect, including both self-discipline and moral considerations. Its purpose is to help your child like himself. And it does this by training him how to cope with all the daily situations that put his self-respect on the line. But you cannot indoctrinate a child with integrity—command him to behave according to a predetermined set of rules. Rather, integrity develops through behaving in self-disciplined and decent ways.

Acquired in this substantial manner it can serve as a solid power base from which to deal with the tough issues of life. Most of all, it's a process of helping your child live by the fundamental imperative for self-love, namely that we can love and respect ourselves only to the extent that we treat others well.

Every child occasionally will misbehave due to inexperience, ignorance or downright selfishness. Although you must confront his transgressions, try not to dwell on these failings. Put your emphasis on teaching him to deal effectively with the difficult pressures and temptations he must face. In this way you will help him meet one of his basic psychological needs—the need to value and love himself. This is what integrity is all about.

TABLE V

Integrity Issues of Emotional Development

I-1 Self-control: Showing Power and Pride

I-2 Patience: Waiting Willingly

I-3 Truthfulness: To Tell the Whole Truth

I-4 Fortitude: the Power to Endure Unpleasantness

I-5 Perseverance: Seeing the Job Through

I-6 Fairness: Living by a Single Standard

I-7 Neatness: Wearing Your Self-respect

I-8 Reliability: "You Can Count on Me"

I-9 Genuineness: "I Am for Real"

I-10 Blaming: "I Didn't Do It—He Did It"

I-11 Stealing: Temptation versus Self-respect

I-12 Work: "Doing My Share"

I-13 Drugs: an Escape from Pain—and Life

I-14 Sex: Caring or Using?

I-15 Leadership: Service or Exploitation

I-1 Self-control: Showing Power and Pride

To mature, your child must develop self-control over his various impulses. He cannot succeed or relate well to others if he is continually dominated by his impulses. Behavior of this kind inevitably will lead him into conflict with others. As he experiences his inability to control himself, his self-respect will diminish.
Internalizing control will be one of the most difficult lessons for your child to master. He cannot gain self-control merely by denying or downgrading his feelings. Any real and valid feeling he denies will submerge into his subconscious only to re-emerge later as a destructive behavior. To gain healthy self-control, he needs to check the impulse to act—but still accept the feeling. He will require considerable help from you.

Pam, six, has a love for music and a fascination with her older sister Vanessa's records. To date, she has broken one and scratched several, much to the consternation of Vanessa and their mother.
The conflict is a common one: the property rights of one sibling versus the self-control of the other. Arriving home from school earlier than Vanessa, Pam has just followed her urge to invade Vanessa's room to play music. She is listening to a record when Mother interrupts:

Mother: Pam, I thought you understood the rule about not touching your sister's records.

Pam: I know but I just wanted to hear this one.

Mother: (*Stopping the record player*) **Apparently you haven't got the message yet.** (*Pam looks put upon.*) Don't look so put out. This isn't a punishment. I want it quiet so you'll be able to listen to me.

Pam: You cut off the middle, the best part.

Mother: Pam, you have to understand that this record is your sister's. If Vanessa finds you here on your own, playing her records again, she'll be very upset. I know how much you like music, this music especially. That's

perfectly normal. But you have to learn you can't always just use what you want.

Pam: It's only an old record.

Mother: There's a lot more involved here than that. You have to learn how not to do something you want to do: how not to play a record you like so much. This is Vanessa's personal property.

Pam: I'd let her hear my record if I had one.

Mother: I doubt it but that's not the point. The point is that you very much need to learn self-control.

Pam: All I want is to play one old record. Why do I need self-control?

Mother: We all need it. I have to control myself all the time. Remember the bubble bath you and I both like so much? There was just enough for one bath so I bathed without it because I was thinking about the fun you would miss in the tub tonight. I may feel bad about not having had a really relaxing bath, but I also feel good because I know I've done something for your pleasure. And I'm proud because I controlled my impulse.

Pam: You did that?

Mother: Yes, and I'll admit it wasn't easy. Self-control is always hard. But it's important if you want to respect yourself and make other people happy.

Pam: You mean it's good NOT to do something you want to do?

Mother: Yes. Sometimes. But about this record, Pam. Let me suggest this. Whenever you have an urge to hear your sister's records, come and ask me. I'll put one on for you, if I'm not busy.

Pam: O.K. Are you busy now?

Instead of reacting with the usual punishment, Mother smoothly introduces the issue of self-control and helps Pam to understand what it means: personal power and pride. Had Mother reacted by yelling at, threatening or hitting Pam, the child would have ended frustrated and alienated. But Mother makes a point of showing Pam what can be gained from self-control. The self-denial implicit in self-control is set out clearly against its positive aspects. Pam can now feel good in one way about not doing what she wants. Based on this encounter and many others like it, she'll eventually develop self-control.

How to Build Self-control

Tell your child about the need for self-control: "You can't go through life just acting on impulse. I want you to learn to control yourself." Let your child verbalize his feelings, especially any resentments. Say, "Go right ahead. I'm prepared to listen to how you feel." Then tell your child that what he is doing will have a bad effect on someone else's feelings. And tell him who that is; let the child know he has more power than he realizes to produce bad feelings in this other person.

Sympathize with your child's urge and how difficult it is to control himself: "I know. It's hard to resist the urge to hit when you're mad." "It's not easy not to do something you want so very much. But, when you have trouble controlling yourself, come to me for help."

Relate your own experience: "When I want to do something, there are many times when I have to say no to myself. I've been through the same thing you've been through. It's not easy for anybody."

Let your child know that the basic issue in self-control is his self-respect: "If you learn not to do absolutely everything you want to do, you'll feel better about yourself. Because if you do something that hurts someone, something you wouldn't want anybody to do to you, you can't like yourself, no matter what the excuse." When he shows good self-control, tell him how proud you are.

In developing your child's self-control, try to learn the feeling behind the impulsive behavior. Quite often, you can head off the behavior by encouraging him to talk to you, thus lessening the pressure on him to act out the impulse. Don't expect your child to gain instant self-control. It will take time and many patient repetitions of this process before you will see much result from your efforts.

I-2 Patience: Waiting Willingly

Patience is the ability to wait willingly for something we want very much. It is related to self-control and is equally difficult to acquire. Many people never acquire it at all. Literature's classic example of patience is Penelope, who waited 20 years for the return of her beloved Odysseus. Obviously, such steadfastness was uncommon even then and is less so now. A wait of a few minutes will provoke many people into a rage. This is especially true of young children. The sense of urgency your child experiences is a factor of the intensity of his desire.

Patience is the mark of a mature, developed person. One reason it is so hard to acquire is the old-fashioned method many people use. Trying to impose an iron will over strong instinctual cravings seldom works. A far better way to develop patience in your child is to help him become more realistic about what to expect.

Consider Josh, five, who is demanding that Father fix a toy truck. Father is busy filling out a complicated report he must finish for a business conference next day:

Josh: Daddy, fix my truck. The wheel came off.

Father: Josh, I'm sorry. I'm busy doing something awfully important just now.

Josh: But I want to play with it.

Father: I know, Josh, I know. You want me to fix it right this minute. And I'm telling you that I can't.

Josh: You mean you won't fix it for me?

Father: Josh, please pay attention to what I'm telling you. I must have this report ready for work tomorrow. It's very, very hard to do and I'm mighty worried about it.

Josh: But the truck will only take a few minutes.

Father: Yes, I know. But I simply don't have a few minutes. You can help me by playing with something else till I'm finished here.

Josh: You just don't want to fix my truck.

Father: That's not true. I want to and I will

after I've finished this report. Waiting is hard, Josh, I know. For both you and me. But I want you to do something for both of us, son.

Josh: Like what?

Father: Help me by waiting. It will show us that you're growing up. If you can wait patiently without feeling terrible about it, it will show me how strong you're growing. It will show me you really understand that sometimes I have things to do that can be very important too.

Josh: O.K. But you do promise to fix it, don't you?

Father: That's right. As soon as I finish. And I want you to know that I'm proud of you for being understanding and for being able to wait patiently. And you can be proud of yourself.

Had he obliged the boy at once, Josh's father would have sanctioned and encouraged his son's impatience, self-centeredness and unrealistic expectation that others should immediately drop whatever they are doing just to respond to his desires. As a result of this exchange and others like it, Josh will be more able to wait and will feel a little less denied and neglected. At the same time, because he is acting in a helpful, reasonable way, he can experience himself as a more worthwhile and respected person.

How to Help Your Child Wait Willingly

A good method is to *use a timer as a game device.* For children who have a severe struggle acquiring patience, such a gadget helps make time a more concrete, definite thing, thereby making patience more tangible. Waiting becomes a test of skill. For example, challenge your child to remain silent for one minute. Set the timer and see if he can do it. In almost every instance, you'll find that the child can master his impatience. He "succeeds" and feels confident and powerful. Later, increase the waiting period to two minutes, five, ten and even more. The greater the challenge, the more powerful your child will experience himself as being. To deepen his sense of power, praise him each time for his

accomplishment, both in the game and whenever else he demonstrates his patience. There will be times when your child will behave impatiently. How can you handle these situations constructively?

Recognize the urgency of his feelings. Tell your child that what he wants is causing him to feel urgency, "a feeling that it's very important for it to happen right now."

Decline his request: "I'm sorry but I can't do it for you right away." Give him a reason that focuses on what your feelings are and how your needs are more important than his from a larger viewpoint. Keep it simple and don't become defensive.

Make and keep a definite time commitment. Then tell him that his waiting with a good attitude took a lot of understanding and tolerance, traits he can feel proud of. Remember that your child's attitude toward waiting is the most important facet of patience. You can ease things by emphasizing how much time things take if you do them really well. A child is generally unaware of this. Simple information will help improve his understanding.

I-3 Truthfulness: To Tell the Whole Truth

Lying is a deliberate falsification or distortion of reality, calculated to misinform and mislead. As such it is intended to influence and manipulate the behavior of someone else. It can be a protective device to avoid discovery and punishment. The lying child invariably is trying to avoid harmful consequences or to produce unmerited benefits for himself.

Before the age of three, your child has a very limited ability to lie to you. Between three and six, you'll have trouble determining when he is lying about things or merely confused by them. After age six, he will be able to lie deliberately in order to avoid work or responsibility, protect himself from punishment or get something he wants. When he reaches adolescence, he will have still more ability to falsify.

The internal consequences of lying are

inescapable. The lying child knows that he is manipulating the opinion and behavior of those to whom he lies. He knows he's doing something fundamentally wrong; as a result, he suffers in his self-esteem. Even though he may brag about his ability to dupe others, he never can feel good about himself nor escape the knowledge that he is being dishonest. At the same time, he faces the censure of others and the loss of social credibility and acceptance.

You can help your child develop into an honest person by removing the dangers of his being open with you. This should be your goal in every situation: to create a climate of acceptance that will keep him open and honest.

Never let a falsehood pass unnoticed. Gently suggest the truth really is otherwise. Gentle confrontation in an accepting climate will help your child become and remain a truthful person.

Despite the best efforts of Jenny, seven, something always seems to go wrong. She's a little clumsy and accident-prone. Today Jenny has just reached for a cereal bowl. It slips and breaks with a resounding crash:

Mother: What happened?

Jenny: I was getting a cereal bowl down and it slipped.

Mother: What do you mean "slipped?" You dropped it. You're always dropping things because you're so damned careless. I'm tired of this sort of thing. I've had it!

Jenny: I'm sorry. I didn't mean to.

Mother: Being sorry doesn't put that bowl back together. Get to your room where you'll be out of my way. I've got enough work to do without your making more.

Next day, Mother hears the crash of a glass. Jenny has done it again:

Mother: Now what have you done?

Jenny: (*Frightened by the tone of her mother's voice*) I don't know.

Mother: You don't know? You're standing right beside a broken glass.

Jenny: I was watching television and didn't see what happened. Maybe the cat knocked it over.

Mother: And maybe you're a liar, Jenny. Next time, I'll be watching you like a hawk. If I've told you once, I've told you a dozen times: I don't want you to take drinking glasses into this den. Now clean up that mess.

A week later, Mother goes into the bathroom and finds water on the floor. Playing there earlier with their bubble pipes, Jenny and her brother Kent have left the water running:

Mother: All right, children. Which one of you left the water running?

Jenny: I didn't do it.

Kent: I didn't, either.

Mother: One of you is lying. If I can't find out who did it, you'll both get a spanking. Now tell the truth—who did it?

After several minutes of threats and accusation, Mother still cannot pin the blame for the bathroom flood. Jenny knows it's her fault but she's not about to open up and be punished. She knows that in her house it's not safe to be open and honest. Being so afraid of her mother, Jenny opts for survival. As a result, she's becoming a deceitful, evasive person.

Raised with a great deal of strictness, Jenny's mother firmly believes that children are naturally inclined toward "evil" and must be disciplined for their misdeeds. In her mind, the principal function of a parent is to administer punishment. Her intentions are sincere—she really wants to raise children with good character. But her methods are destructive. They are driving Jenny and Kent into a protective shell. The children are becoming more and more convinced that their parents (the father is also a severe disciplinarian) are "the enemy." Faced with anger, scolding and physical threats, the two children instinctively resort to lying and elaborate evasions in order to survive.

The problem could be mitigated if Jenny's mother had a better understanding and tolerance of her children's mistakes. But she is unable to cope in a constructive way and—even worse—she has created a climate in which lying is the only "safe" alternative. How might Jenny's mother have handled the little girl's clumsiness?

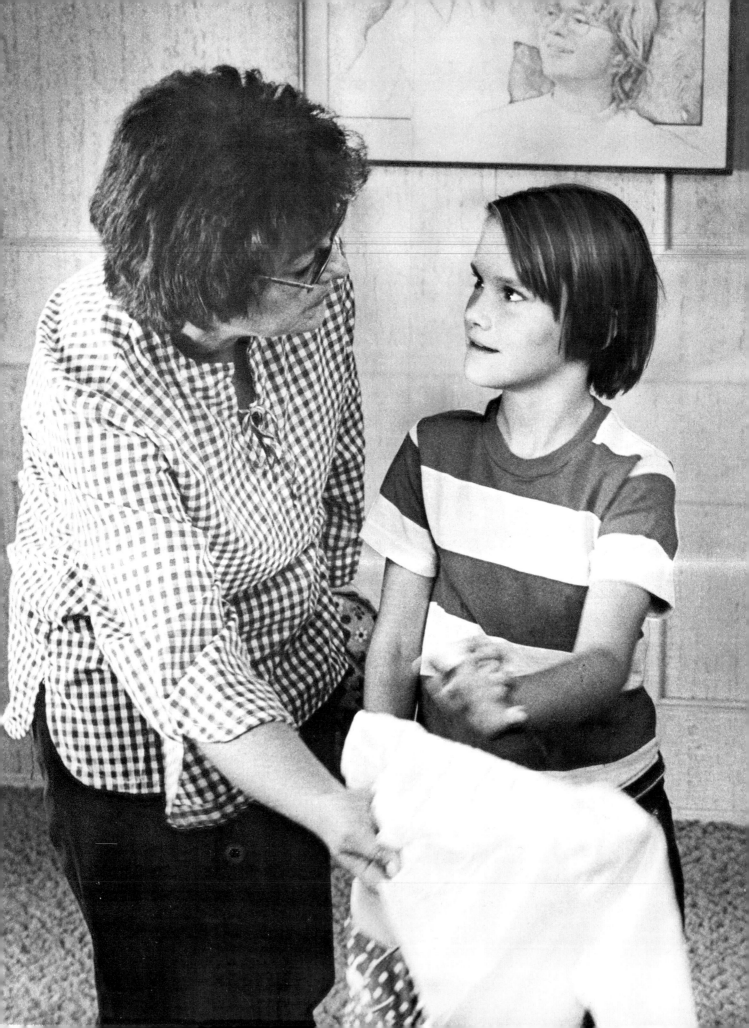

Mother: What happened, dear?

Jenny: I guess I broke something.

Mother: Things like that will happen. Don't worry about it. But do me a favor, please. I'd feel better if you'd promise to try harder to be careful in the house and not break things.

Jenny: O.K. I'll try to be more careful.

This less strident approach should not be confused with permissiveness, which can be almost as destructive as being overly punitive. Here Jenny's clumsiness is met with acceptance and faced with gentle confrontation; both are then followed by a serious request for more-careful performance. It is the tactic of a parent who understands certain basic realities about children:

Children tend to be clumsy till they become better coordinated.

Children can become so keenly involved with whatever interests them at the moment that they accidentally break things or knock them over.

Becoming so engrossed also causes children to forget peripheral things like turning off the water. Much reminding will be necessary.

All children try to avoid punishment and many do so at the expense of being honest. They would prefer to tell the truth if they can do so with safety.

How to Increase Truthfulness

Creating a climate in which your child can be open and honest with you is crucial to his development. When it becomes dangerous for him to admit to you how he feels or has behaved, gradually he loses his awareness because of the protective devices of distortion and denial. He begins to experience things not as he truly feels them but as he perceives it "safe" to feel them. He begins to shade the truth, deny responsibility and look upon himself as a perpetually innocent, falsely accused bystander.

He lives and functions within the narrow confines of a double shell. The outer shell protects him from the dangers posed by his parents; the inner shell walls him off from the anxiety of his own true feelings and experience. Cast adrift in a hostile environment, without any connection with himself or reality, he in time becomes an emotional isolate, a chronically defensive liar.

How can you sidestep this pitfall without falling into the trap of permissiveness? Or, put another way, how can you foster your child's openness and honesty in the face of his tendency to lie his way out of punishment?

The answer can be found in taking a long-range view of your child's development 10 to 20 years from now. With such a goal in mind, everyday mistakes and mishaps will seem a little less earth-shaking. Once you accept your child for the fallible creature he is, you can set about helping him become more responsible, and more honest.

When your child admits something he's done wrong, tell him you admire and respect his honesty. Also tell him you appreciate having his trust, and that you want to keep it.

Point out the value of truthfulness. Ask your child what he thinks he did wrong. Remind him that the basic issue is his self-respect. A person who lies cannot like himself. A person who tells the truth will like himself and feel proud.

When you believe he is lying:

Gently tell him. Say you find it hard to believe him.

Acknowledge that you know he wishes what he says is true.

Tell him that you want to hear the truth. Then explain that everyone makes mistakes. Add that he won't feel good about himself if he knows he isn't telling the truth.

Make it clear your main interest is not punishment, that you want his trust so you can solve problems together.

I-4 Fortitude: the Power to Endure Unpleasantness

Your child needs fortitude if he is to mature. Otherwise, he will be intimidated by the prospect of any unpleasantness, and will tend to become passive and escapist.

It is normal for any child to want to evade

both tedium and pain. There are two different philosophies your child can formulate about the discomfort associated with these everyday challenges. One is the notion that he can pass through life without having to cope with any unpleasantness; this belief is wishful thinking and represents the most common resistance to Emotional Maturity. A more realistic attitude is the acknowledgement that unpleasantness, like death and taxes, is certain. It's the price we all have to pay for the good feelings we get in life. Fortunately, the "ecstasy is worth the agony."

Sammy, nine, just missed the school bus by two minutes. It is 7:40 a.m. as he returns home:

Mother: I thought you left for school?

Sammy: I missed the bus by two minutes.

Mother: Then why didn't you walk?

Sammy: I would have been late.

Mother: That's better than missing the whole day.

Sammy: Fourteen blocks is too far to walk.

Mother: Not for someone who is willing to put up with a little discomfort.

Sammy: It's too cold out today.

Mother: Not that cold.

Sammy: It's too cold for me.

Mother: Sammy, are you proud of yourself?

Sammy: Don't blame me.

Mother: In my opinion, you've just given me a poor reason for not going to school, just to try to escape a little unpleasantness. I don't see how you can have much self-respect if you're going to chicken out so fast when life gets a bit tough. I'm going to sit down and write a note explaining that you missed the bus. So get into your coat again, and off to school you go. I want you to act in a way we both can be proud of.

Sammy is glad to have gone off to school. Instead of shame, he feels self-respect. He is coping with life head-on instead of running away.

Betsy is six. Her mother took her to the dentist for a filling. As Betsy was about to be X-rayed, she hopped out of the chair and ran screaming from the dental office. At home, Mother is now confronting Betsy, who refuses to go back:

Mother: Betsy, I'm sorry about what happened at the dentist's.

Betsy: (Distrustful of polite approaches) You aren't going to get me to go back there.

Mother: I realize now I didn't fully prepare you for what to expect.

Betsy: I knew what to expect. My friend Johanna went to the dentist, and she told me how much it hurt.

Mother: Yes, there's going to be some pain. But not so much that you won't be able to bear it. The dentist is going to rub some painkiller on your gums. Then he is going to give you a shot of more painkiller. That will still hurt a little for a minute. But what you and I have to deal with right now is your big fear of a little pain.

Betsy: O.K., so I'm afraid. But I'm not going back!

Mother: Betsy, this toothache you have is going to get worse if it isn't treated. It will hurt a lot worse than what can happen at the dentist's.

Betsy: But, Momma, I'm scared.

Mother: This time I'll be right at your side and never leave you for a minute.

Betsy: Well, if you promise to stay with me . . .

How to Increase Fortitude

Fortitude combines a measure of courage, strength of purpose and plain grit. Generally you can help your child develop these qualities by your own example, and by encouraging him as early as possible to undertake challenges involving pain and difficulty. Through advance preparation, you can make things a little easier and help your child be more willing to face up to pain and unpleasantness. Whenever you can anticipate his apprehension, explain or describe to him what he is going to undergo. A simple and matter-of-fact approach will reduce excessive imaginings.

Do not allow your child's escapism. When he dodges or balks at the prospect of difficulty, unpleasantness or pain, say, "You don't want to face the fact that you have to put up with some painful things in life." Telling him that you have to cope with pain and adversity and that you don't like it any more than he does will emphasize you're both in the same boat. This will reduce some of your child's antagonism toward you for facing him into something disagreeable. *Remind him that by being brave he will increase both his self-respect and your admiration of him.*

I-5 Perseverance: Seeing the Job Through

All of us know the difficulties, distractions and drudgeries which can be part of finishing some effort. We know how compromise, procrastination and discouragement often keep us from accomplishing our goals. Your child faces these same obstacles. To him, because he is not yet emotionally strong, they seem greatly magnified. Whether he's doing a puzzle, building a model or playing chess with a friend, he tends to become quickly discouraged and upset at the first sign of difficulty.

Perseverance is the determination to maintain one's efforts until an obstacle is overcome. As such, it combines endurance with patience and tenacity. It means being willing and able to tolerate difficulty and perhaps pain in order to achieve a certain goal. Some children are constitutionally more inclined to this kind of tenacity. But every child can improve.

Unless he has perseverance, your child will end without any accomplishments; his self-image as a productive, effective person will suffer. You can help him primarily by your example, and with assistance and advice as needed. If you put him off when he needs help, he's likely to give up in the face of difficulty. If he knows, you are backing him, he's more apt to approach problems with a sense of hope and optimism. Then, once he's experienced some of his own accomplishments, he'll realize that he has the determination to finish a project he starts.

Andy, eight, made a contract with his father to pull all the weeds in the front yard. After working about 10 minutes, Andy now just sits and watches cars go by:

Father: How's it going?

Andy: Oh, I'm tired.

Father: Tell me about it.

Andy: Well, at first it was kinda fun. But then it got more like work. I just didn't feel like doing it any more. It's a drag.

Father: Hard work, huh?

Andy: Yeah.

Father: Even so, I want you to finish it. We have an agreement and I'll be disappointed if you don't carry out your end of it.

Andy: But it's a drag!

Father: I know, Andy. Work is like that. Sometimes it's fun but lots of times it isn't. Still, we have to stick to it. Do you remember the day I fixed your Flexie?

Andy: Yeah. Last week.

Father: You wrecked it so badly it was very hard to fix. I had a tough time getting the wheel back on. I was mad enough to quit. But I knew you were counting on me.

Andy: But, Dad, I'm already tired out today.

Father: I was tired, too. If I gave up so easily, you wouldn't have a Flexie to ride. How would you have liked that?

Andy: I wouldn't.

Father: So how do you think I'll feel if you don't finish pulling the weeds?

Andy: You said you'd be disappointed.

Father: And so will you. Nobody likes a quitter, especially the quitter himself. When you've rested, go finish up.

Andy: O.K. I'll try again.

Father: Good. I'm proud of you for sticking to it.

Father gently prods Andy to finish the job by confronting his son's readiness to give up and by bringing up his own efforts on the boy's behalf. Father doesn't overplay his hand by insisting Andy return. Father understands every child has a deep wish to finish things and accomplish goals; therefore, he emphasizes the benefits Andy's perseverance will have for both of them.

How to Improve Perseverance

When your child is not seeing a job through to its conclusion, confront him. Remind him how often you have to persevere, especially on his behalf. (Obviously, it's vital that this be the case. If you habitually cop out, he'll know it and your argument will fall flat.) Remind your child it's natural to want to quit: "Everybody is tempted to give up when things get hard. I know I am, sometimes." Raise the issue of self-respect, and how copping out will affect it. Say you know he really wants to accomplish what he's set out to do, and will feel better about himself if he finishes.

You may need to give him a half-time pep talk. Quite often a youngster will become thoroughly discouraged halfway through. And it's especially true of children in competition. Whether it's checkers or soccer, if he's lagging behind he'll tend to give up in the face of an outcome that looks dim. You will need to encourage your child to persevere even when results don't seem very glowing. You will have to emphasize the importance of finishing as well as that of winning. By persevering, he gains valuable strength to help him improve future performance. Without perseverance, he'll remain inadequate.

I-6 Fairness: Living by a Single Standard

Your child has a very acute sense of justice which he shows by his rebellion against anything he thinks unfair. You hear it every day: "His piece is bigger than mine." "How come I have to go to bed and she can stay up?" "You always make me pick up my dishes after dinner. Why don't you make Nick pick up his?"

Fairness means acting in accordance with The Golden Rule—treating others as you would wish they would treat you. To your child, fair treatment offers assurance that he won't be the victim of discrimination. But children are more eager to get fair treatment than they are to give it. They incline toward a double standard, demanding fairness for themselves but allowing less of it to others. Like other maladaptive behavior, this takes its toll. Invariably, the child who acts this way denies his awareness of what he's doing. Or he invents an elaborate set of excuses and rationalizations for his behavior. Consciously or not, he knows he's acting inconsistently with the standards he values. He cannot like himself for treating another person in a way he himself would not want to be treated.

Lynn, eight, customarily plays with the dolls, toys and books belonging to her little sister Hope. When the situation is reversed, Lynn becomes quite agitated. Today Lynn has just plucked her own favorite doll from the arms of Hope, who is crying as Mother enters:

Mother: What's going on?

Lynn: Hope did it again. She was playing with my favorite doll. So I took it back.

Mother: Were you trying to make her cry?

Lynn: No. But she deserves to cry. When she plays with anything of mine, she breaks it. I just don't want her touching my things.

Hope: But you always play with mine.

Lynn: That's different. I'm careful.

Mother: That may be true. But do you think it's fair to Hope?

Lynn: As long as I don't break anything.

Mother: That's how you look at it. How do you think your sister sees it? Does that seem fair to her?

Lynn: I don't know.

Mother: Let's look at this thing for a minute. You and I realize you're more careful than your sister. But I don't think Hope is ready to recognize that. All she understands is that, if you play with her things, she ought to be able to play with yours.

Lynn: But I'm very careful. And she's careless.

Mother: But we're talking about the issue as Hope is able to see it. And she sees you taking over all her things without ever giving her a chance at yours. Now, is that fair?

Lynn: I think so.

Mother: Then, you have a double standard.

Lynn: What's that?

Mother: It means you have two standards. You give yourself the right to do things that you won't let her do. To be fair, there can be only one standard for everybody.

Lynn: Oh.

Mother: In this case, the single standard would say that you two either play with each other's things, or you each play only with your own.

Lynn: *(Not liking it, but seeing the point)* All right. I don't want her touching my things, so I won't touch hers any more.

Mother: You can try that for a while and we'll see how it works. Hope, do you understand the rule? Lynn won't play with your things any more. And you won't play with hers.

Hope: O.K.

In this encounter, Mother focuses Lynn's attention on the little girl's self-serving double standard. When Lynn tries to rationalize her behavior, Mother questions the excuse. Then, she confronts Lynn with her unfairness. In this way, Lynn is made aware of her inconsistency. Although she will need many more such confrontations before she learns to act fairly, one important step has been taken and for the time being Lynn's drift toward habitual unfair behavior has been slowed.

How to Foster Fairness

Ask yourself how fair you are with your children. Do you enforce rules equally, being alert to and guarding against favoritism? Fairness should govern your actions as well as your child's.

Question his behavior. Point out the discrepancy. If he is confused or doesn't understand, ask him if he is treating the other child (usually a sibling) in the way he likes to be treated: "If I did this to you, would you like it?" Then, ask your child if he believes in fair play. Ordinarily, he will say yes. This mostly means he thinks *he* should be treated fairly, although he's theoretically committed to a belief in fair play. Ask him again, "Do you believe there should be fairness for one person, or for everyone?" He will have to say, "For everyone." Confront him with his inconsistency, the discrepancy between his belief in fairness and his unfair behavior. Appeal to your child's ability to work out a more mature solution to the problem: "If there's something that seems unfair, let's see what we can do to make it right."

I-7 Neatness: Wearing Your Self-respect

One of the crosses parents bear is that of trying to keep their children clean and reasonably tidy. It can be exhausting work, physically and emotionally. Your child will eat with dirty hands, go to school with uncombed hair and wear his clothes for a week unless you strip them from his back. The cute little fellow who clutters up the family room with his block forts and then walks off and leaves them for you to trip over will in just a few years be concealing his room under a layer of dirty T-shirts, old underwear and last week's sweat socks. When you try to do something about it, he will fight you tenaciously every step of the way, day in and day out.

Usually he attaches no real importance to being neat and clean. In an older child, a preference for squalor can be a rebellion against growing up; it may demonstrate a lack of personal pride, an unwillingness to face the few rigors and the self-discipline involved.

With either the older or the young child, the foremost issue here is self-respect. If he likes himself, he will take care of himself. If he doesn't, he won't. He may even try to sanctify his dirty jeans and unwashed hair by representing them as a "value," a "different life-style." Don't buy this. Wearing jeans and long hair can be a value if they are kept clean. Anything less is an affront to the human spirit, not to mention to health standards. The same applies to littering. The solution is continuing confrontation.

Nick, nine, has just finished an after-school snack and is about to leave behind him a kitchen table littered with dirty dishes and orange peels. Mother, who has steadfastly refused to let Nick get away with his littering and lack of neatness, intercepts him as he is about to exit:

Mother: Just a minute before you leave, Nick. Did you forget something?

Nick: I'm in a hurry. Randy will be waiting.

Mother: You're trying to slip out, aren't you?

Nick: Aw, just this once, Mother, won't you clean up after me? Please?

Mother: No. You've slipped up a couple of other times lately, and I didn't mention them to you at the time. That was enough.

Nick: But I want to go out and play.

Mother: I know. So do I. Instead, I'm going to stay here in a hot kitchen and make dinner for you.

Nick: I'll clean everything up when I get back.

Mother: Then I'd have to look at this unsightly mess all the time you're gone. I won't buy it. You're inconsiderate. Don't I do things I don't really want to do—like cleaning, cooking, doing the laundry?

Nick: Oh, sure. I guess so.

Mother: You know I do, Nick. And I willingly do those not-so-fascinating things because I care about you. How do you show you care?

Nick: I care.

Mother: Then how do you show it?

Nick: (*Starts to clean off the table.*)

Ordinarily, laziness prompts children to leave things lying about. They tend to spend energy only for fun and for getting their immediate needs met. Once the need is satisfied, cleaning up doesn't seem to matter.

This is precisely Nick's problem. But Mother doesn't let him escape. She shows him how she faces unpleasantness for his sake, and challenges him to face some for her. This same kind of confrontation can work for you.

How to Upgrade Neatness

Enforce the law that things must be picked up or put away when not in use. *Confront your child gently about his littering. Do not accept evasiveness,* such as "I have to leave," "It was already a mess," or, "Something else is more important right now."

Role-reversal can help him see the point. If he insists that he doesn't care about your feelings, ask him if he wants you to care about his. Usually he will reply that he does, unless he is lying as a further elaborated evasion. Say that you know he wants you to care about his feelings but that you aren't convinced he cares much about yours. Depending upon what applies, tell him he is unkind, unfair, inconsistent or self-centered, and that he cannot possibly like himself. Say you don't respect him and that you feel sorry for him because he shows that he doesn't respect himself very much. Lean heavily on him by showing your irritation and low opinion of his poor behavior. The same kinds of confrontation can be used to foster his personal cleanliness. The underlying reasons are identical: either he is lazy or is not much aware of your feelings. Don't permit yourself to be sidetracked by smoke screens. The core issue is his pride and self-respect, not the length of his hair nor the fact that he wants to go around in jeans, T-shirt and sandals. As long as he keeps them and himself clean, he's entitled to wear the fashions of his generation.

I-8 Reliability: "You Can Count on Me"

One of the simplest ways to define good character is: the ability to make and keep commitments. Most children find it hard to make a commitment and even more difficult to keep one. When your child can't commit himself, his inability will undermine his self-respect.

In today's moral climate there is a prevailing reticence, if not aversion, about commitments. They are seen as a "hassle," a "bummer" or "too heavy." Despite this attitude, the dependable, committed person is more highly valued than ever in the face of this trend toward noncommitment. Reliability—making and keeping commitments—is not a matter of vogue. It is one of the cornerstones in building self-esteem. It is synonymous with performance. A reliable person can be counted on in a pinch and trusted to meet his obligations. He is not a slave to obligation but understands that his value as a person is involved. And he knows that someone else's feelings are involved in the matter, too. For this reason, he's an extremely desirable person to have around.

Angel, 12, has been asked by her mother to babysit younger brothers aged three and five. Angel agreed to look after them and the house while Mother shopped at the supermarket. It's an hour later and Mother has just returned to find the boys missing. She also notices a stove burner turned on. All the while, Angel had been talking on the phone to a school friend. After some anxious moments, the boys turn up in a neighbor's yard. Now, Mother turns her attention to Angel's unreliable behavior:

Mother: Angel, would you say you're the kind of person who can be counted on?

Angel: But everything is all right now and the kids are O.K. They were only up the street.

Mother: But you had no way of knowing that they were just up the street and all right, did you?

Angel: They're so hard to keep track of.

Mohter: Of course they are. That's why they were your special job—for one hour.

Angel: I'll watch them closer next time.

Mother: I certainly hope so. But it bothers me that you act as if nothing much went wrong. I want to talk about it.

Angel: You're making something too big out of it.

Mother: That's not true. It *is* big. Has it ever occurred to you that your brothers might have been hurt while you were neglecting them?

Angel: I . . . suppose.

Mother: Or that, with the stove left on, there might have been a fire?

Angel: But there wasn't.

Mother: There wasn't because I came home in time to turn off the burner. I can see you're not admitting what you did—or, rather—what you didn't do—because you think I'm attacking you personally.

Angel: Well, aren't you?

Mother: No. It's your reliability I'm concerned about. You're just not dependable enough to take on the little job I gave you. I feel let down, disappointed. Today I overestimated you, and I feel rotten about it. How do you feel?

Angel: Sorry.

Mother: I'm sure you had good intentions. But that isn't enough. You fail to see the possibilities of your undependability. The boys could be in the hospital. The house could be in ashes.

Angel: Now you're making me feel bad.

Mother: If it helps you wake up, then it won't hurt you to feel bad for a while. It may help you learn the importance of keeping commitments.

Even though this confrontation—like any other—is painful, Angel is fortunate. Her mother knows that Angel's character will be undermined if such unreliable behavior goes unnoticed and unchecked. Her mother's supportive attitude makes the difference between Angel's listening to her mother instead of becoming defensively entrenched.

How to Encourage Dependable Behavior

Giving your child responsibility and freedom to function are crucial for developing his reliability. You must let him take risks and help him overcome his mistakes:
Praise him when he behaves dependably.

Be dependable in the way you deal with him. If you make him a commitment, be sure to keep it. Our children are more likely to do as we do than as we ask or tell them to do.

Oppose any lack of dependability. Don't let any broken commitment go by without comment. Your child may regard your silence as tacit approval of his irresponsible behavior. Instead, in a serious but supportive way, inquire into his understanding of the bad feelings he's caused, the possible harm to people or property and, especially, the damage to his budding self-esteem. Ask your child if his behavior is the kind that makes him feel proud or ashamed.

Adjust your expectations to his present ability to deliver. Ask your child if he feels you expect too much of him. If he does and you concur, adjust your expectations more closely to his demonstrated level of reliability. Perhaps you have been expecting a little too much.

If you are concerned about the risks involved when allowing increased freedom, ask yourself these questions:

Is he aware of the major risks, and can he tell you what they are?

Is this only a small increase in the amount of freedom he has been responsible for before?

Will you feel reasonably at ease about his exercising this new freedom?

Does his request seem based more on his own strivings than upon some external pressure?

Will he give you a definite commitment about the extent of his participation and the time of his return?

Does his request correspond reasonably well with what you have seen done responsibly by other children with his maturity level?

The more affirmatives, the more reason you have to allow his request for additional freedom.

I-9 Genuineness: "I Am for Real"

In our age of image-making, promotional gimmicks and the exaggerations of advertising, it's refreshing to meet someone who is genuine and sincere, a person who just tells it like it is. With such an individual, you don't have to be on guard; you don't have to discount what he says in order to get at the truth. You know exactly who he is, what he stands for and just how much you can count on him. More than anything else, you appreciate his essential honesty.

Genuineness is a mixture of spontaneity, openness and honesty. It means being sincere rather than phony. Most of all, it means showing yourself to others as you really are—blemishes and all, no false facade, no dissembling, no hiding behind the pretense of superiority. Because a genuine person is in touch with his feelings, he will have no truck with pretensions of any sort. He doesn't have a hidden agenda or scheme. Neither is he a Pollyanna nor an incompetent hiding behind good intentions. He is a person who knows and values what he is and openly shares himself with others. All the things you do to make your child feel good about himself play a part in helping him become a genuine, sincere person. Recognition, frequent praise, a positive atmosphere, plus support for overcoming his limitations—all these help to build the foundation of self-esteem that makes such genuineness possible. Although some children are more or less naturally inclined to be genuine, every child has a very high potential.

Ian, 12, is on his way to becoming a con man. He's tricky. He knows how to make other people feel appreciated and important, no matter how he feels about them. Ian has just returned home from his latest exploit:

Ian: Dad, you know that newspaper route I got last week?

Father: Yes. I was very proud of you for going out and getting it.

Ian: Yeah. Well, I found out it's more work than I thought. But now I've got a way to take care of that. Do you remember Alan, the guy who was over here a couple of times?

Father: Vaguely.

Ian: Alan's not too bright. He sort of

186

believes everything you lay on him. I told him how smart he is and how much I like having him for a friend. Alan got so turned on, he's delivering the papers for me. And he thinks he's got a good deal!

Father: What is the deal?

Ian: I get 35¢ a month for each house. I give Alan 15¢ and keep the difference for setting up the deal.

Father: But he could get his own route and keep the full 35¢.

Ian: Sure he could. But he doesn't know that.

Father: In other words, you're telling me that you lied, flattered and cheated him.

Ian: Well, he doesn't look at it that way.

Father: Ian, do you think of yourself as being sincere—an honest person?

Ian: I'm not hurting anybody. And Alan thinks he's doing great.

Father: I'm not interested in Alan and what he thinks about you, but what you think about yourself.

Ian: To tell you the truth, I think I'm pretty smart.

Father: We both know that. But I'm talking about honesty and sincerity. When you told Alan he was smart, did you really believe it?

Ian: No way. I mean, he's O.K. but—

Father: How would you like it if I gave you a big line and conned you into something? Would you respect me or trust me?

Ian: Nobody trusts a con artist. I wouldn't like it and I wouldn't stand for it. But what has this got to do with Alan?

Father: Ian, didn't you con Alan?

Ian: Yeah, I guess maybe I did, in a way.

Father: Do you still think you're a great guy, sincere and honest?

Ian: I just thought I had a good thing going.

Father: But how do you feel about it now? Can you really respect yourself for what you did to Alan?

Ian: I guess not. But I didn't think about it like that till now.

Father: Not consciously, maybe. Underneath, though, you knew all along that you were being a phony.

Ian: Well, you've made me see it now. And you're not making me feel very good.

Father: I'm glad. There's nothing wrong with trying to get ahead. But you pay the price of your own self-respect if you're insincere and try to exploit other people. It's not worth the price. I'm glad your bad feeling about yourself has surfaced, instead of being buried.

How to Encourage Your Child to be Genuine

The more you show your child that you appreciate his spontaneity, naturalness and sincerity, the more genuine he can become. Using all the developmental techniques that contribute to his good self-image—particularly acceptance, approval and affection—will help develop the inner strength and image he needs in order to keep the genuineness he was born with. Your own genuineness is vital. So is confrontation when he begins to put on airs.

To deal with your child's pretensions: Tell him whenever he is exaggerating, dissembling or being pretentious. Ask him if he's aware of what he is doing, and if it's deliberate. If he admits to the latter, inquire what he was trying to prove. Ask him what his object was.

Tell him his behavior caused bad feelings in other people. Find out what he thinks of phoniness in other people. Inquire if he's proud of himself for what he did. End by asking, "How can you like and respect yourself when you do such things?"

I-10 Blaming: "I Didn't Do It, He Did It"

Blaming usually is caused by your child's fear of punishment. He imagines it's worth the loss of respect he suffers by telling a lie. As his loving guide, you know better. Blaming is very much like projection. In both cases, your child is trying to get rid of some unwanted feeling. In projection, he is trying to assign the cause of failure elsewhere. In blaming, he is trying to assign his guilt to another person. Both are forms of externalization. There is, however, a notable difference between them. In projection, your child is unaware at the conscious level of the true cause of his failure. As he interprets it, some external factor caused him to fail. Such is not usually the case in blaming. That's why the distinction must be made. Blaming is fully conscious.

When your child tries to pin somebody else with the blame of his own misdeed, he almost always is lying and very well knows the truth. In projection, you first have to make him aware of his motivation. In blaming, the awareness already exists. Your task is to make your child feel secure enough with you so he can afford to admit his guilt. Help your child understand how blaming undermines his self-respect. When you confront him, try to avoid calling him "bad." Labeling him will tend to confirm his fear that he is not an acceptable person. It's best to deal with his evasiveness for what it truly is, a symptom of his insecurity with you.

Justin, 11 and bored, has gravitated to where his two younger brothers are at play. Tad and Ty have been erecting a large and elaborate "boat" of blocks. Justin interferes, angering his brothers by knocking over the blocks. When Tad throws a block in retaliation, Justin hits him and the screaming begins. Mother rushes to the scene:

Mother: Who started the fighting?

Justin: Tad did.

Ty: Justin started it. He knocked our boat over.

Mother: Just a minute, and one at a time. *(Mother proceeds to question each boy until she has a pretty accurate picture of what took place.)* Justin, why did you do it?

Justin: Because he threw a block at me.

Mother: That's not what I'm talking about. Why did you blame Tad for starting it?

Justin: Tad's lying. I didn't do anything. I just touched him, and he says I hit him.

Mother: Justin, we all do wrong things from time to time. But I'm concerned because you knew you were at fault all along and still you made it worse by blaming

somebody else. It wouldn't hurt you to admit you behaved badly. I'll have much more respect for you if you admit you are wrong. You'll feel bad for a little while but you'll feel better in the long run. Did you blame Tad because you thought I'd punish you?

Justin: Yeah. I guess so.

Mother: Do you think I should?

Justin: I don't know.

Mother: Would you feel good if Tad blamed you for something he did?

Justin: No, I wouldn't.

How to Change Blaming to Admitting

Create an open climate in which there is little fear of being honest and owning up to misdeeds.

When you think your child is blaming: Determine the facts. They won't be easy to nail down. Do the best you can. When you are sure you have correct information, directly confront the blaming.

Ask your child how he expected to benefit from his blaming. Because blaming so often is a conscious process, he will probably have a ready excuse. Gently disagree with his evasion. Say, "Were you afraid I'd punish you?" Then, deal with his fear of you by telling him that punishment concerns you less than more important considerations, such as his treating others with kindness and consideration. Also, say you want him to feel safe enough to be truthful with you. Last but most of all, you wish him to understand he can keep his self-respect only by admitting he has done wrong.

I-11 Stealing: Temptation Versus Self-respect

Young children have very inadequate concepts of what property rights are and what stealing means. These concepts are beyond a small child's intellectual understanding and his limited life experiences. To your child's mind, everything interesting should be available for his own use. His first understanding of property rights may come when he is asked to share toys with another child. His fear of losing a favorite truck or teddy bear teaches him the concept of who owns what.

The notion of stealing comes later, after the mental age of five or six has been attained. By this time, the child can understand what stealing is and what its implications are. A child who steals at this age is prompted by uncontrolled desire or the belief that he's not getting something he deserves or needs. In middle childhood and adolescence, stealing is usually motivated by envy of another child or by anger over parental neglect. In some cases, it can be a form of revenge against someone who has hurt him— a way to hurt them by depriving them of something they enjoy. Sometimes, of course, an adolescent steals in order to win the acceptance of a gang.

Stealing is socially destructive. It undermines the meaning of another person's honest work. Even worse, it is destructive to the thief himself. No matter how he rationalizes or excuses his stealing, he suffers from feelings of guilt and a severe loss of self-esteem. In the end, he will dislike himself intensely. As he steals material things, he literally robs himself psychologically of his self-respect.

Amy, aged nine, has been at the corner drugstore where she saw a 25¢ ring that appealed to her. She slipped it into her jeans and sauntered out the front door, pretending innocence. Just outside the door, the assistant manager caught up with her. He didn't call the police over such petty pilfering but he did call Amy's mother. Now it's reckoning time back home:

Mother: Why did you take that ring?

Amy: Are you mad at me?

Mother: Damn right I am. But I haven't decided how to punish you.

Amy: I won't do it again.

Mother: What else have you stolen?

Amy: Well, just a few little things, like rings. But the store has lots of them. I'm sure nobody would miss them.

Mother: If I thought it would do any good, I'd spank you. I don't know what to do with

you. But you should be punished.

Amy: I won't do it again.

Mother: I wish I could believe you.

Mother is expressing her inability to understand Amy, who is simply trying to avoid punishment. But the deeper problem goes unstated and thus neglected. As a result, Amy is likely to steal again.

Neither parent is aware of the fact that Amy feels emotionally deprived and isolated. Her father, a manufacturer's rep who is on the road most of the time, is a virtual stranger. Mother is busy with three younger children; she never really has been able to establish a close relationship with Amy. Like many parents, Mother deals with her child at a surface level, responding only to the child's physical needs.

Lacking the close relationship she needs and wants, and unable to confide her basic concerns, Amy feels completely left out of her family. Daily, Amy's sense of deprivation grows, a deep feeling of social isolation. She feels no one understands her. This is true. Psychologically, nobody even knows her. With such an emotional background, Amy is vulnerable to temptation. The ring becomes an attractive, albeit extremely poor substitute for the better relationship she wants with her mother. Feeling emotionally deprived as she does, Amy is almost inexorably programmed to steal. Until her sense of deprivation is dealt with and diminished, she probably will continue to relieve her bad feelings by petty thievery. Since Amy hasn't much human involvement, she feels she hasn't much to lose.

What could Mother do about Amy?

Mother: What would you say if somebody stole a shell from the beautiful collection you like so much? Would it be O.K. to take one from you just because you have so many?

Amy: But that would be different.

Mother: Stealing's stealing. I'm sure you wouldn't like it if somebody stole from you.

Amy: I won't do it any more, I promise.

Mother: Promises don't seem to be the answer, Amy. For one thing, happy people don't steal. So I assume you haven't been happy.

Amy: Oh, I guess I've been all right.

Mother: Does that mean you've been feeling good?

Amy: Well, not right now.

Mother: Do you think you can talk to me about the things that bother you?

Amy: How can I, when you're always busy with the other kids or keeping house? You never have much time. And Daddy never is around.

Mother: I agree. You feel I've neglected you in the past, and you're right. It's no wonder you feel lonely and deprived. That's one problem. But the second problem is that you're stealing things.

Amy: I'm not as bad as some of the kids. You should see the things they do.

Mother: Do you admire those other kids?

Amy: Well, I wouldn't trust them in my room.

Mother: When you steal something, do you think of yourself as a nice, decent person?

Amy: No, not really.

Mother: You can't steal and still feel like a friend to yourself. Everyone has to like himself, has to think of himself as a good person who deserves fair treatment and respect.

Amy: What difference does it make how I feel about myself, if no one pays any attention to me? Being lonely feels just as bad as worrying about stealing.

Mother: I think you and I need to spend time together like this every day, so you won't be lonely. When you feel my love more, Amy, you'll be less tempted to take things.

How to Discourage Stealing

The surest way to prevent your child from stealing is to head off the emotional neglect that causes it. This means giving the attention, acceptance, approval and affection he needs. Your objective: to prevent him from developing a sense of deprivation.

When your child steals, use this method: Establish the facts. Be sure a theft really has occurred and that your child is responsible. If this cannot be determined with almost complete certainty, wait for a time when it can.

Determine the cause. Tell your child he stole for a reason, and you want to know what it is. If he can't tell you, offer your own opinion, Say, "Your inner self is telling you that life is bad. You feel you deserve to take something that will make you feel better." Point out the emotional price of stealing: "The good feelings produced by stealing don't last. And, because you know you did something wrong, you really end up feeling bad about yourself—worse than before. You lose your own self-respect and can't like yourself. That's a terribly high price."

I-12 Work: "Doing My Share"

Work is necessary for your child's emotional well-being. It pays emotional bonuses which often outweigh the actual financial rewards. Even if it's only a minor chore around the home, work is the most impressive way your child can satisfy his need to feel useful and productive. Without it, he cannot realize his full potential nor become, as he must, independent and self-sufficient. His self-image as a capable and contributing person depends upon work.

The difficulty is that many American children have little or no concept of work's value. This is not surprising. For years, the average child is relatively isolated in educational institutions which keep him from the world of work; consequently, useful work and its rewards are largely alien to his daily experience. For the most part, he simply doesn't know how the work of other people contributes to his own welfare.

All of this feeds the child's tendency to be unmotivated; ultimately, it plays havoc with his self-image, leading to a series of misperceptions about life and work. He assumes, because he's experienced nothing else, that his needs will always be met without any effort on his part. This notion is a serious miscalculation, inevitably colliding with the hard realities of life and leaving the child surprised, disappointed and confused. Meanwhile, without any concept of work as a personal necessity and fulfillment, the child opts for the uncertain comforts of idleness. Even here, he can't escape. His own aversion to work merely heightens his feelings of guilt about living off the efforts of others. He loses self-respect.

You can help counteract this situation by making him aware of what you and others do for his benefit. Once he is old enough, insist he do useful work within the family circle or—more impressive to him—at a part-time job. This will help him develop a realistic attitude about the necessity for work, plus an appreciation of its satisfactions. One of these is the feeling of being useful. Another is an improved self-image.

Boyd is 12 and energetic, always on the go doing things that interest him. His self-centeredness blinds him to the feelings and needs of others. He balks at any work not directly related to what he wants for himself. The family has just finished dinner. Boyd is on his way out the door:

Mother: Wait a minute, Boyd. Where do you think you're going?

Boyd: To play basketball with Dino.

Mother: Get back here and take out the trash.

Boyd: I'm in a hurry.

Mother: So hurry and take the trash out.

Boyd: You're always finding something for me to do.

Mother: And you're always making work for me to do. Do you think it's fair that everybody but you in this family works hard? You're not carrying your share of the load.

Boyd: You're always complaining.

Mother: Does it make you feel good about yourself to know other people have to do your work?

Boyd: I do it sometimes.

Mother: Sometimes isn't enough. You can't respect yourself if you're fair only sometimes.

Boyd: All right, all right. I'm taking the trash out.

Mother: That's fine. Now, show me you understand and appreciate what others do for you. I want you to make a commitment to pitch in and help around here on a regular basis.

Boyd: What do you want me to do?

Mother: Take the trash out every day without being told. When you pull your own weight without having to be yelled at, then I'll be impressed.

Mother's effort in this episode is part of a long-term campaign to help Boyd develop some understanding of the necessity for work—and, eventually, of its value. She simply could have insisted Boyd take out the trash and let it go at that. Instead, she uses the incident as a chance to raise his awareness of the benefits he receives from others and of his own failure to reciprocate. By appealing to his self-respect and sense of fairness, she has him make a commitment to useful work on a regular basis.

At the same time, Mother is realistic about the commitment. She realizes that one encounter is not sufficient to develop Boyd's character. She also knows it's better to teach Boyd this lesson early than for him to learn it from the harsh realities he will face in later life.

How to Increase the Willingness to Work

Recognize and praise your child's efforts. *Start your child when he is relatively young.* The four-year-old who wants to vacuum the den is telling you that he's ready for work. The result won't be a professional job but the value to his self-image will be immeasurable. The eventual outcome in terms of responsibility and willingness to work will be well worth the few minutes you take to show him how to use the vacuum cleaner.

Invite your young child to see many activities as fun rather than as work. Don't discourage his interest even if it means you'll be slowed down a little. *Because he'll appreciate your companionship, the work you do together will be more enjoyable.*

If your child rebels against work, don't

hesitate to point out how the work of others benefits him. If he's given a job to do and shows hesitance—as though he's being put upon—offer to work along with him. When he puts forth a reasonably good effort, show your respect and appreciation for his contribution.

I-13 Drugs: an Escape from Pain—and Life

Today, every parent is concerned with the problem of drugs. It's difficult to avoid because our adult society is so alcohol- and pill-prone. Modern science, along with ages-old alcohol, has almost conspired to make the fairy tale come true: Swallow the magic potion and immediately you will feel and look better. The assortment of chemicals we put into our bodies has become a modern form of the witch doctor's magic. Our children quickly catch the message. After watching thousands of TV commercials promising "instant relief" at the popping of a pill, is it any wonder that many children who feel neglected or unloved should turn to drugs for relief from their sadness or loneliness?

Drugs can be a chemical crutch, an attempt to escape from unpleasant reality. This escapism is epitomized in the phrase "happy hour." The drawback is that chemicals can never change outer reality; they only alter the user's perception of it. His problems still are waiting for him when happy hour is over and the drug effect wears off.

You can help your child stay free of the escapism of drugs by strengthening his ability to cope with trying and unpleasant situations. At the same time, be sure that he is also developing a strong positive self-image. A child who respects himself is unlikely to become an addict. A child who has a negative self-image is a likely candidate for drug addiction or alcoholism.

Even under the best of circumstances, children like to experiment. It is best to react calmly. You can be more effective if you emphasize the underlying issues and calmly discuss what the perils are. If your own example is not exemplary—if you drink, smoke or rely on tranquilizers—you will not be 100% convincing.

When trying to establish the underlying reasons for drug use, ask yourself:
• Is your child sensitive and shy—a loner?
• Does he have insufficient constructive or active interests?
• Is he doing poorly in school?
• Is he subject to a great deal of peer pressure?
• Might he be feeling neglected and rebellious toward you?

How to Deal with Drug Use

The best way to deal with your child's drug abuse is to prevent its happening. Start in early to build a robust, healthy self-image. This means plenty of one-to-one time and special attention to his fortitude. All that has been said previously about challenge, effort, constructive activities, coping, perseverance and problem-solving apply here. But your effort, your taking the time will make the deciding difference. As will your example. *Before your child is 10, explain the worst thing about drugs:* They retard the development of self-reliance and the courage to tolerate discomfort and uncertainty. Point out that, in your opinion, drug use distinguishes the weakling coward from the brave. If you've been giving your child plenty of one-to-one time, you'll have his attention and he will listen to you seriously.

Teach him the effects of drug use. Tell him the use of drugs would change the person he is: "As soon as you add a chemical to your body, you change. You don't feel the same. You don't think the same as you did before. Somebody who keeps on adding these chemicals to his body may never be able to return to being the same person he used to be." Be specific about the harmful effects of drugs:
• Weakened judgment
• Further inability to cope
• Loss of self-respect because of becoming drug-dependent

Ask your child the reason for his drug use. Don't accept such superficial answers as, "My friend insisted," "Everybody else was doing it," "It won't hurt you," or, "I just wanted to try it."

194

Find out the true facts and then confront him whenever he uses drugs. Stress all the hazards involved. If your child is susceptible to drug use, ask him how you can help him with the underlying problem. Then, work closely on solving it together.

Don't delay seeking professional help. If the drug-use problem doesn't show steady improvement, admit your limitations and seek professional assistance. When the relationship between you and your child is improved, the drug use will lessen or stop.

I-14 Sex: Caring or Using?

Sex questions children ask pose a problem for every parent. How much to tell, whether to delay until the child is older or to tell him now, whether to be completely honest about your own sentiments—these problems are faced by every parent. Since your true sentiments will be revealed, it's wisest to be open and direct about your own personal views and values regarding sex. If you start early being candid with your child, you will find that—even as differences of opinion may develop—the openness to discussion of the issues will remain a permanent part of the parent-child relationship. Even if he disagrees with you, he still will respect you and your viewpoint. He will always appreciate your willingness to listen as well as his easy access to your honest opinions. Many misconceptions can be prevented by his being able to obtain his information and attitudes from you, rather than by being forced to rely on his inexperienced and misinformed peers.

For children, sex can be very perplexing and troublesome. Because of so much ignorance, and differing attitudes about sex, a child can undergo a lot of difficulty and embarrassment just trying to assemble the basic facts. Even sex education, with its penchant for anatomy charts and films about menstruation and VD, often neglects the essential human dimension—mutual caring. By itself, when only an instrument of pleasure, sex invariably is incomplete and involves exploitation. Men have used women only for pleasure. And women have used sex as a coin of exchange with which to exploit and dominate men. Neither posture is honest, healthy nor likely to be emotionally fulfilling.

Mature sex is more than a game. It touches our most intimate feelings of self-worth. In its best sense, it is the ultimate in acceptance, affection and affirmation. As such, mutual caring is an essential ingredient. It elevates the relationship to an affirmation of each other's worth. If there is no caring, a kind of emotional rape takes place. The Lothario who pursues his own pleasure while only professing to care robs his partner of her self-esteem. His falseness, when revealed, shatters her sense of personal worthiness at the deepest, most intimate level.

As your child approaches puberty, you will want to help him develop a positive attitude toward sex. That attitude involves one basic issue—learning to use sex in a caring rather than exploitative way. Be sure your child understands the importance of caring in relation to sex. Explain the emotional hazards—the loss of self-respect and esteem—that go with using someone else for one's own sexual pleasure. On the other hand, teach your child to know when he is being exploited sexually and when not. If he doesn't understand this, he may be destined for some very real heartbreaks.

Gabrielle, 16, is typically obsessed with boys. Recently she broke through her shyness and apprehension to make friends with Cal, whom she met in history class. Gaby's parents were pleased that she brought Cal home so they could meet him. They took a liking to the boy because he is friendly and easy to have around. Yet they are aware they don't know his true character and intentions. Neither does Gabrielle.

On a Saturday morning, her mother notices Gaby in a pensive mood:

Mother: A penny for your thoughts?

Gaby: I was thinking about the party last night.

Mother: Did you have a good time?

Gaby: Yes . . .

Mother: Yes, but what?

Gaby: But, Mom, how do you know if a boy really likes you?

Mother: By the way he treats you.

Gaby: How can you be sure that it's you he likes, and not what you're doing together? Do you know what I mean?

Mother: I think so. Sometimes that's hard to figure out, especially when you're 16.

Gaby: Just how do you tell?

Mother: Are you worried about what you did?

Gaby: Not about what we did. But about the way he feels about me.

Mother: Would it embarrass you to tell me what you were doing?

Gaby: Not really. They put the lights out and we were kissing . . . well, for a long time.

Mother: Is he the first boy you've ever kissed?

Gaby: Sort of. Do you think it was wrong?

Mother: Only if somebody's feelings get hurt.

Gaby: How can kissing hurt anybody? I think it's great.

Mother: Then, what are you worried about?

Gaby: Well, suppose he doesn't really like me? Suppose he's just pretending so he can get it on with me?

Mother: Is that what you think?

Gaby: I don't know. I just wonder if he really likes me. I like Cal so much, yet I really don't know a lot about him. Is it love, when you like to be with someone so much?

Mother: It's one of the signs, Gaby, but you can't be sure this early. It takes time to know.

Gaby: I just wish there were some way I could be sure he's sincere.

Mother: Usually you can tell by the way a boy treats you. If he's grabby, doesn't care about how you feel, or is in a hurry to get it on, then chances are he's not very much interested in you as a person. If he's patient and considerate, if he enjoys talking to you as well as touching you, he probably cares about you.

Gaby: I really hope he cares about me.

Mother: There's no way to make someone care a lot about you, whether he's sincere or not. That's something that just happens. So try not to worry about it. Just be careful your friends don't pressure you into something you don't feel you want to do.

Gaby: What do you mean?

Mother: When the lights went out last night, wasn't that a message to the couples to get more intimately involved?

Gaby: I guess so. I didn't think much about it at the time. But I guess you're probably right. Everybody else was getting physical.

Mother: That's what I mean. In a situation like that, your friends may be pushing you toward more physical intimacy than is called for so soon.

Gaby: I'm really happy I have you to talk to. None of my friends can talk to their mothers. It's always a hassle.

Mother: I'm glad, too, Gaby, Trying to sort out the difference between sex and love is hard to do, especially when you're young. And it's an important thing to know.

Gaby: It's sure hard, though.

Mother: It just takes time to see the difference. Where do you think you stand with Cal now?

Gaby: It's just going to take time for us to be really sure how we feel about each other. There's no way to rush it.

That same Saturday, one partygoer is not discussing last night with his parents. They really wouldn't want to hear about it anyway. Every now and then, they have made some fleeting remark to him about not making a girl pregnant or catching VD. But they have never talked to Chet about the issue of boys and girls caring about each other. It makes them too nervous—they really don't know what to say. Ironically, this under-advised young man is now counseling his friend Cal.

Chet: Did you see the fox I brought to the party last night?

Cal: Yeah. How did it go?

Chet: All the way, man! Out of sight! How

194

about you and Gaby?

Cal: Not that much. But she seems to like me . . . I think we could have gone as far as I wanted.

Chet: You mean you didn't want to?

Cal: Sure, I did. But—she likes me more than I think I like her.

Chet: Then why not make the most of it?

Cal: Gaby's a really sincere and serious person, Chet.

Chet: So she's got class. So much the better.

Cal: Chet, to you a girl is—well, like having another dish of ice cream. But Gaby has made me stop and think. I can see she has a lot of feeling for me.

Chet: Listen, girls like to get it on, too, you know.

Cal: But I think there's more to it than that.

Chet: What are you trying to say?

Cal: Suppose she likes me a lot, and we go all the way. Then, she's probably going to think I like her as much as she likes me. But I'm really not all that sure how I feel about Gaby yet.

Chet: You sure make a lot of problems for yourself, don't you?

Cal: If a serious girl like Gaby thinks that I care about her that much, she could fall in love with me. And, if I'm not in love with her, she's going to get hurt.

Chet: She'll get over it. So enjoy, enjoy.

Cal: You don't understand. I don't want to treat somebody badly. Even if Gaby wants to, I don't think I should do it if I don't really care.

Chet: But it's not that big a deal. Besides, you said you like her.

Cal: I respect the kind of person she is but I'm not sure yet that I'm all that excited about her. She's easy to be with, like a good friend. But I don't want her to think I'm completely stoked on her and then have her get hurt.

Despite the self-centered sexual attitudes advocated by friend and confidant Chet, Cal sees there's more to sex than just sex.

How to Talk About Sex

Remember how important your attitude is when you are discussing sex with your child. Your child will regard sex as normal and from an early age will ask you questions about it. The more honest you are from the start, the more likely it is that he'll continue to confide in you and seek your guidance. Always convey a positive attitude, one that recognizes sex as a natural and loving human activity.

In response to his questions, make available to him material at his appropriate age level. Some books you will find useful are:

Answers to Questions Children Ask About Love, Sex and Babies, Leokum Arkady, Grosset and Dunlap, New York, 1974.

The Sex Handbook: Information and Help for Minors, Heidi and Peter Handman, G. P. Putnam and Sons, New York, 1974.

Your Child and Sex: a Guide for Parents, Wardell B. Pomeroy, Delacorte Press, New York, 1974.

Don't try to hide the facts. It's best that he find them out from you and not from some sandlot acquaintance. Remember, the most important "fact of life" is the degree of genuine liking between the two people involved. Clarify the difference between sex and love. New and exciting, both often happen to young people at the same time. Explain to your child how very difficult it is to sort out the difference between the two feelings, which can confuse an experienced person, let alone a child in or approaching the early teens. Tell your child that sex is not love and love is not sex, and sex alone without a deep liking for the other person becomes very boring. But when there is sex with someone you love, the attraction and the mutual caring can last forever. And this really is what everybody is looking for. *Raise the issues of caring and exploitation.* Mention that both boys and girls are capable of fooling themselves about how they really feel. They also have to contend with the problem of whether each partner in a relationship is genuinely cared for or being used sexually. A girl sometimes will bestow sexual favors to keep the attention of a boy whom she really doesn't care about too much in order to prove to herself that she is appealing. A boy sometimes will deliberately mislead a girl who likes him and cause her to think he likes her more than he does in order to enjoy physical intimacy with her. This is dishonest and disrespectful. Point out that in each case the exploiter will suffer personal guilt.

Give your child guidelines for his protection, ways for gauging the sincerity of friends. For instance, if a boy is too eager and physical, a girl should know that, no matter what he says to the contrary, his foremost interest probably is himself and his own pleasure. And if a girl is too easy and complaisant or a bit too eager, a boy can be reasonably sure that she may have some motive other than a personal liking for him.

I-15 Leadership: Service or Exploitation

Many parents fall into the trap of categorizing their child as either a leader or a follower. If you label your child as a follower, you may in effect be writing off his aptitude for potential leadership. This can be a disservice to him, since research in the classroom has shown that the age of readiness for acquiring leadership skills usually lies between seven and eight. It was found that almost every child has leadership ability; the main requirement for its emergence is the opportunity to lead at his age of readiness.

This research (Harold Bessell and Uvaldo H. Palomares, *Methods in Human Development, Theory Manual;* Human Development Training Institute, La Mesa, California, 1973) has dispelled the myth of the so-called "born leader." Rarely, however, are children given the opportunity for leadership at an early age. What typically happens is that they aren't offered leadership opportunity till many years after they are ready for it. Then children are beyond their optimal time and this aptitude has diminished. In those classrooms where the

Human Development Program or a similar program is used, the child is likely to be offered a chance to lead at the age of readiness. And in those homes where the parents are aware of this potential the child is likely to have some leadership role in family affairs.

There are two kinds of leadership, diametrically opposed: service and exploitive. The first is characteristic of the dedicated leader who gives of himself to benefit his fellow man. The second characterizes the exploitive leader who is self-seeking, self-centered and self-serving. With this distinction in mind, it is wise to consider ways for your child to develop as a service-oriented leader:

• Recognize his leadership potential when it surfaces around age seven to eight.
• Teach him the concept that genuine leadership means serving others, not himself.
• Give him actual experience in performing a leadership role within the family.

Barry, nine, had two full years of the Human Development Program during the second and third grades. His parents have some familiarity with the program and wish him to practice service-oriented leadership at home as well as at school.

Dinner is over, and his parents have begun talking about Father's two-week vacation, coming up next month. Each family member has a dream vacation, including Valerie, aged 12:

Mother: Have you all been thinking about our vacation trip?

Barry: Yeah. I want to go fishing.

Father: I want to play golf. Shall we fight about it, Barry, or would you like a chance to lead the discussion?

Barry: I want to be the leader.

Mother: Is that O.K. with Valerie?

Valerie: Only if he does a good job and lets us tell him afterwards what we think of how he did.

Barry: O.K. I will. And I promise to let everybody talk.

Father: Well, I sure would like to be able to play golf every day.

Valerie: I want to see the Grand Canyon.

Barry: How about you, Mom?

Mother: I just don't want any cooking or laundry. That will be my vacation.

Barry: I really would like to fish but I wouldn't be able to on a golf course or at the Grand Canyon. It looks to me like someone's going to be dissatisfied.

Valerie: Looks like you're going to bomb out, brother. How you gonna solve this?

Father: I don't say I have to play golf every single day.

Valerie: And I guess I don't have to spend every day at the Grand Canyon.

Barry: Who has a good idea so everyone will at least get some of what he wants?

Mother: I saw an ad for a place that claims to have something for the whole family. It's in western Colorado, not too far from the Grand Canyon. How many days of driving would that be?

Father: Not more than two each way—and that's my limit for 16 days off. Does this place have a golf course?

Mother: Yes. And fishing is only an hour away.

Valerie: What would I do there?

Mother: Well, you could swim and hike. And we might put in a day or two at the Grand Canyon.

Valerie: Sounds like a winner.

Barry: Is there anyone not happy about this plan? Then, it's all settled.

Father: I have no complaints—how do the rest of you think Barry did?

Mother: You're an excellent leader, Barry.

Valerie: You're O.K. You let everybody say what he wanted. And you helped us to find a good solution.

The time is four years later. Barry, who has been experiencing and delivering service-oriented leadership since the third grade, knows the difference between service and exploitation. He is now 13, as is Biff, who recently moved into the neighborhood. Biff is an experienced baseball player. Because of his ability and aggressiveness, Biff was spontaneously chosen to captain the newly formed neighborhood team before anyone had a chance to know his character. He has been making the most of it in a subconscious effort to bolster his sagging ego. Biff needs all the reassurance he can get but until now no one ever has discussed this issue with him. Barry loves baseball and doesn't hate Biff but he has had to hear the team's complaints about the newcomer's self-serving ways. Barry understands what Biff's ego problem is and is determined to save the situation if he can. The team has just played its third game of the season:

Barry: Biff, can you come over to my house for awhile?

Biff: Sure. Say, how about that home run I hit in the top of the sixth?

Barry: (*Wanting to give Biff some reassurance, yet not wishing to endorse the idea that acceptance can come only through grand-slam performance*) We're lucky to have you on our side, all right.

Biff: I had that pitcher psyched from the first ball he threw.

Barry: (*Wishing to change the subject tactfully*) I wish I could read pitchers the way you can . . . You know, Biff, I'm kind of interested in what you think is the difference between a good captain and a bad one.

Biff: (*Defensively*) Has anybody been complaining about me?

Barry: Yes, and that's what I want to talk to you about.

Biff: What's the gripe? We've won every game.

Barry: Oh, everybody likes that part.

Biff: Sure they do. Winning is what counts.

Barry: Well, your attitude is coming across to the guys as, "Win with Biff—that's all that matters." I agree it's fine to win. But it's just as important that we all have a good time and like one another.

Biff: The guys are ungrateful. They don't appreciate me.

Barry: Another complaint is that you've been the only one to pitch. So you get to play more than anybody else.

Biff: Well, who can pitch better than me?

Barry: Maybe nobody. But Ned and Rob are pretty good.

Biff: Maybe. But why take an outside chance?

Barry: The trouble is that, to the other guys, the game is baseball. To you, it's Biffball. You hit first, you pitch, you pick the time, the place, the teams we play and the line-up. You make all the decisions. It's like everybody else exists just to make you look good. What's in it for the rest of the guys?

Biff: They're on the winning team. What more do they want?

Barry: Biff, if you keep making all the decisions yourself, you're not going to have a team. Or any friends, either.

Biff: (*A bit stung by the truth*) Do you think it's that serious? You mean the guys might quit the team? Or dump me?

Barry: If you're willing to let them share in the decisions and play more, I think we still may get it to hang together.

Biff: Yeah. That makes sense. Maybe I'll try it.

Despite Barry's best efforts at friendly confrontation, two weeks later the team does fall apart. The narrow, self-seeking habits to which Biff is accustomed have become too deeply entrenched. Nothing short of psychotherapy will provide Biff with enough sustained confrontation and guidance to convert his self-defeating patterns to more mature ways of getting his needs met.

How to Foster Service-oriented Leadership

Recognize your child's leadership potential at his age of readiness (about age eight). Let him begin by leading discussions in which he is the moderator. Teach him to seek and hear out the view of each participant. Show him how to try to develop some kind of consensus. In advance, have him agree to listen to and accept a critique of his leadership. Insist that all criticism must include his strong points and not just his limitations. This will give him the feedback he needs for improvement.

To avoid his exploitation of other people:

Tell your child that a leader has been given a trust and should serve the interests of others. Discuss the emotional hazards of exploitive leadership.

Tell your child that some leaders exploit passive, frightened or inexperienced followers. Tell him these leaders would dislike being treated in the way they treat others, and would never respect the person who treated them so badly. Therefore, it's inevitable that exploitive leaders must dislike themselves. (This may surprise your child, since leaders who misuse people are experts at hiding their self-loathing from themselves and others.) Praise your child's sincere efforts. Let him know you recognize and respect him for a service-oriented approach to leadership whenever he shows this kind of self-respecting, mature behavior.

Epilogue

This book is a call to action. It presents a plan, a blueprint to help you raise an emotionally mature child. But like every plan, it needs implementation. You are the key. Your consistent use of these methods and concepts, your tenacity and devotion are vital to the outcome. It won't be easy. There will be days when you'll feel deeply discouraged. But you can be assured that parents who are using these methods and concepts are getting good results.

In the years ahead, Emotional Maturity will take its deserved place as one of the basic concerns and goals of child-rearing. We are all going to come to realize what psychotherapists already know, namely that many of society's problems and inadequacies stem directly from our individual and collective emotional immaturities. Once this happens, the institutions that deal with children and their well-being will begin to foster Emotional Maturity with the attention and resources it deserves.

In the meantime, you have a role to play. You play it every day in your encounters with your child. By using the methods and ideas suggested in these pages, you can give your child a precious heritage—the inner strength of Emotional Maturity. And despite the difficulties and effort involved, in those brief, fleeting years you will build a loving relationship with your children that will last a lifetime.

A Selected Bibliography of Theoretical and Research References

The principal author would like to give reference and to express appreciation to those who have contributed most notably through theory or research to the present construction of what he believes to be a comprehensive system of emotional maturation. The system draws considerably from three of the major theories of personality, the Freudian, Skinnerian and Gestalt, and to a lesser degree from the Rogerian and Transactional Analysis. From the Freudian school has been drawn the mechanisms of defense as elucidated by Sigmund and Anna Freud, and most especially from the neo-Freudian contributions of Adler, Sullivan and Horney. If there is one most powerful influence it is Karen Horney, especially for her work, *Neurosis and Human Growth,* in which she gives an outstanding description of how the self-concept functions.

From the Skinnerian or Pavlovian school has come the simple, yet impressive and effective concept of reinforcement, or in lay terms, reward or praise. From the Gestalt school as presented by Fritz Perls have come the simple, but very useful devices of role-reversal and role-playing. Through Carl Rogers, Eric Berne and Thomas Harris have come the emphasis on the fundamental human need for acceptance.

Many, many others have contributed, and only a partial list can be given. All have helped to make this book possible, what we believe is a simple and organized scheme, one that can give any parent of the young child a map to the territory of emotional maturation, and the few core methods necessary to assure that it can become a reality for their child.

ADLER, Alfred, *Understanding Human Nature,* Fawcett Publications, Inc., Greenwich, Connecticut, 1965.

ARKADY, Leokum, *Answers to Questions Children Ask About Love, Sex and Babies,* Grosset and Dunlap, New York, 1974.

AXLINE, Virginia Mae, *Play Therapy,* Houghton Mifflin Company, Riverside Press, Cambridge, Massachusetts, 1947.

BARUCH, Dorothy Walter, *New Ways in Discipline,* McGraw-Hill Book Company, Inc., New York, 1949.

BERLO, David K., *The Process of Communication,* Holt, Rinehart, and Winston, New York, 1960.

BERNE, Eric, *Transactional Analysis in Psycho Therapy,* Grove Press, New York, 1961.

BESSELL, H. and PALOMARES, U.H., *Methods in Human Development, Theory Manual,* Human Development Training Institute, La Mesa, California, 1973.

BLOOM, B.S., *Stability and Change in Human Characteristics,* John Wiley and Sons, Inc., New York, 1964.

BLOOM, B.S., *Taxonomy of Educational Objectives, Handbook No. 2,* "Affective Domain," David McKay Co., Inc., New York, 1956.

BRAYFIELD, Arthur H., "Human Effectiveness," *American Psychologist,* pp. 645-65, 1965.

BRIDGES, Katherine, *Social and Emotional Development of the Pre-School Child,* Kegan Paul, London, 1931.

BRILL, A.A., *The Basic Writings of Sigmund Freud,* Random House, Inc., New York, 1938.

CAPLAN, Gerald, *Principles of Preventive Psychiatry,* Basic Books, Inc., New York, 1964.

CRUTCHFIELD, Richard, "Conformity and Character," *American Psychologist,* X, pp. 191-198, 1955.

DOBZHANSKY, Theodosius, *Mankind Evolving,* Yale University Press, New Haven, 1962.

ERIKSON, Erik H., *Childhood and Society,* W.W. Norton and Co., Inc., New York, 1950.

FENICHEL, Otto, *The Psychoanalytic Theory of Neurosis,* W.W. Norton and Co., Inc., New York, 1945.

FREUD, Anna, *The Ego and the Mechanisms of Defense,* Hogarth Press, London, 1937.

FREUD, Sigmund, *The Ego and the Id,* Norton, New York, 1961.

GESELL, Arnold, and ILG, Frances L., *The Child from Five to Ten,* Harper and Row, New York, 1946.

GESELL, Arnold, et. al., *The First Five Years of Life: A Guide to the Study of the Preschool Child,* Harper and Brothers, New York, 1940.

GLASSER, W., *Reality Therapy,* Harper and Row, New York, 1965.

HANDMAN, Heidi and Peter, *The Sex Handbook: Information and Help for Minors,* G.P. Putnam and Son, New York, 1974.

HARRIS, Thomas A., *I'm OK You're OK—A Practical Guide to Transactional Analysis,* Harper and Row, New York, 1963.

HOLT, John, *How Children Fail,* Dell Publishing Company, Inc., New York, 1965.

HORNEY, Karen, *Neurosis and Human Growth,* W.W. Norton, New York, 1950.

ILG, Frances, L., M.D. and AMES, Louise Bates, Ph.D., *Child and Behavior,* Harper and Brothers, New York, 1955.

ISAACS, Susan, *Social Development in Young Children,* Routledge and Kegan Paul, Ltd., London, 1933.

LE BOYER, Frederick, *Birth Without Violence,* Alfred A. Knopf, New York, 1975.

LORENZ, Konrad, *Evolution and Modification of Behavior,* University of Chicago Press, Chicago, 1965.

MAZZANTI, V.E. and BESSELL, H., "Communication Through the Latent Language, *American Journal of Psychotherapy,* Vol. X, No. 2, pp. 250-260, April, 1956.

MONTAGU, Ashely, *The Biosocial Nature of Man,* Grove Press, Inc., New York, 1956.

MONTESSORI, Maria, *The Secret of Childhood*, Orient Longmans, Bombay, Calcutta, Madras, New Delhi, 1962.

PERLS, Fritz, *Gestalt Therapy Verbatim*, Bantam Books, New York, 1969

POMEROY, Wardell B., *Your Child and Sex: A Guide for Parents*, Delacorte Press, New York, 1974.

RAPAPORT, David, *On the Psychoanalytic Theory of Motivation: A Systematizing Attempt*, University of Nebraska Press, Lincoln, Nebraska, 1960.

ROGERS, Carl R. *Client Centered Therapy*, Houghton Mifflin, Cambridge, Massachusetts, 1959.

RUESCH, Jurgen, M.D., *Therapeutic Communication*, W.W. Norton and Company, Inc., New York, 1961.

SCHRAMM, Wilbur, et al., *The Science of Human Communication*, Basic Books, Inc., New York, 1963.

SCHUTZ, William C., *A Three-Dimensional Theory of Interpersonal Behavior*, Holt, Rinehart, and Winston, New York, 1960.

SKINNER, B.F., and FERSTER, Charles B., *Schedules of Reinforcement*, Appleton-Century Crofts, New York, 1957.

STONE, L. Joseph, and CHURCH, Joseph, *Childhood and Adolescence*, Random House, New York, 1957.

SULLIVAN, Harry Stack, *Conceptions of Modern Psychiatry*, 2nd edition, William Alanson White Psychiatric Foundation, Washington, D.C.

SULLIVAN, Harry Stack, *The Interpersonal Theory of Psychiatry*, W.W. Norton and Company, Inc., New York, 1953.

SZASZ, Thomas S., M.D., *The Myth of Mental Illness*, Hoeber-Harper Book, New York, 1964.

VAN DER BERG, J.H., *The Changing Nature of Man*, Del Publishing Co., Inc., New York

WATSON, Robert I., *The Great Psychologists from Aristotle to Freud*, J.B. Lippincott Company, New York, 1963.

WHITE, Burton L., *The First Three Years of Life*, Prentice-Hall, Englewood Cliffs, New Jersey, 1975.

WHITE, R.W., "Motivation Reconsidered: The Concept of Competence," *Psychological Review*, pp. 66, 297-333, 1959.

WHITE, R.W., "Ego and Reality in Psychoanalytic Theory," *Psychological Issues*, 1963.

WOODWORTH, Robert S., and SHEEHAN, Mary R., *Contemporary Schools of Psychology*, The Ronald Press Company, New York, 1964.

Suggested Children's Literature

The following list of stories give dramatic presentations of the various emotional issues of development presented in the System.

A-2   GEORGE AND MARTHA (story #1), James Marshall; Houghton Mifflin Co., Boston, 1972.

A-3   ERIC AND MATILDA, Mischa Richter; Harper & Row, New York, 1967.

A-6   THE LITTLE HOUSE, Virginia Burton; Houghton Mifflin Co., Boston, 1952.

A-7   PETUNIA, BEWARE!, Roger Duvoisin, Knopf, New York, 1950.

A-8   YOU'RE THE SCAREDY CAT, Mercer Mayer; Parents' Magazine Press, New York, 1974.

A-10   THE THREE FUNNY FRIENDS, Charlotte Zolotow, Harper & Row, New York, 1961.

A-12   YOU LOOK RIDICULOUS, Bernard Waber, Houghton Mifflin Co., Boston, 1966.

A-14   THE DOG WHO THOUGHT HE WAS A BOY, Cora Annett; Houghton Mifflin Co., Boston, 1965.

     WHY CAN'T I BE WILLIAM?, Ellen Conford; Little Brown & Co., Boston, 1972.

A-15   A SPECIAL TRICK, Mercer Mayer; Dial Press, Inc., New York, 1970.

A-16   WHERE THE WILD THINGS ARE, Maurice Sendak; Harper & Row, New York, 1963.

A-17   PETUNIA, Roger Duvoisin; Knopf, New York, 1950.

A-18   IN THE NIGHT KITCHEN, Maurice Sendak; Harper & Row, New York, 1970.

R-1   GEORGE AND MARTHA (story #4), James Marshall; Houghton Mifflin Co., Boston.

R-2   BEDTIME FOR FRANCES, Russell Hoban; Thomas Y. Crowell Co., New York, 1975.

R-3   GEORGE AND MARTHA (story #2), James Marshall; Houghton Mifflin Co., Boston, 1972.

R-4   THE MILLER, HIS SON AND THEIR DONKEY, Roger Duvoisin, McGraw-Hill, New York, 1962.

R-5   GEORGE AND MARTHA (story #5), James Marshall; Houghton Mifflin Co., Boston, 1972.

R-6   DINNER AT ALBERTO'S, Russell Hoban; Thomas Y. Crowell Co., New York, 1975.

R-7   I WONDER IF HERBIE'S HOME YET, Mildred Kantrowitz; Parents' Magazine Press, New York, 1971.

R-8   PETUNIA, I LOVE YOU, Roger Duvoisin; Knopf, New York, 1965.

R-9   THE MILLER, HIS SON AND THEIR DONKEY, Roger Duvoisin; McGraw-Hill, New York, 1962.

R-11   FINDERS' KEEPERS', William Lipkind & Nicolas Mordvinoff; Harcourt, Brace & World, New York, 1951.

R-15   I AM BETTER THAN YOU, Robert Lopshire; Harper & Row, New York, 1968.

     I DON'T LIKE TIMMY, Joan Hanson; Carolrhoda Books, Inc., Minneapolis, 1972.

R-16   HARVEY'S HIDEOUT, Russell Hoban; Parents' Magazine Press, New York, 1969.

R-17   THE HATING BOOK, Charlotte Zolotow; Harper & Row, New York, 1969.

     BEST FRIENDS, Myra Brown; Golden Gate Junior Books, San Carlos, California, 1967.

     I'M NOT OSCAR'S FRIEND ANY MORE, Marjorie Sharmat; E. P. Dutton & Co., New York, 1975.

R-18   THE WHITE MARBLE, Charlotte Zolotow; Abelard-Schuman, New York, 1963.

C-1   HERMAN THE HELPER, Robert Kraus; Windmill Books, New York, 1974.

C-4   NOTHING TO DO, Russell Hoban; Harper & Row, New York, 1964.

C-5   CHANGES, CHANGES, Pat Hutchins; Macmillan Co., New York, 1971.

     MY MAMA SAYS THERE AREN'T ANY, Judith Viorst; Atheneum, New York, 1973.

C-6   LEO, THE LATE BLOOMER, Robert Kraus; Windmill Books, New York, 1971.

C-7   HERMAN THE HELPER, Robert Kraus; Windmill Books, New York, 1974.

C-8   WILLIS, James Marshall; Houghton Mifflin Co., Boston, 1974.

C-9   PETUNIA, BEWARE!, Roger Duvoisin, Knopf, New York, 1950.

C-10   HERMAN THE HELPER, Robert Kraus; Windmill Books, New York, 1974.

C-12   WILLIS, James Marshall; Houghton Mifflin Co., Boston, 1974.

C-13   HOWIE HELPS HIMSELF, Joan Fassler; Albert Whitman & Co., Chicago, 1975.

C-14   WILLIS, James Marshall; Houghton Mifflin Co., Boston, 1974.

C-15   THE BOY, THE BAKER, THE MILLER AND MORE, Harold Berson; Crown Publishers, New York, 1974.

C-16   CHANGES, CHANGES, Pat Hutchins; Macmillan Co., New York, 1971.

C-18   WILLIS, James Marshall; Houghton Mifflin Co., Boston, 1974.

I-1   WHAT'S THE HURRY, HARRY?, Charlotte Steiner; Lothrop, Lee & Shepard Co., New York, 1968.

I-2   WHAT'S THE HURRY, HARRY?, Charlotte Steiner; Lothrop, Lee & Shepard Co., New York, 1968.

I-3   SAM, BANGS AND MOONSHINE, Evelyn Ness; Holt, Rinehart & Winston, New York, 1966.

I-4   WHEN VIOLET DIED, Mildred Kantrowitz; Parents' Magazine Press, New York, 1973.

I-5   THE LAZY DOG, John Hanberger; Four Winds Press, New York, 1971.

I-9   THE DOG WHO THOUGHT HE WAS A BOY, Cora Annett; Houghton Mifflin Co., Boston, 1965.

I-12   WILLIS, James Marshall; Houghton Mifflin Co., Boston, 1974.

I-15   HERMAN THE HELPER, Robert Kraus; Windmill Books, New York, 1974.

Index A

Index B

Index B provides the reader with a list of common symptoms which are not mentioned in THE PARENT BOOK. In order to learn what the underlying developmental deficiencies are the necessary system sections and chapters are given.

About the Authors

HAROLD BESSELL, Ph.D., is a Clinical Psychologist. After graduating from Purdue University in 1952 he worked at the Wichita Guidance Center and at the Wichita V.A. Mental Hygiene Clinic. For the past 18 years he has been practicing family therapy in La Jolla, California. He has taught at Wichita University, San Diego State University, and The California School of Professional Psychology, where he currently teaches courses in Prevention and Child Development. Dr. Bessell is the creator of The Human Development Program (better known as The Magic Circle), a curriculum for emotional development widely used in the public schools. Dr. Bessell's articles have appeared in Psychology Today, The American Journal of Psychotherapy and elsewhere. He and his wife, Pat live in Poway, California, and are the parents of three children.

THOMAS P. KELLY, Jr., is a writer, film maker, and teacher with a broad background in child development issues. As a film maker he has written and produced films for O.E.O., Headstart, and most recently, the Children's Bureau. In 1969 he was nominated for an Academy Award for his film about the Upward Bound program, A SPACE TO GROW. In 1974 he was nominated for an Emmy Award as writer of a TV Special, THE METROPOLITAN WASHINGTON DRUG ABUSE TEST. Together with Dr. Bessell, he has created an affective television program for children, presenting the concepts in this book, HERE COMES GALLAGHER. He is married and the father of seven children.

THE PARENT BOOK By Bessell and Kelly

May be Re-ordered from: **JALMAR PRESS, INC.**
6501 ELVAS AVENUE
SACRAMENTO, CA 95819

OTHER JALMAR PUBLICATIONS

T.A. FOR TOTS (and other prinzes) A. Freed $5.95
T.A. FOR KIDS (and grown-ups, too) A&M Freed 4.95
T.A. FOR TEENS (and other important people) A. Freed 7.95
T.A. FOR MANAGEMENT: Making Life Work Novey 6.95
JOY OF BACKPACKING: People's Guide to the Wilderness Look 5.95
A TIME TO TEACH, A TIME TO DANCE M. Freed ....(reduced) 8.95
WARM FUZZY TALE Steiner...3.95
REACH FOR THE SKY: The Romance And Techniques of Hang Gliding Severance 7.95

SEND FOR COMPLETE JALMAR CATALOG OF BOOKS, AUDIO/VISUAL MATERIALS, CASSETTES AND RECORDS
TRADE DISCOUNTS AVAILABLE ON REQUEST

ORDER FORM

JP JALMAR PRESS INC.
6501 ELVAS AVENUE
SACRAMENTO, CA 95819
(916) 451-2897
THE WARM FUZZY COMPANY ®

Purchase order, check or
money order must accompany your order.

Special Instructions
All materials F.O.B. Sacramento. Include payment of shipping and handling charges with all orders. Calif. residents must add 6% sales tax. Prices subject to change without notice.

Minimum order $5.00
Shipping, handling and insurance:
under $15.00 — $1.75
$15.00 to $20.00 — 2.25
over $20.00 — 2.75

QUANTITY	TITLE (Checks from Canada and other foreign countries should be marked "Payable in U.S. Funds")	UNIT PRICE	TOTAL

Ship to _____

	Sub-Total (Calif. residents 6% sales tax)	
	Handling & Shipping	
	Total	